THE LAST
ATLANTIC
LINERS

The largest liner ever built, Cunard's 83,673-ton Queen
Elizabeth, *arriving at New York in the early fifties.*

THE LAST ATLANTIC LINERS

William H. Miller

CONWAY
MARITIME PRESS

© William H Miller 1985

First published in Great Britain in 1985 by Conway Maritime Press Ltd,
24 Bride Lane, Fleet Street, London EC4Y 8DR

ISBN 0 85177 320 6

Designed by Tony Garrett

Typesetting and page make-up by Witwell Ltd, Liverpool

Printed and bound in Great Britain by R J Acford, Chichester

AUTHOR'S NOTE

Just over two hundred passenger ships sailed the North
Atlantic in the years since the Second World War. Some
made one or two crossings; others survived for merely a
single season. Still others were the now largely forgotten
emigrant, austerity or freighter-combination types.
Because of the limited amount of fresh, perceptive
material and also, more obviously, the size of this work,
some of these ships have not been included.
Approximately half have been mentioned. Hopefully,
some of those other ships may find a place, or at least a
mention, in a future volume. Such a projected title would
also include some of the liners on the more distant trades,
away from the North Atlantic.

CONTENTS

8: THE TOURIST AND IMMIGRANT SHIPS

9: THE LAST SHIPS OF STATE

10: THE EMPTY NORTH ATLANTIC

APPENDICES

INTRODUCTION

On 24 July 1947, a year or so before my birth, a special, quite historic meeting took place off Cowes. The giant *Queen Elizabeth* – crisp, fresh and one of the most beautiful-looking liners of her time – was approaching England's South Coast. She had just sped across the Atlantic from New York with a full load of passengers. She had made a brief detour to Cherbourg and transferred to tenders those passengers bound for a Continental destination. She then dashed across the Channel for her call at Southampton. On the same day, the stately *Queen Mary* – dressed in commercial livery for the first time since the autumn of 1939 – left Southampton for brief trials, a prelude to her post-war maiden run. Roland Montgomery was at Cowes for the meeting of the ships, their first rendezvous in Cunard colours. 'It was difficult to decide which was the more beautiful: the sleek rake of the *Elizabeth* or the regal style of the *Mary*. Freshly painted, both glistened. Their throaty whistles seemed to bellow for minutes on end. It was a thrilling occasion: a chorus of salutes momentarily brightening the post-war British gloom. They were the supreme ships, the ultimate ocean liners, sheer genius. The Atlantic Ferry seemed now to be officially reopened.'

A decade or so later, in the summer of 1958, the *Queen Mary* was part of one of those frequent processions of liners, a maritime parade, if you like, at New York. During my school holidays, I often stood along the Hoboken shore, just across from Manhattan, as the liners came and went, like characters in a play. The ships were all as familiar as the cast in a long-running serial. It was a busy, but fairly typical day. Cunard's *Britannic*, with her squat stacks in their original White Star colours, came down river first from 'Luxury Liner Row'. From my select, very private vantage point, I could peer along the Hudson and see the liners as they moved from their berths to be turned by a team of tugs and eventually head southward. Twenty or so minutes after undocking, they would pass before me, seemingly larger than life. As the *Britannic* passed that morning, the usual escort tugs were missing. They had returned to another berth, to assist with another liner. The Greek *New York* soon followed, her upper decks lined with passengers. She made her way past a string of other tugs, often with barges in tow, as well as railway carfloats, floating cranes and an inbound

freighter. Whistles, all different in tone and power, pierced the air. The *New York* signalled that she was clear and well underway, while even throatier sounds vibrated from the Uptown docks. The French *Liberté*, with her enormous red and black stacks, and towering pole masts, was next to sail. As she steamed past Hoboken, she momentarily blotted out the New York City skyline. Then the Greek *Olympia* approached from the opposite end of the river. She slipped behind the *Liberté* and then reappeared as she headed up river, to occupy the berth that had been vacated by the French ship. A set of frenzied salutes passed between the liners. The three Moran tugs that had undocked the *Liberté* lingered in mid-river and would soon assist the Greek flagship. The noontime sailings included four other liners: American Export's *Constitution*, United States Lines' *America*, Italian Line's *Saturnia* and National Hellenic American's *Queen Frederica*. The final member of this mid-day flotilla was, in fact, the largest of all. The *Queen Mary* began to leave her berth at precisely 12.30, manoeuvred by five tugboats. As she slipped past, the steam whistles on her first and second funnels signalled their farewells.

All of these liners were part of the transatlantic fleet. They were working their customary, often hectic relays, into port, offloading passengers, turn-round and replenishment, on with a new set of passengers and then outward on another voyage. The pattern was well established, seemingly unalterable. Then in October, just a few months later, the first commercial jet crossed the North Atlantic. It departed from Idlewild Airport, just twenty miles east of 'Luxury Liner Row'. Life for the great Atlantic passenger ships was to change entirely.

Ten years later, on a magically crisp autumn afternoon in 1967, I was aboard a chartered spectator boat for one of New York Harbour's more historic occasions, the final sailing of the *Queen Mary*. Three other liners were docked nearby, the *Independence, United States* and *Franconia*. They were running short of time as well. The *Mary* was finishing thirty-one years of Cunard service in which she had seen a thousand crossings and over two million passengers and earned an estimated $600 million in revenues. Few liners left a more successful legacy. But, by the mid-sixties, the *Queen* was in debt, sometimes shabby, certainly no longer in step. The jet had crushed the Atlantic liner. The *Mary*'s final departure, more than any other single event, symbolized this blunt succession. Tugs, barges, fireboats, ferries and pleasure craft hooted, honked and screeched – farewell gestures to abdicating royalty. Majestically, she steamed off on her last run, disappearing in a shadowy midday light.

In the summer of 1983, with another stretch of years past, I spent a quiet Sunday roaming about the rubble of the Southampton Ocean Terminal. It had been built in the late forties, especially for the Atlantic superliners. Now, with its purpose long gone, the space was better suited to a new breed of ships, the Japanese car carrier. Bulldozers sat momentarily in silence, but positioned for levelling the last remaining two hundred feet of the structure. Those long, empty gangways that once connected with the likes of the *Queens, United States* and *Île de France*, were soon to be hauled-away to some scrap pile. Ironically, not very far from this site, a small shop specializes in memorabilia from

A jubilant occasion: the Queen Mary *arriving at Southampton in August 1945 on her first visit since the peace-breaking summer of 1939. Although victory was finally in hand, the big Cunarder is still dressed in her grey war colours.*

long gone liners: silverware from the Cunarders, menu cards from Canadian Pacific, sepia post cards from the French Line. The trade is almost always brisk.

From that first post-war meeting of the two Cunard *Queens* to those summer gatherings at New York, that last sailing of the *Queen Mary* and finally to the demise of long deserted terminals, this work is dedicated to the ships, their owners, the operations and the personalities that have been a part of the past forty years on the North Atlantic. This has been the era of THE LAST ATLANTIC LINERS.

William H Miller, Jersey City, New Jersey Spring 1984

Victor Scrivens Collection

ACKNOWLEDGEMENTS

This book has been inspired, to a certain extent, by my conversations with Captain Cornelius van Herk at The Hague in the summer of 1982. The Captain freely offered his detailed, exact and vivid recollections of the Holland-America liners, mostly during transatlantic service. I am deeply indebted to him for the many memories and impressions that he shared with me.

I am also fortunate in having been granted interviews with a rather remarkable group of shipboard personnel and personalities. Their names are listed in alphabetical order: Captain Eric Ashton-Irvine, formerly with Cunard; Frank O Braynard; Michael Cohn; Captain Narciso Fossati, formerly with the Italian Line; Brenton Jenkins, formerly with Cunard; Christian Kloster, then managing director of the Norwegian-Caribbean Lines; John Havers; Len Houghton, of Cunard; William Prins of Holland-America Line; Captain Boleslaw Rakowski of the Polish Ocean Lines; Fred Sarver, formerly of American Export Lines; Captain Harvey Smith of Cunard; Cees-Jan van Herk; and Captain Robin Woodall, also with Cunard.

I am also indebted to George Devol and the World Ocean & Cruise Society; Peter Eisele, editor of the journal *Steamboat Bill*; Arnold Kludas, historian at the German Shipping Museum at Bremerhaven; and author C M Squarey.

I must also thank, especially for their kind use of treasured photographs and other memorabilia, the following: Erwin Abele, Frank Andrews, Ernest Arroyo, Claire Bottino, J K Byass, John Catrambone, Luis Miguel Correia, John Draffin, Frank Duffy, Alex Duncan, Louis Gardella, Herbert G Frank, Pat Havers, Fred Hawks, Doreen Heywood, Peter Lancaric, Robert Lenzer, Vincent Messina, A Michaelson, Richard Morse, Hisashi Noma, Ralph O'Hara, Fred Rodriguez, Robert Russell, Richard Sandstrom, Sal Scannella, A Scrimali, Victor Scrivens, Ken Seeman, James Shaw, Roger Sherlock, Willie Tinnemeyer, Thomas C Young, V H Young, Everett Viez and Barry Winiker. I must also acknowledge the gracious assistance of the American Export Lines, Canadian Pacific Steamships, Companhia Colonial, Cunard Line, French Line, Hapag-Lloyd Shipyards, Holland-America Line, Norwegian America Line, Polish Ocean Lines, Port Authority of New York & New Jersey, Port of Le Havre Authority, Skyfotos, Southern Echo Newspapers, Swedish-American Line, United States Lines and Zim Lines.

In conclusion, warmest appreciation and thoughts to my family and other friends, who have been so wonderfully supportive and encouraging.

CHAPTER ONE

THE QUEENS AND OTHER CUNARDERS

CUNARD LINE

The QUEEN MARY *and the* QUEEN ELIZABETH

The Cunard *Queens*, the illustrious *Mary* and *Elizabeth*, were the best known superliners of all time. They were popular, prestigious and immensely profitable for most of their lives. They led the post-war Cunard Line fleet, assuredly the biggest on the Atlantic. No company could offer more sailings, more berths or ships of greater distinction and repute. In those years, and until the mid-sixties, Cunard was legendary and its ships unsurpassable.

The *Queen Mary*, designed in the twenties, was the first thousand-foot ocean liner, the first to reach 75,000 tons and, moreover, the first intended to run a five-day schedule (and thereby allow a timetable that depended on two rather than three big liners). A great deal of experimentation was required.

Laid down in December 1930 and then subjected to a long delay on the stocks because of the Depression, the *Queen Mary* was not ready for launching until September 1934. There is a pleasant myth attached to the choosing of a name for the new Cunarder. Supposedly, the company was overwhelmed with suggestions – everything from *Britannia* and *Galicia*, to *Hamptonia* and *Clydania*. Among the royalist proposals were *Princess Elizabeth, Princess Margaret Rose* and *Marina* (after the popular Princess Marina, Duchess of Kent) but the story goes that Cunard directors favoured *Victoria*. It was certainly pleasing to the ear and fitted in with the firm's policy of selecting names ending in 'ia'. Lord Rydon, a Cunard director and personal friend of King George V, supposedly requested His Majesty's permission to use his late grandmother's name: 'Would His Majesty consent to our new great liner being named after the most illustrious and remarkable woman who has ever been Queen of England?' The King is said to have replied, 'This is the greatest compliment that has ever been made to me or my wife. I will ask her permission when I get home.'

In reality, Cunard had decided at the outset to name their new liner (Shipyard Number 534) the *Queen Mary* and entered into protracted and highly secret negotiations with the Royal Household concerning the ship's name and arrangements for her launching. It seemed sensible, in view of their recent merger with the White Star Line, to abandon their 'ia' nomenclature, a considerate gesture to the ships and heritage of both firms. The name achieved a compromise. Furthermore, a large Government loan for completion of the *Queen Mary* prompted consideration of a nationalistic and inspiring name. The monarchy was the perfect stimulus for patriotic fervour, especially in the lingering austerity of the Depression. And, very

importantly, 1935 was to be Silver Jubilee Year in Britain. King George V and Queen Mary, by then nearing their seventies, had inspired enormous respect, and even to the little Princess Elizabeth, future Queen, her bearded grandfather was 'Grandpa England'. Queen Mary, with her erect carriage and a style in dress that made no concession to changes in fashion, was also a symbolic figure. Her Majesty was delighted that the new flagship was to bear her name. The liner herself had taken on unintended significance. As Britain's brilliant 'ship of state', she was a project of fortitude and determination, completed by a nation overcoming the difficulties of the worldwide Depression. She was the focus of superb workmanship, of advanced design, of power, of combined effort and, hence, enormous pride. Her planning brought together various levels of British society from the Royal

The two Queens *at Southampton on 27 September 1946. The* Mary *was about to begin her reconversion for luxury service while the* Elizabeth *was completing her commercial outfitting.*

Family and Government ministers to artisans, designers and dock labourers.

Once fitted out and ready for commercial service in mid-1936, the *Queen Mary* was also ready for appraisal. Despite touches of modern art placed mostly in the public lounges, the new *Queen* was a conservative liner, one very much in the tradition of a fine hotel. She was a warm and comfortable ship, with far less of the massive grandeur of France's *Normandie*, her arch rival, which had been completed the year before. The Cunard ship lacked the innovatory glitter, the almost pretentious extravagance, of her Gallic rival. The *Queen Mary* followed very much in the spirit of the earlier Cunarders, typified by the big *Aquitania* of 1914. She was equipped with soft upholstery, brass handrails and, everywhere, chrome, glass; and glossy veneers. There were velvet curtains, carpets with swirling floral patterns, trumpet-shaped pylon lamps, traditional fireplaces, wood-framed clocks, murals, and a marble medallion depicting Queen Mary. Above all, the liner was unmistakably British, assuredly a Cunarder. She was the

perfect evolutionary ship, far less revolutionary than the company sometimes liked to suggest.

A rich Texan, seated in the Verandah Grill Restaurant on board the *Queen Mary*, is reputed to have been so delighted with the ship that he asked if he might buy her. A rather surprised *maître d'hôtel*, so the story goes, responded, 'I'm terribly sorry, sir, but you see, she's part of a set!' The *Queen Mary* and *Queen Elizabeth* were always thought of as a pair, most often simply as the '*Queens*', and in fact, many passengers thought they were identical. In reality they were entirely different ships. The *Mary* was the three-stacker, the older ship, possibly even beginning to date, but a speed champion, and very grand. The *Elizabeth* was a twin-stacker, raked, more modern in design, and perhaps just a little less grand.

If the second Cunard express liner had been called *King George V*, as rumour suggested, in honour of the well-loved monarch, who had died in January 1936, the liners would have become 'the King and Queen of the Atlantic'. Instead, however, they became 'Queens of the Atlantic', a far more attractive pairing and balance. In February 1938, still two years from her completion (the ship's commercial maiden voyage was set for April 1940), Cunard revealed that *Queen Elizabeth* was the chosen name, after the popular Duchess of York, who had become Queen when her husband ascended the throne as George VI.

While the *Mary* had already been in service for four years, the incomplete *Elizabeth* had to flee for safety in February 1940. She was the perfect bomb target while still at the John Brown shipyard. An elaborate concealment began with the deliberate spreading of a rumour that she was to go to Southampton for further dry-docking. Assuredly, the *Luftwaffe* would be waiting for her in the Channel. However, once she had cleared Greenock at the mouth of the Clyde, she sped west and not south for the safety of New York. She reached New York on 7 March and berthed across from the already grey-painted *Queen Mary*. It was the very first meeting of the two liners. Two weeks later, the *Mary* steamed off to Australia, on the start of her wartime service. No two ships have ever performed so well or heroically as did the two *Queens* during World War II. Liveried in grey, they sailed almost every ocean, zig-zagging, in blackout and always with radio silence. They transported whole divisions – and often more – to various battle-fronts. In 1942, they were moved to the North Atlantic – on a precisely timed, top-secret run between New York and Gourock in Scotland. Sailing week after week, almost as Cunard had intended for them in peacetime, they helped more than any other ship to prepare for the invasion of Normandy and the eventual peace in Europe. Winston Churchill paid the highest compliment to the two giant Cunard troop ships: 'The *Queens* helped to win the war in Europe by at least a year!'

In all, the *Mary* carried over 810,000 wartime passengers; the *Elizabeth*'s total passed 811,000. Neither liner docked in Southampton, their intended British terminal port, until August 1945. The *Mary* had last been there in August 1939, the *Elizabeth*, never. The locals were delighted and proud to see them, even if they were both still in faded greys. Cunard funnel colours were added a month later.

In the latter half of 1945, the Atlantic relay was reversed, at least temporarily. For example, the *Mary*

The Queen Elizabeth *outbound along the Hudson River at New York – with the liners* Liberté, United States *and* Constitution *in the background.*

arrived at Southampton on 31 August with 11 troops and 93 passengers on board, but returned to New York on 5 September with 14,083 troops. Figures for the *Elizabeth* were similarly unbalanced: 100 passengers on arrival at Southampton, followed by a westbound trip to New York with 15,830 aboard. Cunard's first fare-paying passenger after the war, an American businessman, crossed on the *Elizabeth* that August. His fare was $200 and he boarded the liner from a tender carrying troops. He later commented on the voyage to New York: 'What a pleasant trip. We passed some Nazi U-boats waiting to surrender.'

In early 1946, it was decided that the *Elizabeth* would be the first of the two *Queens* to be restored. She was released from war service on 6 March, after landing her final military passengers, 1709 in all, at Berth 101 in Southampton. Then, after she had been stripped down, it was planned that, as the largest ship of any kind then afloat, she would go to the Tail of the Bank, at the mouth of the Clyde, for her full refit. The narrow, often shallow river bed prevented her from returning to her birthplace at Clydebank.

Some 2000 workers, many of them living aboard and receiving supplies from barges and workboats, transformed the *Elizabeth* while she sat at anchor off Gourock. The liner maintained steam at all times, and a

Port Authority of New York & New Jersey

special 200-unit fire brigade was posted to the ship. Over thirty tons of fresh, commercial colouring replaced the battered wartime paints. The 2000 portholes and windows were scraped and then cleaned, and 4000 miles of electric wiring surveyed. Simultaneously, the furnishings for the *Elizabeth* came out of wartime storage. The *Aquitania* delivered pieces from America, others came from Lancashire warehouses or by freighter from Australia. The total came to 21,000 items, including the likes of 4000 mattresses, 2000 carpets, and 1500 wardrobes and dressing tables. The liner returned to Southampton in mid-June for the final stages of her restoration.

The *Queen Elizabeth* was a symbol to a post-war Britain in the same way that the *Queen Mary* had inspired the nation in the middle of the Depression. She was floating brilliance in a time of austerity and lingering gloom. Beautifully decorated, albeit somewhat less grandly than the *Mary*, she seemed even more of a modern liner.

Cunard enthusiastically reported the details of her delivery, listing everything from the 50 or so woods spread over her 13 decks to the 37 public rooms, 30,000 lamps, and 700 clocks.

Her Majesty Queen Elizabeth, accompanied by the Princesses Elizabeth and Margaret, was on board the liner for her trials in the Firth of Clyde, on 7 October 1946, soon after their visit to the battleship HMS *Vanguard*. Captain Eric Ashton-Irvine, who later served as Staff Captain on both of the great Cunarders, was aboard for the occasion. 'I especially recall the Captain asking one of the junior officers to explain the new radar system to Princess Elizabeth. The officer turned white. He wasn't familiar with the brand new equipment, which had just been installed. But, following orders, he gave a valiant try. In the end, however, it was the Princess who did the explaining. She had just been shown a similar system aboard the battleship HMS *Vanguard* one week before.'

Port Authority of New York & New Jersey

Captain Ashton-Irvine also recalled the delight with which officers and crew greeted the ever-gracious Queen. 'We asked if she might give us a special portrait photograph for the Officers' Ward Room. She agreed readily. Several weeks later, a beautiful, very original portrait was delivered to the ship. There was one stipulation, however. If the ship was to be retired or sold, the portrait would revert to the Queen. Indeed, in 1968, when we retired the *Elizabeth*, the picture was, in fact, returned to the then Queen Mother.'

Cunard was delighted with the liner's first set of official trials, recalling that there had been no trial runs at the time of her secret delivery and her maiden dash to New York in March 1940. The *Elizabeth* managed 30 knots without straining. There has always been debate over the actual top speed of this second *Queen*, especially since the *Mary* alone took the Blue Riband, in 1938, at 31.6 knots. Captain Ashton-Irvine insists that the *Elizabeth* was the

The stately and majestic Queen Mary *has just departed from New York City's 'Luxury Liner Row'. Berthed at piers in the background are the* Kungsholm, Britannic, Mauretania, New York *and* United States.

faster. 'During a wartime crossing, in top secret, we reached 36¼ knots. However, this never occurred again. The *Queens* were designed for service speeds of 28½ knots, which meant consuming 1,000 tons of fuel per day. If they went beyond this speed, the fuel consumption climbed to 1500 or 1600 tons. After the War, it was simply too expensive to push the *Elizabeth* to absolute maximum speed. One record-breaker was quite enough and that was the *Mary*.'

The *Mary* was released from war duty at the end of September 1946, just as the *Elizabeth* was preparing for her post-war maiden crossing. The *Mary*'s return was not to come until midsummer in the following year. Like her slightly larger running-mate, she had to undergo stripping-down and then extensive restoration and refitting. However, there was a last-minute change. The *Queen Mary*'s conversion to a luxury ship was carried out entirely at Southampton, rather than at the intended anchorage off the Clyde. Simultaneously, in a newspaper report, the US Government revealed that it had paid Cunard close to $91 million for the wartime transport of American soldiers in the two Cunarders.

When the two *Queens* met off Cowes, both dressed in their commercial colours for the first time, on 24 July 1947, the post-war transatlantic liner trade had officially opened. The *Queens* then reigned, twin leaders of the best ocean liner express service ever offered. Even better days were ahead, with the boom of the early fifties. However, Cunard could not have envisaged the eventual swift slaughter of the Atlantic fleet by jet travel. The *Queens* were to have both good and bad times.

As intended, the paired liners maintained the first two-ship luxury shuttle service on the North Atlantic, crossing between Southampton and New York, with a call at Cherbourg in each direction. Generally, they sailed from Southampton on Thursdays, crossed the Channel and made their brief call at the French port (where there was only tender service until 1952) and then headed into the open Atlantic and sped across to reach New York the following Tuesday. Moored at Pier 90, at the foot of West 50th Street, they had a very basic, but very busy 24-hour turn-round. On Wednesdays, they would sail again, with a new load of passengers, some priority cargo and a fresh supply of provisions and fuel, for the eastward leg of their round trip. According to Captain Ashton-Irvine, 'We always averaged between 27 and 28 knots, but when we reached Nantucket, we cut two boilers. We dropped our speed to 20 knots for that last two hundred miles into New York.

At New York, because of their 39-foot draught, the *Queens* were forced to move with the changing tides. At times, there was just a mere two or three feet between their keels and the muddy bottom of the Hudson River. As they proceeded along the River to Pier 90, groups of Moran tugs would begin to gather, as if forming a royal procession. Should any problems arise, help would be nearby. The docking process for such mammoth liners, which usually lasted about thirty-five minutes, often required as many as eight tugs. Almost always, the *Queens* used the north berth of Pier 90, where the gangways and openings were best suited to the ships and where their departures could be made more efficiently.

Consequently, because of the tide charts at New York, it was often difficult to predict the exact arrival and departure times for these largest of ships. One week, for example, the *Queen Mary* might arrive at seven in the

morning on Tuesday and then sail at eleven on Wednesday morning, whereas the *Queen Elizabeth*, arriving the following week, might dock at noon on Tuesday and then sail at midnight on Wednesday. As the peak summer months began to pass and change into the autumn season, the two liners gradually relaxed their balance of sailings so that they would leave New York on Thursdays, then Fridays and, by mid-winter, even on Saturdays. I can vividly recall waiting patiently along the Jersey side of the Hudson, on a frosty morning in mid-December, for the *Queen Mary* to make a 10.30 departure.

Of course, on occasion, the ships were delayed by bad

Southern Echo Newspapers

At Southampton: the Queen Mary *at the Ocean Terminal, the* Mauretania *in the inner berth and the* United States *just arriving in the background. Opened in 1950, the Ocean Terminal was replaced in 1983 by parking for imported Japanese cars.*

worked with near-superhuman effort so as to get the liners out again as close to their posted sailing time as possible.'

In the peak summer months, between June and September, the *Queens* were often filled to absolute capacity. Their passenger accommodations were balanced between three classes, the normal arrangement for most major liners after the War. Berths on the *Elizabeth* were listed as 823 in first class, 662 in cabin class, which Cunard enthusiastically described as 'the happy medium', and 798 in tourist class, making a total of 2233. The *Mary's* accommodation was put at 711 in first class, 707 in cabin, and 577 in tourist, a total of 1957. Minimum single fares for the 1949 season were listed as £130 for first class, £80 for cabin and £59 for tourist.

The *Queens* worked a prescribed, annual timetable, with very little deviation, especially in those immediate post-war years. They provided a schedule that was useful to tens of thousands of passengers – film stars, diplomats, industrialists, and budget tourists – who knew that there was a weekly departure for most of the year in two large, extremely fast, safe and comfortble 'floating cities' of excellent repute.

The *Queens* were designed to endure heavy, strenuous schedules, but it was decided, at least during their commercial years, that they should undergo two periods in dry dock each year. Each winter, usually in January or February, they would take a turn in the huge King George V Graving Dock at Southampton. This was the full refit and survey that covered all aspects of the ships, from the boilers and refrigerators to lifts, lifeboats and anchor chains. Of course, their bottoms were scraped, the propellers and rudders checked, and fresh coats of paint applied overall. Then, in the summer, usually in early August, they would each miss a round trip and spend five or six days in the same Graving Dock for general maintenance and emergency repairs.

By the mid-fifties, Cunard was at its post-war peak. The Company was said to be carrying one-third of all passengers that crossed the Atlantic. In 1957, there were twelve Cunard liners in service: the *Queen Elizabeth, Queen Mary, Mauretania, Caronia, Britannic, Media, Parthia, Scythia* and four brand new ships for the Canadian run, the *Saxonia, Ivernia, Carinthia* and *Sylvania.*

Brenton Jenkins, who served as a purser aboard all of the larger Cunarders, joined the firm in 1946. 'In those years [the late forties and fifties], Cunard was the epitome of shipping lines. It was like working for the Bank of England. In fact, family connections were necessary just to be hired. Fortunately, I had my uncle's service from the twenties and thirties. [The earlier Jenkins was chief engineer aboard the *Berengaria, Majestic* and *Lancastria.*] It worked. I was hired as a junior assistant purser, a counter

weather. Captain Robin Woodall, who served aboard the *Elizabeth*, recalled this aspect of their operation. 'Mostly, I remember the dreadful North Atlantic weather: the snows, gales, winds and fogs. It was absolutely evil. Fortunately, liners like the *Queens* were basically "indoor" ships. On those instances when the *Queens* were delayed the crew, coupled with Cunard's shoreside staff, often

A typical scene on a summer's day in the mid fifties at the Southampton Ocean Terminal. The Queen Elizabeth *is at berth, resting between voyages to New York.*

boy, on the grand old *Aquitania*. This was the beginning that led me to the mighty *Queens*.' Captain Ashton-Irvine recalled that seniority and an established procedure provided the only path to serving on the *Mary* and *Elizabeth*. 'When you joined Cunard as a junior third Officer, you were assigned to ships by class, working upwards. One started with the *Media* or *Parthia*, then went to the *Ascania*, then to the *Scythia* class, then the *Britannic* and finally on to the *Mauretania* or *Caronia* before being placed aboard the *Queens*. They were the ultimate plateau.'

World War II became more and more of a distant memory for the *Queen Mary* and the *Queen Elizabeth*. All of those hectic and heroic sailings with thousands of anxious troops on board seemed long past. For several years afterward, the teak rails on the *Elizabeth* retained the carved initials and markings from her wartime passengers. In the late forties, the *New York Times* reported, 'There are names of many strains on board, among them Isaki, Mullins, Carnavale and Knicos – mingled with plain Ben, Joe, Pat and Molly, the latter whom may have been a service woman on board the great transport or just a wistful memory for some soldier at sea.' The article continued, 'More ambitious pen-knife artisans had carved bold strokes along the rails with the names and numbers of companies, regiments, divisions, squadrons, groups and

other units.' The rails were removed in the early fifties, and at least one was sent to the US Government archives.

However, while the *Queens* were the most popular, successful and profitable pair of superliners ever built, they did have their share of troubles and embarrassments. On 14 April 1947, six months after entering commercial service, the *Elizabeth* was about to complete another eastbound run round the Isle of Wight and steam up to Southampton. On board were 2246 passengers (including the Duke of Marlborough, Randolph Churchill and Bea Lillie), £13,000 worth of express cargo, 649 bags of mail, 34 diplomatic pouches, 1500 bon voyage parcels, 1689 pieces of heavy baggage, 8992 of stateroom baggage, 26 cars, 113 containers of cinema film, 479 bars of gold bullion valued at £148,000, and 1 dog. While rounding the Brambles, in the approaches to the Solent and eventually to Southampton, the liner ran aground on a sharp turn. Such embarrassment and annoyance! She sat for twenty-six hours, locked tight in a holding position, awaiting the sixteen tugs that would be needed to pull her free. Even the Admiralty at Portsmouth sent help. The tanks were pumped out to lighten the 83,673-ton liner – 1065 tons of

Bellboy inspection on the Queen Mary *in 1947.*

fuel oil went into barges and 2610 tons of fresh water went over the side. One passenger, among the many whose plans had been disrupted, sent a one-word telegram message to friends ashore: 'Stuck!' Press coverage of the incident was quite harsh, and many passengers became annoyed at the failure of the liner's staff to keep them informed. By way of appeasement, the first class passengers and their baggage were finally taken ashore in tenders. The *Queen Elizabeth* was finally pulled free on the evening of 15 April and towed stern-first down the Solent. She anchored seven miles off Calshot. A thick fog had then set in and further complicated the delay. The liner had to wait the night before proceeding to her Southampton berth.

Later, there were still other problems. The *Queen Mary* went aground off Cherbourg in January 1949, and then had to make an emergency return to Southampton, where 100 tons of concrete were put in her damaged stern. On a number of occasions, both ships were forced to dock or sail without tugboat assistance, particularly during strikes at New York and Southampton. They also endured any number of protests and strikes by dockers, which often resulted in delayed sailings and required careful handling by Cunard's shore personnel.

The elements played their part as well. In March 1956, the *Queen Mary* was tossed about in one of the North Atlantic's worst storms. Some 40 passengers and 50 crew members were injured. Three years later, in August 1959, in a thick afternoon haze, the *Elizabeth* collided with the 8500-ton *American Hunter*, a freighter of the United States Lines, in the outer reaches of New York Harbour. The smaller ship was said to have 'bounced off' the mighty Cunarder and then disappeared in the mists. With 2246 passengers on board, the *Queen* was forced to return to Pier 90 for inspection and possible repairs. Two holes along the starboard side were plugged temporarily with ten tons of cement. The *Elizabeth* sailed off on the following night The freighter finally docked with a dent in her bow.

Fire was another hazard, especially for such vast, intricate liners. The *Queen Elizabeth* was nearly destroyed on 8 March 1946, while berthed at Southampton for the beginning of her post-war refit. While the ship's entire fire brigade was ashore, a blaze erupted in a small storage room and smoke was soon pouring from the Promenade Deck windows. The Southampton Fire Brigade were summoned, but found that their ladders were too short to reach the upper-deck. In response, several of the ship's lifeboats were lowered to act as lifts for firemen and their hoses. Within three hours, the fire was finally under control. The damage consisted of some flooding, blistered paint, and several warped steel beams. Another fire broke out on the *Elizabeth* in September 1960 on her aproach to the English Channel from New York. Three first class staterooms were damaged as the ship stopped to allow fire crews to fight the blaze. Faulty electrical wiring was found to be the cause.

Another reason why the *Queens* were almost constantly in the news on both sides of the Atlantic was the seemingly endless parade of celebrities they carried. The famous and nearly famous were always 'on their rosters. Winston Churchill crossed on the *Queen Mary* at the end of 1951, travelling with a staff of 40. Just as on his wartime crossings, when he had an accompanying party of 160, part of the Main Deck was reserved for the Prime Minister. His apartments included a specially created dining room and communications centre. Churchill used the *Queen Mary* again in January 1953 for a visit to Washington and meetings with President Eisenhower. On this round trip, however, the Churchill party dined more often in the Verandah Grill Restaurant.

The Duke and Duchess of Windsor were frequent passengers, particularly in the late forties and early fifties, before they developed an allegiance to the new *United States*. They often boarded at Cherbourg, and one Cunard Captain recalled a blustery night-time sailing from France aboard the *Queen Mary*. On the bridge, he suddenly spotted a rather small man in an oversized coat peering down at the harbour activity from the bridge wing. The Captain barked to one of his assistants that passengers were not permitted on the bridge without an invitation, but was promptly advised that the passenger was, in fact, the former King of England. The Duke and Duchess were probably the best known, most often photographed Atlantic passengers of the post-war era. Captain Robert Arnott, in his memoirs, *Captain of the Queen*, recalled the royal exiles in the late forties. 'On one of their trips with Cunard, I counted seventy-five cases going into their luxurious suite on Main Deck, and then they had seventy additional trunks in the hold. During the voyage, the Duchess would phone the bridge every morning at eight-thirty, inquiring about the weather forecasts. In this way, she planned her wardrobe, which often meant changes several times each day.'

In October 1954, Her Majesty Queen Elizabeth the Queen Mother sailed out for a goodwill visit to North America in the *Elizabeth*, the liner she had named in September 1938, and home a month later in the *Mary*. At

A portion of the first class dining room on board the Queen Mary. *The large map of the North Atlantic on the background wall included electric lights which outlined the ship's progress as she steamed between continents.*

A restaurant scene aboard the Queen Mary *in October 1966.
Captain Eric Ashton-Irvine is seated in the centre.*

the Ocean Terminal at Southampton, the *Elizabeth* had
been irregularly docked stern-first, a precaution against a
rumoured dock and tugboat strike. What if Her Majesty's
sailing was delayed or, far worse, cancelled? In the end,
the strike was delayed in deference to the beloved Queen
Mother. The Queen, the Duke of Edinburgh and Princess
Margaret came down to Southampton for the sailing,
travelling from London aboard a special five-coach train
and later joining the Queen Mother for a farewell supper
in the Verandah Grill. Once at sea, Her Majesty, on her
first full voyage in the liner that bore her name, made
daily tours of the ship, frequently dined in the Main
Restaurant, and attended a special children's tea party.

Other voyagers included former President Eisenhower,
the King of Arabia, Earl Mountbatten, the former kings of
Rumania and Yugoslavia, Aristotle Onassis, Lord
Beaverbrook (who so feared delays caused by fogs in the
Solent that he always disembarked at Cherbourg and then
flew on to London) and, of course, a nearly endless list of
names from the worlds of Hollywood and the theatre,
who included Mary Pickford, Clark Gable, Humphrey
Bogart, Laurel and Hardy, Laurence Olivier, Merle
Oberon and Elizabeth Taylor. In his recently published
diaries, Noel Coward recounted numerous crossings
aboard the *Queens*. On one trip, he recalled Evelyn
Waugh, Coco Chanel, and Lord Beaverbrook as fellow
passengers. On another, there were Alfred Lunt, Lynn

21

The huge bow section of the Queen Mary *seems headed directly into the* Britannic *during this view of an arrival. The* Mary *was being gently manoeuvred into the north side of New York's Pier 90 while the* Britannic *was at berth on the south side of Pier 92. The distance between these piers equalled two New York City blocks.*

Fontanne, Lord Montgomery, Debbie Reynolds, Eddie Fisher, and Madeleine Sherwood.

Steward Len Houghton also recalled grand days with illustrious passenger lists. 'In those years [the fifties], Cunard was running a very deluxe transatlantic shuttle. It was indeed still the Palm Court days. We could cater for any nationality and, in first class, a full breakfast could be ordered, specially cooked and then promptly served even at three in the afternoon. Of course, I think the *Queen Mary* was the most favoured. She had the grandest atmosphere. We had famous passengers on almost every crossing. I remember that we were given special instructions on how to speak when the Queen Mother sailed with us in 1954. In the end, however, only one engineer fumbled. Instead of the customary "Your Majesty", he referred to the Queen Mother as "Your Queenship"! We also had Princess Marina of Kent, the Shah of Iran and his Queen Soraya, and Emperor Haile Selassie of Ethiopia. But to us, the staff members, it was always very much like *Upstairs, Downstairs*. There was never, ever a sense of familiarity.'

Purser Brenton Jenkins also witnessed a great celebrity parade on the *Queens*, particularly in the fifties. 'Mae West travelled with us very often. She was my personal favourite. She was a highly intelligent woman, who was especially kind to the staff members. Near the end of each crossing, she would give a special luncheon party just for the Purser's Department. When we arrived at New York, usually at seven or eight in the morning, the press would come aboard [by launch in outer New York Harbour] and always ask to meet with her. Unfailingly, she agreed – and always dressed in that incredible style that belonged only to her.'

'The Duke and Duchess of Windsor were always very friendly, no matter what hour or where on board one might run into them. They were both very concerned with physical fitness and more particularly with dieting. The Duchess maintained a magnificent figure, which so suited her exceptional wardrobe. However, on Sundays, in the middle of the five-day crossing, she would indulge completely and order a bowl of chocolate sauce.'

'Liberace came aboard in the early fifties, for his first concert tour of Europe. He travelled with a party of twenty-five, including one little man who seemed to do nothing more than to carry those famed gold lamé dinner jackets. Liberace himself was wonderfully undemanding, yet I recall how that vast three-deck high Main Restaurant on the *Queen Mary* came almost to a complete halt at dinner as he made his entrance, bejewelled and glistening.

Hail and farewell: the Queen Mary *leaving Southampton for the last time, on 31 October 1967. Note the 310-foot long paying-off penant flying from her mainmast.*

Once, we mustered the courage to ask him to give a concert in the Main Lounge. He quickly agreed, but with the stipulation that all passengers, from all classes, be invited. Noel Coward was sitting in the front row, applauding as loudly as everyone at the end of the performance. Afterward, the Commodore presented the pianist with a fine Scottish woollen travelling rug. When we reached Southampton, there was a special train down from London, carrying a huge banner that read "Welcome Liberace".'

But life, especially that grand life, was slowly changing for the *Queens* and for Cunard itself. A new, quite different competitor, the jet aircraft, had arrived by the late fifties. Travel time across the Atlantic suddenly dropped from six days to six hours. Cunard managers at first regarded transport in such new, considerably less comfortable craft as just a fad. After all, 'real travellers' would still prefer ships like the *Queens* – or so they thought. Within a year after the first commercial flight to London in October 1958, the airline industry had secured 63% of all Atlantic passenger traffic – 1.5 million by air, against 882,000 by sea. The difference increased steadily. Life was never again to be the same for the *Queens* or almost any other passenger ship then working the North Atlantic.

The *Queens* began to make a loss in 1961, just three years after that first transatlantic jet passage. Of course, the problem was not entirely this competition, but also the age of the two huge Cunarders, which were appearing increasingly dated in comparison with the more modern *France, Rotterdam, Bremen* and others. (Almost ironically, several years later, as they were being retired in 1967–68, the two Cunarders were reappraised with great fondness and interest as 'floating museum pieces'. Fascination with the thirties and, in particular, with the Art Deco movement was then just beginning to emerge. The *Queens* were looked upon as great statements, 'monuments' if you like, to that period.) Cunard did occasionally attempt to upgrade and redecorate the liners, but often in the most hideous taste, with loud colours, coloured lights, even plastic flowers. One loyal passenger complained. 'The *Queen Elizabeth* is beginning to look like a Blackpool dance hall.'

In February 1963, the *Queen Elizabeth* made the first pleasure cruise in the history of the two ships. It was a five-day run between New York and Nassau, with fares beginning at $125. A voyage arranged particularly for nostalgic and enthusiastic travellers who wanted a trip in at least one of the famed Cunarders, and with all tickets sold, it was able only barely to make ends meet. The

Queens were never intended to go cruising, never designed to visit tropical ports with inadequate harbour depths and ill-equipped docks. Consequently, when the *Elizabeth* and later the *Mary* went on cruises, they generally had to anchor miles from shore, which necessitated inconvenient, time-consuming trips in big tenders for passengers who were bound for the attractions of land.

The *Mary*'s first cruise was from Southampton to Las Palmas in the Canaries, in December 1963. It was, in fact, Cunard's first cruise from a British port since 1939. Again, nostalgia echoed throughout the sales efforts. It was a last chance to sail in one of the world's greatest ships. Despite some inconveniences, including the lack of air-conditioning, outdoor pools and lido areas, most passengers returned thrilled with their unique experience. 'It was something to tell the grandchildren', as one passenger happily reported.

By late 1966, however, Cunard had slipped further and further into the red – and into mismanagement. Quite simply, the Company had kept the *Queens* and several other Atlantic liners in service far too long. Ideally, in perfect hindsight, such ships should have been retired very soon after registering their initial losses. By December 1966, the *Queens* were each losing nearly £750,000 annually. The Company's treasury was being drained. Scheduling had become near to impossible. While the occasional cruise was still offered, mainly with weak financial results, the transatlantic trade was in rapid decline and decay. On one midwinter crossing, the *Elizabeth* steamed into New York with 200 passengers and 900 crew members aboard! *The Times* called the liners 'limping leviathans'. Another critic referred to their operations as 'Cunard-on-Sea' – comparable with any faded English seaside resort. The good old days had indeed passed.

The *Queen Elizabeth* underwent a million-pound face lift during the winter of 1965–66, which included the addition of full air-conditioning, private plumbing in most of the cabins, and the creation of a large lido deck with outdoor pool. She was supposedly a 'new ship', intended to last until at least 1975, according to Cunard's projections. Specifically, she would be the early partner to the new superliner (the *Queen Elizabeth 2*) then being built as a replacement for the *Mary* and destined to come into service in 1969. Cunard planned to continue its two-ship Atlantic express run well into the seventies.

Such a plan was, at the very least, misguided. Even schedules which depended on a single big liner, such as the *France* or the *United States*, were unprofitable. Cunard could not expect to continue running two large liners, especially two ships so obviously ill matched as the *Elizabeth* of 1940 and a brand new *Queen*. Soon afterwards, further problems included the devastating six-week

The Queen Elizabeth *on her final sailing from New York in October 1968. Half of the student dormitory ship* Stevens *can be seen to the left. She was the former* Exochorda *of the American Export Lines and was berthed for some years at Hoboken, just across from the New York City skyline.*

British Maritime Strike in the spring of 1966. The *Queens*, temporarily withdrawn, sat idle alongside the Southampton Docks with a large assortment of passenger ships from various British firms. When the *Queen Elizabeth* set out on a special autumn Mediterranean cruise from New York, she carried a scant 600 passengers. It had all become cruelly obvious.

On 9 May 1967, bitter – yet in some cases unexpected – news came from the Cunard headquarters: 'The Chairman of Cunard yesterday pronounced the death sentence on the two most famous ships the world has known.' The *Queen Mary* would leave service almost immediately, at the conclusion of her current Atlantic season in September. The *Elizabeth* was to have one more lonely year, until October 1968. Cunard's two-ship express service was to end. The pioneering, imaginative plan from the late twenties that was finally put into

operation in 1947 was now anachronistic. The *Queens* had performed as a commercial team for twenty-one years, fourteen of which were financially profitable.

During 1967, just as it was announced that the *Queen Mary* and *Queen Elizabeth* were to be withdrawn, the entire Cunard Company shook. Captain Robin Woodall recalled that tense period. 'It was like a great crash. Suddenly, we dropped from 135 to 35 officers. There was a special panel within the Company that decided who went and who stayed. Beginning in that autumn, a member of the management would come aboard upon arrival at Southampton and discuss the future with each officer. I was the only survivor of ten officers then on the *Carinthia*. We suddenly had very few ships, in fact just three remaining liners – the *Elizabeth* until October 1968, and the cruise-ship sisters *Carmania* and *Franconia*. Of the hundred redundant officers, some went to cargo ships, some were paid-off and some simply retired. The only bright hope at this time was the new superliner then building on the Clyde. Fortunately, the traditionalist three-class *Q3* design had been abandoned in favour of a more practical blend of Atlantic liner and worldwide cruise ship. This was the *Q4* project or, as she is better known these days, the *QE2*.'

The gracious, beloved *Queen Mary* sailed from New York for the last time on 22 September 1967. The Port had never given such a busy send-off. Tugs, ferries, pleasure

The charred, twisted remains of the Seawise University, *the former* Queen Elizabeth, *at Hong Kong, in 1973.*

boats and charter craft escorted the liner to the Verazano-Narrows Bridge, at the mouth of the open Atlantic. Not only was the liner's sea-going career ending, but the event marked the official farewell to the heyday of transatlantic liner travel. Those northern sea lanes had grown quite empty, and in due course only the *Mary*'s successor, the *QE2*, would regularly ply the same service between New York, Cherbourg and Southampton. The old *Mary* was leaving behind a brilliant, unparalleled record: 1001 crossings, 3.7 million miles, 2.1 million passengers and revenues that totalled some $600 million. Except in those final years, she was a superb success, profitable, popular, totally distinguished.

Cunard had received several bids for the liner. The most persistent at first was made with the intention of converting her for the Australian immigrant run, between Southampton and Sydney via the Cape of Good Hope. She would have become an all-tourist class ship with some 2500 berths. Another firm wanted her for a floating hotel at Gibraltar. Officials of the City of New York thought of using her as a high school, docked along the Brooklyn waterfront. Japanese buyers wanted her for scrapping. Fortunately, however, the highest bid came from Long Beach, California, a city rich in harbour oil moneys. The historic ship was to be the perfect tourist attraction – museum, shopping centre, hotel and convention complex. Long Beach bought the *Mary* for $3.45 million.

Cunard chartered the liner to a New York City travel firm for a last, melancholy run to her new home in California. She sailed from Southampton, south to Lisbon and the Canaries, then across to Rio before rounding the South American continent and heading northward to Panama, Acapulco and, finally, Long Beach. It was a forty-day cruise, the longest commercial voyage of her career. She reached California on 9 December and, two days later, was stricken from the British Register of ships and transferred to local ownership. (Several years later, following her extensive conversion, the *Mary* was reclassified as a 'building' rather than a ship, as she is now permanently moored, unable to sail and draws all of her support from shore.)

The 'Hotel *Queen Mary* ' opened in May 1971, after nearly four years of rebuilding and refacing, which cost some $72 million. She was moved by a fleet of tugs from a local shipyard to her permanent berth, secured to the wharf by a series of cables, pipes and gangways, and surrounded by a specially-built breakwater. At first, there were mixed reviews. Many people were shocked to see the beloved *Mary* as a tourist gimmick. Her upper decks were lined with stands selling hamburgers and souvenirs. Others were grateful and delighted that she had been saved. Her lower decks were converted to a museum, which not only outlined the ship's career, but was a tribute

to ocean liners in general. She seemed to be the ideal liner for permanent preservation, the most illustrious and successful of them all.

Unfortuantely, by the late seventies, it became clear that the *Queen Mary* was not the great success that the City Fathers had predicted. In fact, she was again losing money. Although she was located in one of the world's busiest tourist areas, she often lost potential visitors to other attractions in southern California, such as Disney Land and the Hollywood film studios. Late in 1980, the City Government reconsidered the liner's future. At first, it was arranged for the Wrather Corporation to manage the former Cunarder, giving her the improvements required to safeguard her years ahead. Soon afterward, however, she was sold outright to Wrather. By 1982, the Corporation had spent $10 million in bringing back to life the complex around her. Part of the money was spent on the flying boat *Spruce Goose*, which has now been moored nearby. The *Mary* is now part of an improved, more attractive tourist site, which may, with luck, ensure her future.

Sadly, the *Queen Elizabeth* did not fare as well. After being retired in October 1968, with another well recorded send-off from New York, she was dispatched to Port Everglades, Florida (despite earlier suggestions of Philadelphia). It was intended that she should become the American East Coast version of what the *Queen Mary* was to be in California, hotel, convention centre and museum. However, on this occasion, Cunard wanted a share. They retained an 85 per cent interest in the project. In fact, the entire venture was a dismal failure. Amid mismanagement and financial difficulty, the *Elizabeth* sat at her Port Everglades berth, neglected, rusting, indeed very forlorn. Two years passed before, the liner was placed on the sales lists, in the summer of 1970. Again, Far Eastern scrappers were prominent among the bidders. Dismantling the liner and recycling her remains would have repaid the long, expensive tow to Taiwan. However, C Y Tung, who was then assembling one of the world's largest merchant fleets, had other ideas. He outbid the scrappers, partly for nostalgic reasons. His plan was to adapt the ship to form a combination of floating university and cruiseship. Mr Tung aroused interest among the press around the world when he spoke of plans to create 'a floating United Nations', with students of all races on board. The *Elizabeth* was registered in the Bahamas and renamed *Seawise University*, a play on Tung's initials, C Y.

The long-neglected, former *Queen* limped from Florida to a breakdown in the Caribbean, and eventually, via South Africa, to Hong Kong, Tung's working base, where she was to be refitted for $6 million. Much as in her postwar restoration off Gourock in 1946, the liner was anchored in Hong Kong Harbour with work barges and

Everett Viez Collection

ferries secured alongside for the transformation. At the end of this refit, set for early 1972, it was planned that she would go a Japanese shipyard for final dry docking and outfitting.

In the overall plan, Mr Tung intended to use his Orient Overseas Line passenger division as operating agents in sending the liner on a number of noted cruises. Advertising literature described such schedules as 'the rebirth of a legend'. A Circle Pacific Cruise, set to sail from Los Angeles on 24 April, was to visit Honolulu, Suva, Sydney (her first call there since 1942), Fremantle, Bali, Singapore, Hong Kong, Kobe, Yokohama, Honolulu, Vancouver, and return to Los Angeles, all in seventy-five days. Fares were planned at $30 per day, a

Cunard's Mauretania *was a refined, smaller version of the giant* Queen Elizabeth. *Many passengers preferred the former ship's slightly more intimate atmosphere.*

modest amount, even for the early seventies. Later on, the ship was meant to return to the North Atlantic, calling, in the course of another cruise, at New York.

Pathetically, the former *Elizabeth* was never to sail again. On 9 January 1972, the eve of her departure for the Japanese shipyard, she caught fire while still at anchor in Hong Kong Harbour. The fire spread quickly (there were, in fact, five different outbreaks), and the liner soon turned into a blistering, smoke-filled inferno. Nearly nine hundred guests, who were mostly refit workers and their families, escaped to safety, with only nine reported injuries and no fatalities. Arson was never eliminated as a cause of the blaze and some people regarded the fire as an act of sabotage, prompted by the clash between the Communist Chinese and the Taiwanese. The ship suffered structural damage under the weight of water pumped in to quench the fire and capsized on the following day, 10 January. She sat grotesquely in 43 feet of water at an angle of 65 degrees. One newspaper described her as a 'blackened corpse ... a mess of unrecognizable, tangled steel'. Although there were reports, particularly from the C Y Tung offices, that she would be refloated and made good, the damage was too great for repair to be financially possible. The liner was ruined. A Japanese salvage and scrap firm was called in, and within two years the wreck was gone. That second *Queen*, having begun her life with a mysterious maiden voyage, ended it with further mystery. The *Elizabeth* seems to have been deprived of that special touch of good fortune which protected the *Mary*, the luckiest of the last Atlantic liners, still in active retirement in Southern California.

The MAURETANIA

Completed in the summer of 1939 and then almost immediately called to war duty, the handsome *Mauretania* was finally released from service and returned to Cunard in September 1946. Thoroughly refitted, she was back on the North Atlantic luxury run by April 1947. For most of the year, she sailed between Southampton, Le Havre, Cóbh and New York. Her Southampton-New York crossing took seven days. In the slack winter months, she travelled south from New York to the Caribbean on luxury crusies.

The *Mauretania* was intended also to serve each summer as a 'relief ship' when the *Queens* underwent their summer drydocking, usually in late July or early August. Captain Ashton-Irvine disputes this role. 'While the *Mauretania* was a very fine "sea boat" and certainly a scaled-down version of the *Elizabeth*, she was not really an express liner. She simply did not have the extra speed to run a Southampton-New York sailing in five days. At best, one of her regular seven-day passages was scheduled to substitute for the *Queen* that missed the weekly balance in midsummer.'

The *Mauretania* remained as one of the Atlantic Ferry's most popular liners until the early sixties, just as the full effects of the jet invasion were being felt. Captain Robin Woodall did a voyage in the liner in the summer of 1961. 'She was an absolutely gorgeous old girl, but was slipping fast. On an August westbound crossing, which was usually an absolute sell-out voyage, we had 407 passengers [1140 was capacity], 141 tons of cargo and all with a crew of 604. It was all becoming more and more unprofitable – and

The Mauretania was repainted in so-called 'cruising green' at the end of 1962. In her final years, she was used more and more for cruise sailings.

more and more obvious.'

In 1962, she was repainted in Cunard's so-called 'cruising green', with the intention that she would spend far more time in luxury cruise service than as a three-class ship. In the following year, in rather a rushed scheme for survival, she was assigned to a new Cunard service in the Mediterranean, sailing between Naples, Genoa, Cannes, Gibraltar and New York, but looked dated beside the sleek Italian liners. The new service failed, the *Mauretania* lost money, and her owners sent her on more and more cruises. Captain Harvey Smith recalled the liner in those final, desperate years. 'She was ageing and just couldn't pay. She used to miss transatlantic voyages simply through the lack of passengers. I often remember her just sitting at the Southampton Docks, just next to the Ocean Terminal, laid-up for weeks between crossings.'

Eventually, in a rather anxious search for revenue, she was even given out to charter, and on one occasion carried guests to the opening of a new refinery at Milford Haven. The trip was a last echo of the earlier grandeur of the North Atlantic crossings, with gold watches offered as bingo prizes. Like so many of the Atlantic fleet, the *Mauretania* had fallen on very hard times. Her career ended in November 1965, when, some ten days after her last arrival at Southampton, she left for a scrapyard at Inverkeithing in Scotland.

The CARONIA

After World War II, Cunard began planning for yet another major liner, smaller than the two *Queens*, but more compatible with the *Mauretania*, which was seen as something of a loner in the Company's passenger fleet. Then, in a flash of inspiration, Cunard caught a glimpse of the future – a new liner designed almost totally for cruising. This ship emerged in 1948 as the *Caronia*, a liner intended to sail any ocean, any latitude, for any length of time. Alternatively, with a few doors closed and notices posted, she could serve on the regular North Atlantic passenger run, should the occasion arise. Her keel plates were first laid down in 1946, and in October the following year Princess Elizabeth and the Duke of Edinburgh travelled to the John Brown yard at Clydebank for the launch. The *Caronia* was the biggest liner to come off the ways for British use since the end of the war, and the Government used the occasion as a symbol of national recovery (even if the country was still suffering from shortages).

The new liner had a number of design innovations. No other Cunarder had toilet facilities adjoining all the

Eric Ashton-Irvine Collection

cabins, a feature which was particularly dear to wealthy American cruise passengers. She had a permanent outdoor pool, a facility cherished in the tropics. Internally, she was a scaled-down version of the *Queen Elizabeth*, but managed something of a clubby luxury. Her appearance was sleek – a towering tripod mast and one huge funnel on an otherwise serenely balanced hull. She was painted in four shades of green (which inspired her best remembered nickname, 'the Green Goddess'), allegedly for heat resistance in warmer climates, but possibly more in an attempt at distinction. Captain Ashton-Irvine recalled the secrecy surrounding the decision to paint the newest Cunarder in green: 'Early in 1948, I quite accidentally came across a marine artist, who had a special commission from the chairman of Cunard. It was the new ship, then still building on he Clyde. I was one of the very few to see the special colouring. The worried artist asked that I immediately forget what I had seen. I suspect that the painting was something of a test, just to see what an all-green 34,000-tonner would look like.'

Brenton Jenkins, then a junior purser, was aboard the *Caronia* for her sea trials off Scotland in the autumn of 1948. 'On the speed trials, we had the Duke of Edinburgh aboard. He was representing Princes Elizabeth, who was about to give birth to Prince Charles in London. Already, much publicity surrounded the ship, particularly about her standard of luxury and intended worldwide cruising. She was nicknamed "the millionaires' yacht".'

The new ship began service at the beginning of 1949 and immediately went into cruising, first from New York to the Caribbean. As a cruiser, the *Caronia* generally attracted the well-to-do. Her voyages were as long as

A portion of Caronia*'s staff posed on her bow.*

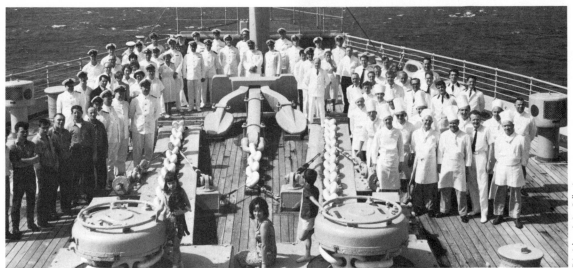

When completed in late 1948, the Caronia *was distinctive as the largest post-war British liner and also as the biggest liner to be fitted with a single mast and a single funnel. For some years, her stack actually ranked as one of the largest afloat.*

they were diverse: around the world, in the Pacific, or around Africa in January, the Mediterranean and the Black Sea in spring, the North Cape and Scandinavia in summer, and the Mediterranean again in the autumn. She was to be overhauled each year in the late autumn and then cross to New York in January, usually via several Caribbean ports, to repeat her annual cruise pattern.

There are many recollections of the *Caronia*. She was unique, even to the Cunard fleet, and left a strong impression. Captain Ashton-Irvine was among those who thought very highly of her. 'She was a superb ship for her time and purpose. She was the result of the continuous designs and ideas that came from the Liverpool head office. Cunard had a design team that produced hundreds of passenger ship proposals. There was even one for a 100,000-tonner with space for 4000 passengers!'

The *Caronia* had the extraordinary ratio of 640 crew members for her 600 cruise passengers. Captain Ashton-Irvine felt that this provided her competitive edge. 'The crew made her. They were mostly older, very loyal staff members. For example, during the long cruises, at the end of a day's touring ashore, the stewards and stewardesses would welcome the returning passengers with stateroom tea for the ladies, cocktails for the gentlemen and then draw their hot baths. It was like coming home to a luxurious manor house. Our most loyal passenger, Clara MacBeth of New York, lived aboard the *Caronia* for nearly fifteen years, spent $20 million in fares and retained the same cabin steward for every voyage.'

Len Houghton served aboard the *Caronia* for eight years. 'Her long, expensive cruises lured a special

Some masquerade ball contestants on the Caronia's *world cruise of 1965.*

on Miss MacBeth in her stateroom. It was a very rare courtesy accorded to a passenger, but then she had been living aboard the liner for years. Another event, during the summer North Cape cruises, was the *Caronia* football match in Bergen between the staffs of the ship's Balmoral and Sandringham Restaurants. First, there would be a parade, which all the passengers would attend. The Captain and Staff Captain – as captains of the opposing teams – drove in open landaus. Even the Mayor of Bergen would attend. There was a silver cup for the winning team.'

The *Caronia* was not without her problems, however. To Captain Woodall, she was a 'crank ship, a tender ship. We were always having trouble with her stability and draft.' Captain Harvey Smith had similar recollections. 'From an operational standpoint, the *Caronia* was always

clientele. We had women on board, like Miss MacBeth and Miss Jones, who joined the ninety-day world cruise in January, then the six-week spring "Meddy" [Mediterranean] and then finished with the summer North Cape. When we reached Southampton, they went up to London, to the Dorchester or Savoy, spent several weeks there and then crossed homeward in one of the *Queens*. [Return first class passage in any Cunarder was included in *Caronia* cruise fares when her voyages ended at Southampton.]

Captain Harvey Smith also has fond recollections of the cruising *Caronia*. 'Mostly, I recall the many older ladies that simply lived aboard – some for months, others for several years. I especially recall one old dear who drank a bottle of brandy a day. You could always tell the level she had reached by the tilt of her bright red wig. The *Caronia* was the most expensive ship of her day. A suite for the ninety-day world cruise in the late fifties could cost as much as $28,000. Even operating the *Caronia* was pure luxury; no expense was too great. We would fly out fresh lobsters to meet the ship at some remote port or, as on one Far Eastern cruise, we even flew in fresh milk from northern Australia.'

A ship such as the *Caronia* had her special rituals and occasions. Captain Robin Woodall recalled that as a young officer he had had among his Sunday duties 'to call difficult to handle. The much larger *Queens* were far easier by comparison. We always had tremendous steering problems with her. In April 1958, during her world cruise, she caught the wind, rammed a lighthouse on the breakwater at Yokohama and pushed it into the sea. We had to go to the big American Naval Base at Yokosuka for repairs. Her wide funnel was another problem. It too always gave us wind problems.'

By the late fifties, the *Caronia*'s sparkle had begun to dim. She achieved a rather dubious position as the first big Cunarder to lose money. One report hinted that she had an enormous appetite for expensive fuel oils, another that she was mechanically faulty and therefore required frequent repairs, and still another that her luxurious housekeeping costs exceeded her income. Whatever the case, Cunard did elect to underwrite her for some years,

since she was something of a 'prestige ship'.

In 1967, Cunard's financial woes were little short of overwhelming. Almost all of the Company's liners were in trouble, ageing, expensive ships competing with jet aircraft and newer liners. The *Caronia* was certainly not excluded. Captain Smith was with her in the end. 'She had lost that devoted following. On her final cruise, in September 1967, we carried only 340 passengers – out of a possible 600 and then with a crew of 550. I also sailed in her

The last of the White Star Liners, the Britannic, *sailing from New York on the morning of 10 July 1958. It was the Port's busiest ocean liner day since the thirties. Eight other liners can be seen in the background: from left to right, the* Ocean Monarch, Queen Elizabeth, Olympia, United States, America, Constitution *and* Vulcania.

Richard K Morse Collection

on her final Cunard voyage, going empty from New York to Southampton. Laid-up, she then went on the sales lists.'

While she was lying idle at Southampton for a time, there was a strong rumour that she would be sold to Yugoslav entrepreneurs for use as a floating hotel along the Dalmatian coast. However, a Greek businessman, Andrew Kostantinides, bought the liner and changed her name – first to *Columbia*, then *Caribia*. She was re-registered in Panama before going to Piraeus and then Naples for a less-than-thorough refit. Her return to cruise service in February 1969 was for two-week jaunts from New York to the Caribbean. After an outbreak of fire in the engine room off Martinique on the second trip, the passengers had to be flown home and the crippled ship was towed back to Manhattan. There began five years of wrangling, a slow, undignified end for the former *Caronia*. First, her 'mixed' crew sued over unpaid wages and then the City government saw her as a safety risk while docked in port. Mr Kostantinides went to court, and won. New York had to provide a safe anchorage.

Idleness breeds trouble, even for elderly ocean liners. In the following five years, the *Caribia* loitered about the Port of New York. She sat, shifting from anchorage to one pier after another, seemingly unwanted. Once, the sleek, new *QE2* greeted her old Cunard relative with three blasts as she slipped past. There was no reply. Huge sheets of paint began to peel from the *Caribia*'s hull and upper decks into the Hudson. There was trouble with the port authorities, Coast Guard and Fire Department, with lingering crew members and repairers, creditors and their sheriffs. The worst embarrassment came when she was docked illegally at a City pier and received a parking ticket from the New York City Police Department. Hope for her revival dwindled. In early 1974, while the ship was berthed at Pier 56, itself a former Cunard terminal, her ballrooms, lounges, staterooms and galleys were opened to an interested and nostalgic public. Price tags were put on all the fittings, from large sections of bruised wood panelling to battered stainless steel from the galleys. Collectors walked ashore with stuffy smoking-room chairs, monogrammed crockery, and even telephones from the suites. The old *Caronia* was stripped practically bare.

Kiki Kogelnik, an artist, decorator and owner of New York City's One Fifth Restaurant, attended the *Caribia* auction. 'I was told that the ship was actually designed in the late thirties, but built in the late forties. She was, in fact, late Art Deco. The most basic change between those two decades was to use much lighter woods. I came ashore with two mirrors, china and some table linens.' A year later, though the *Caribia* had long since departed, a quantity of her furnishings and fittings still remained at the same West Side pier, some of them in containers and crates, others exposed to New York's changeable climate.

Kiki Kogelnik bought some decorative items relatively cheaply and conceived the idea of the One Fifth Restaurant in 1976. 'Using the *Caronia* items seemed a natural, especially since the nostalgic interest in Art Deco and ocean liners was just then beginning to blossom. We even thought of naming it the "Caronia Restaurant".' The entire ambience grew from the use of furnishings from the ship, and the clientele included many former passengers.

In April 1974, the *Caribia* left New York, under the guidance of a powerful ocean-going tug, bound for the scrapyards of Taiwan. At Honolulu, she was said to be taking on water, but it was a mild leak that seemed to warrant little attention, and the slow tow to the East continued. Seeking refuge at Guam during a tropical storm, the tug lost control on the entry into the harbour. The *Caribia* was thrown against a rocky breakwater and broke in three. Local authorities rushed in and dismantled the remains on the spot.

The BRITANNIC

The *Britannic* never seemed quite to fit in with the rest of Cunard's post-war passenger fleet. She looked different, with her long, almost squat profile, and her name lacked the customary ending. Perhaps most obviously, her twin funnels did not bear the usual Cunard black and orange-red colours but always retained the buff and black of her original owners, the White Star Line.

The *Britannic* and her near-sister, the *Georgic*, joined Cunard in 1934, as part of the merger that created Cunard-White Star Limited, the title used until 1950, when the company reverted to the name of Cunard. They were the last vessels for the distinguished, but often troubled White Star firm, whose fleet had included the *Majestic*, the *Olympic*, and the *Titanic*. At the end of the World War II, the *Britannic* was restored to look just as before on the outside. It seemed a wise decision to continue the White Star colours on her short twin stacks (the forward of which was dummy), as Cunard's colours would not have suited their shape. Her passenger accommodation was decorated in traditional style, whereas the *Georgic* had displayed the more modernistic elements of Art Deco. Among the items brought from wartime storage were several fine carpets from the pre-war *Aquitania*. The passenger berthing was modified to an established, post-war design, with 429 in first class and 564 in tourist. Otherwise, the only notable feature of the *Britannic*'s return to service was a collision in New York's Ambrose Channel on 1 June 1950, with the freighter *Pioneer Land*.

Captain Harvey Smith served aboard the *Britannic* as a young junior officer. 'We worked a monthly schedule, sailing between Liverpool and New York [occasionally via Halifax on some westbound trips] and with a call at

Skyfotos

Cóbh in each direction. Usually, we'd put into New York on Saturdays and then remain along the north side of Pier 92, at West 52nd Street, until Thursday or Friday. In addition to the passengers, we had seven hatches of cargo to work, which often included automobiles, whiskies and grain. Each winter, the *Britannic* would make a Mediterranean-Black Sea cruise which lasted roughly sixty days, sailing out of New York, but terminating at Southampton. The cruise fares, which began at $1600 in the late fifties, included return first class passage in any Cunarder, even the *Queens*. On these cruises, we carried an older crowd. There was no air-conditioning nor an outdoor pool, but it didn't matter. The *Britannic* had a club-like following of loyal passengers, who travelled for travel's sake.'

While the *Britannic* was generally considered to be a 'good, solid sea boat', she began to show signs of old age in the late fifties. Captain Smith was aboard for her final transatlantic season in 1960. 'In June, while two days inbound to New York, we found we had a broken crankshaft. At first, we thought of towing her back to Britain for repairs. However, it was later decided to continue to New York. The repair job that followed then rated as the biggest of its kind ever done at an ordinary liner berth. The liner was docked on the south side of Pier 90, often just across from one of the *Queens*, and with many of her crew sent home. It took two weeks just to cut out the fractured crankshaft – a near superhuman task that meant working twenty-four hours a day for the crews from Todd Shipyards, who were supplied from trucks and barges. A special counterbalance had to be placed aboard once the shaft was removed. The final repairs took another nine weeks. The original, thirty-year-old Burmeister & Wain diesels were the largest ever put into a liner.'

Even during her last months, in the autumn of 1960, the *Britannic* faced trouble. Captain Smith recalled, 'We were hard hit by a British seamen's strike, but managed to keep

After heavy damages during World War II, the Georgic was rebuilt considerably, retaining just a single funnel and a stumped forward mast.

sailing. We somehow provided the same high standards of food and service in first class, but had to make do with self-service in tourist class.' Soon afterwards, the *Britannic*, by then the very last White Star survivor, went to the scrappers at Inverkeithing in Scotland. Cunard had seriously considered building a 27,000-ton replacement, especially for the Liverpool trade, but the idea never came to pass. Instead, since the Canadian liner trade was beginning to slump, the *Sylvania* was swung over to the New York run, beginning in April 1961. For several years, she was the replacement to the *Britannic*.

The GEORGIC

Like her slightly older near-sister *Britannic*, the *Georgic* was taken over for troop-carrying, which began in March 1940. While the earlier ship's record was accident-free, the *Georgic*'s military service was rather short. John Havers was at Port Suez, in July 1941, just as the grey-painted *Georgic* arrived with troops. 'She was at anchor and hit in a night time air raid, on the 14th. A bomb went down her elevator shaft and started fires. Crippled, burned and twisted, she was almost completely sunk. To most observers at the time, she was finished, quite useless to the war effort. But, with old-fashioned persistence, she was gradually salvaged and then taken to Port Sudan [later to Karachi and finally to Bombay] for mostly temporary repairs and patching-up. In January 1943, she began the long, slow voyage homeward to Belfast [the Harland & Wolff yard] for thorough rebuilding. Those of us who remembered and helped to save her at Port Suez received an encouraging telegram after she left Bombay: "I am doing 15 knots to Capetown. Thank you and congratulations".'

The *Georgic* would never be the same again. She was

sold outright to the British Government, to be operated by the Ministry of War, but under Cunard-White Star management. She resumed sailing in December 1944 as a greatly altered ship. Her forward dummy funnel had gone, as had the mainmast, and the foremast was cut down. Steward Len Houghton served aboard her at the very end of the war. He remembers that her beams and other parts were still twisted, even after her rebuilding as a 'super trooper'. Damage from the explosion and subsequent fire was still quite evident. 'We nicknamed her "the corrugated lung".'

The *Georgic* was altered by Palmer's on Tyneside in September 1948 into an emigrant ship. Two years later, she began a series of peak season charters to Cunard to assist with the booming North Atlantic trade. Len Houghton was again on board. 'Although she had her White Star colours, she was only under charter to Cunard and sailed only in the summer months. The passengers lived mostly in dormitories. We sailed between Southampton or Liverpool, Le Havre, Cóbh and then across to Halifax and New York. We had immigrants westbound and budget tourists and students eastbound. The restaurant on board was like a cafeteria. Everyone carried trays. Her general condition was such, however, that the London surveyors would not let her sail the North Atlantic in winter. Instead, she then worked the Australian immigrant run out to Sydney via the Suez.'

Cunard never advertised the *Georgic* as one of their regular passenger ships. In fact, she was placed below all of the Company's passenger ships, even the rather elderly single-stackers on the Canadian trade. To Captain Ashton-Irvine, the post-war *Georgic* was a 'third rate motel'. She finished her last Cunard charter in October 1955, and then completed a final stint on the Australian route. In February 1956, she went to the breakers at Faslane in Scotland.

The MEDIA and the PARTHIA

The sisterships *Media* and *Parthia* were unique to the post-war Cunard fleet. They were the Company's only combination liners, carrying 250 first class passengers as well as six holds of cargo. They were originally designed as twelve passenger freighters in 1946, for the Brocklebank Line, a Cunard subsidiary. The building orders were divided. The contract for the first went to an old friend, John Brown at Clydebank, while the other went to Harland & Wolff at Belfast, the first ever for a Cunarder. Then, soon after the start of construction, the designs were reworked. The ships were transferred directly to Cunard and modified for transatlantic passenger-cargo service. Cunard directors thought that such unassuming ships might be well suited to the monthly Liverpool–New York trade, and indeed they were fairly

successful in their dual purpose, but the company did not again make use of such combinations in design.

The *Media* appeared in August 1947 as the first new passenger ship ordered for the Atlantic run after World War II. Captain Harvey Smith later served aboard the *Parthia*, which followed in April 1948. 'This ship and her sister were totally unlike the other large Cunarders. Cargo was very much of a priority. Outwards from Liverpool, we took whiskies and cars, usually 100–125 per trip and mostly Rolls Royces and Jaguars. Homewards, we often made a special call at Norfolk, Virginia, to load tobacco. Being basically cargo liners with rather minimal passenger quarters, these ships had long turn-around stays in port and therefore were terribly costly. They were also very poor sea boats. In fact, we specifically tested the *Media* in 1952 for the first pair of fin stabilizers on the notorious North Atlantic. The results showed great promise and resulted in stabilizers being fitted to almost all of the larger liners. They were even fitted to the giant *Queens*.'

Len Houghton also remembered these Cunard sister-ships. 'For cargo, we often carried thoroughbred horses from Ireland to New York, where they were then trans-shipped to Kentucky. One officer used to log all of the manure for his garden back home.'

By the late fifties, within ten years of their creation, the pair were no longer practical. Freighters with twelve passenger berths were more efficient and profitable. In fact, Cunard was building a new freighter fleet and the *Media* and the *Parthia* no longer suited the Company plans. In 1961, the sisters were put on the sales lists. Captain Smith was with the *Parthia* at the very end of her Cunard career. 'She was hard hit by a strike while in Liverpool's Gladstone Drydock with her bottom plates off. Subsequently, she sat there for 4½ months.'

The *Media* was promptly sold to Italy's Cogedar Line, the Compagnia Genovese d'Armamento SpA, for one of those near incredible, very radical conversions. Taken to Genoa, she was cut down to the hull. A new passenger liner emerged. She was even lengthened with a new bow and stern, reaching to 557 feet, which was 26 feet over her original length. Most of the cargo holds were gutted and replaced with passenger accommodation. The upper decks were built anew and filled out most of the ship. Within a year's alterations, her capacity had increased from 250 first class to 1320 tourist class.

Renamed *Flavia*, she was put on a round-the-world tourist run, sailing from Bremerhaven, Rotterdam, Southampton and Genoa through the Suez Canal and then onwards to Fremantle, Melbourne and Sydney. Homewards, she mostly sailed by way of the south Pacific, Panama and the Caribbean. When the Cogedar Line was bought by another Italian company, the Costa Line, in 1968, the *Flavia* was restyled as a cruise ship, mainly sailing on short trips between Miami, Nassau and Freeport. In February 1982, with reports that her original turbines had finally become faulty, she was sold to Chinese buyers. Renamed *Flavian*, she was sent to Hong Kong and has been laid-up ever since.

The *Parthia* was sold, also in 1961, to other British owners, the New Zealand Shipping Company. Refitted as the *Remuera*, she was placed for a time on the long haul to New Zealand via Panama and the Caribbean. Sold to the Eastern & Australian Steamship Company in 1964, she became their *Aramac* for a triangular service which ran from Australia to Japan via Hong Kong, returning via some Pacific islands. She was finally scrapped on Taiwan in 1970.

Unusual in the Cunard passenger fleet, the combination liner Media *and her sistership, the* Parthia, *carried only 250 first class passengers. Built in 1947, the* Media *was the first Atlantic liner to have fin stabilizers, which were fitted in 1952.*

Eric Ashton-Irvine Collection

CHAPTER TWO

UNDER THE TRICOLORE

The DE GRASSE

The Compagnie Générale Transatlantique, more commonly referred to as the French Line, was in a particularly weak position at the end of World War II. All but one of its notable pre-war liners were gone. The *Lafayette* had burned out at Le Havre in May 1938, the superb *Paris* met a similar end at the same port some eleven months later, the very modern *Champlain* was mined in July 1940, and then, perhaps the saddest loss, the brilliant *Normandie* caught fire and sank at her New York pier in February 1942. All that remained was the celebrated *Île De France*, which had been taken by the Allies during the war, but which was not to be fully restored until the summer of 1949. Otherwise, there was one smallish cabin liner that survived, the 17,700-ton *De Grasse*. For two years from the summer of 1947, she alone maintained the French Line's luxury service to New York.

The *De Grasse* had been withdrawn from transatlantic service in the late summer of 1939 and laid up at Bordeaux, supposedly in safety from the threatening Nazis. In fact, she was captured some months later, during the fall of France, and afterwards used as an accommodation ship. She seems not to have sailed during the war years. On 30 August 1944, as the German army began its retreat, the ship was deliberately sunk by depth charges and abandoned in shallow waters. One year later to the day, the French raised her. The repairs and restoration were to take another two years.

The *De Grasse* sailed alone until she was joined by the much larger *Île de France* in July 1949, and the giant *Liberté* in August 1950. She remained on the North Atlantic until October 1951, when she was transferred to the Le Havre-West Indies route, just as the new *Flandre* was to come into service. The *De Grasse* was paired with another pre-war survivor, the 13,300-ton *Colombie*. However, she was soon displaced again by new tonnage, namely the *Flandre*'s sister-ship, the 19,800-ton *Antilles* (1953). Without further work, the *De Grasse* came out of service that April.

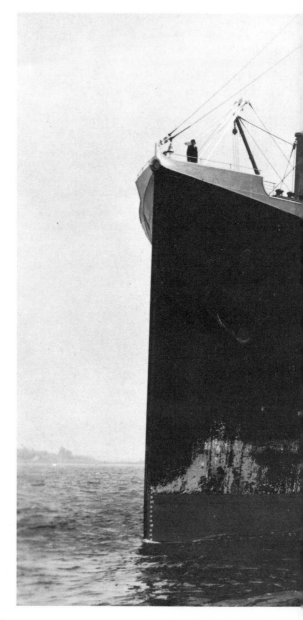

The Île de France inbound at New York for the first time since wartime trooping, in July 1949.

Just as the tricolour was being hauled down, Canadian Pacific Steamships found themselves in rather desperate need of passenger tonnage. Their *Empress of Canada* had just burned and sunk at her Liverpool dock, and the company expected 1953 to be a busy year for the transatlantic ships because the Coronation was to take place in London. The *De Grasse* was hurriedly purchased. With very little alteration, she raised the British flag and became the *Empress of Australia*, immediately starting on the Liverpool run to Quebec City and Montreal. The ship remained with Canadian Pacific until 1956, when she was again replaced by new tonnage. She was bought by the Italian Grimaldi-Siosa Lines. Renamed *Venezuela*, she was refitted extensively for the transport of West Indian immigrants, sailing from Genoa and Naples. She survived until March 1962, when she ran aground at Cannes, suffering damage that was beyond economic repair. That summer, she went to the breakers at La Spezia, Italy.

The ÎLE DE FRANCE
While never the biggest or fastest of Atlantic liners, the *Île de France* is still thought of as one of the dream boats of all

Victor Scrivens Collection

Victor Scrivens Collection

For two years, between 1947 and 1949, the smallish De Grasse *maintained the French Line's luxury service on the North Atlantic. Originally built with two thin stacks, she was rebuilt after war damages with a single, wide funnel.*

time. She was distinctive, stylish, magnificently decorated, and very popular, but was noted most of all for superb service and cuisine. She was often described as 'the cheeriest way to cross the Atlantic'. Her name was mentioned in songs, novels and countless news features. Like Cunard's original *Mauretania* of 1907, the *Queen Mary* and another grand Frenchman, the *Normandie*, the *Île* had that rare combination of ingredients that created the perfect ship.

The *Île* was engaged in war duty for the Allied forces until September 1945. She then turned to 'austerity service', sailing between Cherbourg and New York, as well as to troubled French Indo-China. It was not until the spring of 1947 that she returned to the Penhoet yard at St Nazaire for massive restoration and rebuilding. She inherited some of the *Normandie*'s exquisite furnishings, had her three original stacks replaced by two of more modern proportions, and recovered much of her former glamour. She steamed into New York Harbour in the summer of 1949, on what amounted to a second maiden voyage, to renewed praise.

The *Île* was still very impressive, assuredly one of the finest liners in post-war service. British travel writer and passenger ship expert C M Squarey wrote at the time of her recommissioning, 'Here, indeed, is a romantic ship, a dramatic ship and a stately ship. Striding up what must be the world's longest gangway [at Le Havre], I entered the grand foyer of this ship and, in two blinks, sensed that certain vitality and zest for life that is a product of the French temperament and French way of living. Among the things that struck me were the bellboys in their smart red rig; the boulevard effect of the promenade deck with its rows of bright red deck chairs; the enormous, but

beautifully proportioned cinema, showing technicolor films; the orchestra playing at embarkation time – no union nonsense there; the original design of the cabin class lounge with its curved mezzanine floor, clever and effective; iced water piped around the ship; the corners leading off the alleyways to the cabins that were rubber-lined so that trunks do not damage the paintwork; plug-in facilities lock-controlled so that the steward can check against the wrong voltage razor, etc., being used; mirrors and angular lighting that are so effective in the cabin class saloon. No woman, who considers she has an atom of attraction, will ever use the lift to the first class restaurant, but instead will delight in wending her way down the most elegant staircase ever built into a ship, to sweep into a saloon that is of most dignified design and is so faultlessly furnished; I trow that no man or woman will ever perpetuate the atrocity of dining in this lovely setting in other than the right rig.'

The kitchens were as good as they had been before the war. It was often said that more seagulls followed the *Île de France* than any other ship. The American epicure and author, Craig Claiborne, recently recalled his first discovery of haute cuisine aboard the *Île*, during a tourist-class crossing in 1949. Passenger Michael Cohn was on board a few years later. 'My most vivid memories are of the food. Even in tourist class, we had selections such as skate in black butter. There was even onion soup at breakfast.'

The *Île* settled down to profitable service, teamed with the larger *Liberté* and the tourist-oriented *Flandre*, but still uniquely favoured and still news worthy. On 26 July 1956, while outward bound off Nantucket, she rescued 753 survivors from the sinking *Andrea Doria*. In October of the

Germany's former Europa, *now restyled as the* USS Europa *for the Americans, is seen underway in September 1945, her first voyage since late 1939. Soon afterward, she would be handed over to the French as reparations.*

The Liberté *had a very powerful, romantic appearance. In 1945, her tall funnels were heightened even further by added dome tops.*

same year, she was lashed by a giant Atlantic storm, which flooded six passenger cabins and dented her superstructure. She went aground off Martinique during a Caribbean cruise in February 1957. Her passengers had to be taken ashore and flown home while the liner was towed all the way to Newport News, Virginia for repairs.

The Île, with her passenger lists at last declining, reached retirement in November 1958. The French Line's Paris offices were faced with a decision over their ship's future. The Sheraton Corporation talked of turning her into a hotel, somewhere in the Caribbean. There were suggestions of preserving her as a museum, and one enthusiast wanted to have her cut down and sailed into the heart of Paris. She was eventually sold to the highest bidder, a Japanese firm of scrappers, who sailed her out to Osaka with a crew of sixty as the *Furanzu* (France) *Maru*. Her end was not as tranquil or as dignified as the French Line would have liked. The Japanese chartered the former Île for $4000 per day to a Hollywood film company. Robert Stack, Dorothy Malone and hundreds of others climbed aboard to make *The Last Voyage*, a dramatic account of an aged transpacific liner's final sailing. Technicians blasted away at the lounges, gutted some of

The Embarkation Hall on board the Liberté.

the former suites, and even released the forward funnel into the deckhouse. Was there no respect for an Atlantic legend? The French succeeded in a court action to have the obvious red-and-black funnels at least partially disguised. Months later, with the filming over, the *Île* went back to Osaka for dismantling.

The LIBERTÉ

In May 1945, invading American forces entered the port of Bremerhaven and raced for the docks. Their prize was the third largest liner then afloat, the 49,000-ton *Europa* of the North German Lloyd. She had been one of the queens of the North Atlantic in the thirties, of the same select group as her near sister, *Bremen*, and the *Rex*, *Conte di Savoia*, *Normandie* and *Queen Mary*. They rivalled one another in speed, size, style, cuisine and service. When World War II erupted in the late summer of 1939, the *Europa* was sailing for New York, but received orders to reverse course and returned to her Bremerhaven pier.

The American soldiers who boarded her nearly six years later saw little to reflect the opulence of earlier days. Instead, they found a neglected vessel which had been held from the sea and seemingly passed by during the war. Yellowing signs were posted throughout all decks for the benefit of Nazi troops who had never arrived aboard. Great doors were cut in her sides for an invasion of Britain that had never happened. As the war regressed for the Germans, the likelihood of any role for the *Europa*

The sitting room of the Arromanches Suite on board the Liberté.

diminished. Near the end, an order was issued from Berlin to destroy the liner, but was not carried out.

The Americans seized the ship and quickly reclassified her as AP-177, the USS *Europa*. After cleaning and some brief trials, she was ready to return to sea duty. She left Bremerhaven for New York on her first troop crossing in September 1945, with 4300 soldiers and 960 crew on board. She was then given a relatively short forty-five-day overhaul at the big dry dock in Bayonne, New Jersey, within the confines of New York Harbour. She was fitted out to repatriate troops from Europe, at a rate which was calculated from her size and service speed of 28 knots at 20,000 soldier-passengers per month.

The USS *Europa* completed only a few voyages before the serious problem of fires emerged. The outbreaks seemed unending and one raged a full nine hours. On another day, five different fires had to be put out. A commission of inquiry discovered that the Germans had removed many materials and fittings as shortages developed in the last months of the war and provided inferior replacements. Furthermore, some serious cracks were uncovered in the hull. Unwanted, the ship passed to the United Nations Reparations Commission, who allotted her to the French in place of the superliner, *Normandie*, lost in 1942.

She was renamed *Liberté* (although *Lorraine* had been the first choice), hoisted the tricolour, and then ran into more trouble. Docked at Le Havre, during the very early stages of refitting in December 1946, she was ripped from her moorings by a gale and thrown against the sunken hull of the *Paris*, which had been left untouched since she burned and sank at her pier in April 1939. A gash in the *Liberté*'s bottom caused her to settle, although fortunately in an upright position. Restoration work was temporarily put aside as salvage became the priority. Eventually, the hole was plugged and the ship towed to the Penhoet-yard at St Nazaire.

To become a French liner in the stunning tradition of the *Normandie* and the *Île de France* meant nearly three years of heavy cosmetic surgery for the *Liberté*. She emerged in the summer of 1950 as a grand example of late Art Deco, fitted with sumptuous public rooms, a wonderful array of first-class suites and apartments, and a fine restaurant. She could cross between Le Havre and New York, with a call at Southampton or Plymouth, in just six days. Along her decks walked Elizabeth Taylor, Greta Garbo, European aristocrats, and commuting tycoons. Even after the jet

Another first class cabin on the Liberté, *although this is an inside room.*

invasion in the late fifties, the *Liberté* maintained her following.

The original, flattish German funnels were altered in 1954. New domed tops lent a towering, almost top-heavy appearance, which probably added to romantic images of the enormous size of ocean liners. In the late fifties, as the *Liberté* returned to St Nazaire for her annual maintenance, she passed by her eventual replacement, the 66,000-ton *France*, which was to come into service in early 1962. The *Liberté* sailed from New York for the last time in November 1961, surrounded by a flotilla of tugs and spraying fireboats. At nearly thirty-two years old, she was leaving a distinguished memory. Although there was some talk of using her as a floating hotel at the Seattle World's Fair in 1962, she was broken up at La Spezia, Italy, by the summer of that year.

The FLANDRE

Like the companies who were their rivals on the North Atlantic, the French fleet also increased their passenger tonnage after the war. The first passenger vessels were built for the French colonial service to North Africa, through Marseilles. Then came the designs for two larger liners, one for the New York route, the other for the West Indies run, and both very alike, except that the first, the *Flandre*, had a low, almost squat funnel and a black hull, while the *Antilles* had a higher stack and an all-white hull. Visually, there was little chance of confusing the pair at that time.

The *Flandre* was launched on 31 October 1951, at the Ateliers et Chantiers de France yard at Dunkirk. She was intended basically as an 'intermediate, relief ship', which, though attractively furnished and well served, was not considered to be a serious partner to the much larger *Île de France* and *Liberté*. Her accommodation was first arranged in a rather unusual fashion, with a large number of berths (402) in first class, 389 in cabin class and rather fewer (97) in tourist class. By 1953, however, this was amended to 339 in first, 285 in tourist and 100 interchangeable, according to demand. Further changes two years later resulted in 232 in first class and 511 in tourist. The last figures seemed the most fitting for the mid-fifties Atlantic.

The *Flandre* left Le Havre on her maiden voyage on 23 July 1952. During the seven-day crossing, serious electrical failures and fuel pump disorders caused a loss of power, which was most unfortunate on a maiden crossing, and the ship had to be towed into New York Harbour for her fireboat reception. The French were mortified. The local stevedores, notably lacking in sympathy, afterwards referred to the liner as 'the Flounder'. After returning to Le Havre, the *Flandre* was sent back to her builders, who were still under contract to overhaul and repair her mechanical systems. She spent ten months at the shipyard and did not resume her sailing schedule until April 1953.

Herbert G Frank, Jr Collection

The Flandre *had the misfortune to break down on her maiden voyage, had to be towed into New York Harbour and thereafter became known to the local dockers as 'the Flounder'.*

The *Flandre* became a popular, friendly ship. She ran between Le Havre, Southampton or Plymouth, and New York between April and November, and sailed with her sister *Antilles* from Le Havre to the West Indies in the winter. After the retirement of both the *Île de France* and the *Liberté*, she spent one final season (1962) paired with the brand new, 66,000-ton *France*. The liners formed an ill-matched pair and, in addition, the transatlantic trade was already in decline. The *Flandre* was repainted in tropical white and permanently transferred to the Caribbean trade in October 1962. She returned only briefly to the North Atlantic, during the summer of 1967, for two round trips to Quebec City and Montreal in connection with Expo 67 held that year.

The French sold the *Flandre* in February 1968 to Italy's ever-growing Costa Line, who wanted her for cruising. Taken to Genoa, she was extensively rebuilt with new cabin accommodation for 754 passengers (exclusively first class), public rooms redecorated in a more modern style, and an aft lido deck with two pools. Height was added to the funnel in the process to provide a more efficient exhaust system. She was renamed *Carla C* in tribute to a member of the Costa family.

The Costa Line had hoped initially to use the liner in their own schedules, but received a lucrative charter offer from the Los Angeles-based Princess Cruises. Advertised as the *Princess Carla*, although never formally renamed, she began sailing from Los Angeles to the Mexican Riviera ports of Acapulco, Puerto Vallarta and Mazatlan. Later, she made several Panama Canal cruises, sailing into the Caribbean and back to California. During one of these voyages, Jeraldine Saunders wrote *The Love Boat*, which eventually became a popular television series, and later featured another Princess liner, the *Pacific Princess*.

The *Carla C* was recalled within two years, in 1970, by her Italian owners for the profitable Caribbean cruise trade. She was among the first liners to be based at a Caribbean port throughout the year and linked with aircraft connections for both American and Latin American travellers. She was placed on the weekly seven-day circuit out of San Juan, Puerto Rico, and sailed to Curaçao, La Guaira, Grenada, Martinique, and St Thomas. Except for the occasional crossing to Italy for her annual overhaul, she has been on this trade ever since. In the early 1980s, she made several charter cruises from

The Embarkation Hall on board the Flandre. *Despite being created in as late as 1952, the space has very definite touches of 1930s Art Deco.*

Part of the enclosed promenade on the Flandre.

La Guaira, two of which included visits to New York.

The twenty-year-old turbines were again troublesome in the mid-seventies. In June 1974, the ship was sent to an Amsterdam shipyard and fitted with new, more efficient Stork-Werkspor diesel engines. The *Carla C* was successfully transformed from steamship to motorliner. On 14 February 1976 she collided in San Juan Harbour with the cruiseship *Cunard Adventurer*. Fortunately, the damages were slight.

When I sailed aboard the *Carla C* in April 1983, there was very little evidence of her earlier life as the transatlantic *Flandre*. The public rooms had long since been adapted and redecorated, and the cabins were entirely refurbished. The only remaining French touch was the wood panelling in a small stairwell leading from the passenger accommodation to the bridge.

CHAPTER THREE

YANKEE FLAGSHIPS

UNITED STATES LINES

The AMERICA

The *America* has been thought of as one of the most beautiful of ocean liners, assuredly the best decorated American transatlantic passenger ship. She was certainly one of the finest and most popular liners of her time. Commissioned in the tense summer of 1940, she was soon afterward taken by the US Government and outfitted for her wartime use as the troopship USS *West Point*. She was not released until early 1946, when the American passenger fleet was in urgent need of a new liner on the North Atlantic. Some $6 million were spent on reconditioning her to the highest standards. The *America*, having reverted to her original name, started her first peacetime commercial sailing on 14 November 1946. For several years, the ship worked alone, since intended fleet mates were not restored. The pre-war *Manhattan* went to Government lay-up and her sister, the *Washington*, was reactivated as an austerity ship. However, the design of the *America* was carefully reviewed during planning for the new, fast American superliner, the 53,300-ton *United States*, which was to appear in the early summer of 1952.

The *United States* and the *America* were obviously an unbalanced pair. The newer ship was able to make the Atlantic passage to Le Havre and Southampton in five days. The slower *America* crossed in six days to Cóbh, seven to Le Havre and Southampton and eight to her turn-round at Bremerhaven. However, many travellers preferred the pace of the smaller ship. The addition of two or three days seemed very different from the almost hectic patterns of the giant *United States*.

In the early sixties, as transatlantic trade fell into decline, the *America* sailed on the occasional cruise, to Bermuda, Nassau, or deeper into the Caribbean. However, like so many of her Atlantic contemporaries, she was not ideally suited for such sailings. Among other features, she lacked such cherished amenities as an outdoor pool and sweeping lido decks. In September 1963, the ship was seriously affected by a labour dispute – a disagreement between the American and Hispanic crew members, centred around the use of staff toilet facilities. Hours before the liner was scheduled to sail for Europe,

the voyage had to be cancelled and the passengers sent ashore. There was so little hope of prompt settlement, that the *America* was laid up in the Todd Shipyards in Hoboken, across the Hudson River where she sat without any sign of life. Despite rumours of her retirement, she resumed her Atlantic schedule in the following February, but it was to be her final American season. Falling passenger lists, a threat of labour problems, and Washington's growing reluctance to increase financial aid to liner services combined to make the *America* only one of many American passenger ships rushed into retirement.

United States Lines

The *America* was sold in November 1964 and handed over to new owners, the Greek-registered Chandris Group who assigned her to one of their numerous subsidiary companies. Okeania SA. Renamed *Australis* ('Australian maiden'), she was sent to Piraeus and, while mainly at a harbour anchorage, underwent conversion for the transport of immigrants to Australia. Her accommodation was more than doubled from 1046 berths to 2258, and she was noted as having the largest passenger capacity of any large liner then afloat. Although she was listed as flagship of the Greek merchant navy, and her owners were Greek, she sailed under the flag of Panama. Her new clientele of migrants to Australia and New Zealand, was often balanced on homeward runs by tourists and disenchanted settlers bound for Europe. She was on an extensive route from Southampton and occasionally Bremerhaven and Rotterdam to Gibraltar, Naples, Malta, Port Said, Aden (after the closure of the Suez Canal in 1967, this was altered to Casablanca, Las Palmas and Capetown) and then onwards to Fremantle, Melbourne, Sydney and Auckland. On her way home, she would go via Suva, Tahiti, Acapulco, the Panama Canal, Cristobal, Port Everglades and Southampton. On the very last leg of these three-month sailings, passages were offered eastbound between Florida and England. She also ran frequent cruises, from Southampton to Portugal, West Africa and the Canaries, a Mediterranean trip, and a route from Sydney to the South Pacific islands.

As the *Australis*, the former *America* seemed to be a huge success for the Chandris Company, at least until the mid-seventies. By then, her Greek owners had lost the lucrative contract with the Australian Government for the transport of immigrants, who were, from then on, to fly to Australia. She left Southampton on her last run in November 1977, and was then laid up at a rather remote anchorage at Timaru in New Zealand.

The Chandris Company, along with several American travel firms, decided to reactivate the liner as a New York cruise ship in the summer of 1978. They even decided to capitalize on the ship's heritage and renamed her the *America*. She reached New York in May 1978, and a brief overhaul at Bayonne, New Jersey, revealed that her hull and general machinery were 'quite sound', despite her thirty-eight years, but the ship had been neglected, and was in urgent need of other repairs, as well as cleaning, and improvements in her passenger accommodation. These problems remained unsolved. She ran two short,

Three of America's four largest transatlantic liners at New York together on 14 March 1957: the Independence *is at the bottom, at Pier 84, while the* America *and* United States *share Pier 86. The Greek* Olympia *is just above the American flagship, docked at Pier 88.*

overnight cruises, both of which were unsuccessful and received very poor press. Passengers came ashore complaining of blocked lavatories, dirty, ill-equipped cabins, and generally unsatisfactory conditions. The whole affair was discouraging, and the *America* was fairly soon withdrawn from service.

The ship sat for weeks along New York's 'Luxury Liner

The America *undergoing her annual overhaul and drydocking at the Newport News Shipyard in Virginia.*

Row', just a few blocks north of the berth she had occupied when run by the United States Lines. She was later seized by the local sheriffs for auction. Her short-cruise owners had withdrawn and declared bankruptcy. The Chandris Company, which had actually sold the ship for $5 million to the now bankrupt New York operators earlier in the summer, bought her back at a bargain $1 million and took her to Greece, supposedly for repair in Perama Bay, near Piraeus. I last saw her there, in February 1979, moored in a row of assorted passenger ships, the

Everett Viez Collection

50

former transatlantic *Olympia*, the Chandris *Ellinis* (ex-*Lurline*), the former *Bergensfjord*, Furness-Bermuda's onetime *Ocean Monarch*, and a sizeable group of coastal ships, cruise ships and ferries.

The ex-*America* (renamed the *Italis*) left the Perama Bay mooring for a series of Mediterranean cruises, mainly out of Barcelona, in the summer of 1979. She sailed as a single stacker, with her forward dummy funnel removed.

When the *Italis* returned to an anchorage in Perama Bay late that year, there were reports that she was to become a hotel ship based in West Africa, and the name *Noga* was painted on her bow. However, at the time of writing, she has not yet left her Greek moorings.

The America *berthed at the Columbus Pier at Bremerhaven.*

The former America, *restyled as the Chandris Lines'* Australis, *in a photo, dating from November 1977, at Lisbon, during the ship's last voyage out to Australia.*

The UNITED STATES

Ralph O'Hara, a passenger ship enthusiast from Winnetka, Illinois, recalled his arrival in New York Harbour on a September afternoon in 1952 aboard the Cunarder *Mauretania*. 'At the approaches to the Lower Bay, word spread that the brand new *United States* was ahead of us in the distance. Just about everyone scurried to the upper decks for a closer view.' The vessel with the twin red, white and blue stacks which attracted so much attention aboard the *Mauretania* was, in fact, the *Washington*, a pre-war veteran painted in United States

Lines' commercial colours, but carrying Government dependants and refugees for the Military Sea Transportation Service. In her first summer, the *United States* was the most newsworthy ship afloat. Not only was she the American flagship, but she was also large, and the fastest liner afloat. Everyone wanted to see this triumph of engineering.

Ideas for the design of a ship of great size and speed originated as early as World War I in the mind of her designer, William Francis Gibbs. Plans began in earnest in 1943 and were finally approved after 1945 by the US

Government. Washington officials were deeply impressed with the wartime performance of the two Cunard *Queens* and could therefore see the value of a comparable American superliner in the event of another war. She would also be prestigious as the ultimate American 'ship of state', and a technological show piece. The project was contracted to the Newport News yards in Virginia, and the first keel plates were put in place early in 1950. Day and night shifts followed. The ship was floated in dry dock (rather than traditionally launched) when nearly complete, some fifteen months later. Mrs

Bess Truman, the American First Lady, was to have named her, but a politically sensitive decision was going to have to be made in Washington, about whether to use the liner commercially or send her on Korean War duty. Since her husband elected not to become directly involved, Bess Truman could not accept the United States Lines' invitation. The liner was named by Mrs Tom Connally, wife of the Texas Senator.

The maiden arrival at New York of the superliner United States *in the summer of 1952.*

When 'The Big Ship', as Gibbs lovingly nicknamed her, came into service in June 1952, she made worldwide news. Her maiden crossing (with Margaret Truman on board, representing her father) began at New York on 3 July. The trip was a record-breaker: 35.5 knots eastbound and 34.4 knots westbound. This exceeded the 31.6 knots of the *Queen Mary*'s best record from 1938, and so took the Blue Ribband. (Since so many details of her machinery and underwater hull form were kept a tight secret by her Government sponsors, it was not revealed until the late sixties, in a *New York Times* article, that she had achieved 44 knots briefly during her trials off the East Coast. The article pondered the point and suggested that, at such a speed, she could make Europe in 2½ days. In all probability, that speed could not have been sustained without causing damage to the hull through vibration. At best, the *United States* could make European shores in just over three days.)

The ship's speed was of interest mainly because it would be an advantage if she were to act as a troop ship in time of war. Of course, in peace time, passengers were keen to travel on the world's fastest liner. The British travel writer, C M Squarey, described her as 'Money, skill and imagination – and the greatest of those is, in my opinion, imagination; for above all, this ship is an imaginative ship. I can think of no other country that would have the daring and the imagination to conceive and build a ship of over 50,000 tons that is a dual-purpose job: a money spinner in peacetime and a superb troopship in wartime.' Mr Squarey continued, 'She is a brilliant ship – brilliantly conceived, brilliant in her workmanship and brilliantly American.'

Fortunately, the ship's capacity for conversion into a transport for 15,000 soldiers was never needed, although she was briefly on stand-by during the Cuban Crisis in 1962. For a whole decade the *United States* carried a full load of passengers (including large numbers of American military personnel and their families in the tourist class in both directions across the Atlantic. However, rises in the cost of fuel and labour, and competition from air travel started a decline in her profits by the early sixties. The Government helped with increasingly generous operating subsidies. Despite the fall in the North Atlantic passenger trade, she was still thought of very much in terms of prestige, as a national symbol. The Duke and Duchess of Windsor travelled in the same suite, season after season. Then, there were the Eisenhowers, any number of Roosevelts, Fords, and Vanderbilts, the Queen of Greece, the Emperor of Ethiopia and the Crown Prince of Japan. Some glory remained.

Night-time sailing from Southampton: the United States *is about to begin another five-day crossing to New York.*

The *United States* could take approximately 1930 passengers – 871 in first class, 508 in cabin class and 551 in tourist class. Her interior decoration, while pleasant and often comfortable, lacked the high charm of the *America*. Instead of a series of spacious, high public rooms, the *United States* had comparatively low and broken-up rooms divided into smaller spaces. To some, she appeared too metallic, too grey, too obviously suitable for conversion to a troopship. One of her worst critics called her 'dull early Sheraton', referring to the hotel chain. But, nonetheless, she kept to a precise schedule (aside from the frequent strikes which have so often hindered American ship operations), was impeccably maintained and consistently gave the impression that she was indeed special.

When the *America* was withdrawn and sold-off in 1964, it was merely a matter of time for the *United States*. Her turn-round in ports was accelerated in order to offer more frequent sailings and cut costs. However, by the late sixties, the US Government were looking at passenger ship operations in a new light. Quite simply, they considered them far too expensive. The military value was no longer a priority. At the onset of yet another

A first class cabin with sitting area on board the United States.

United States Lines

painful strike, the *United States* was abruptly laid up in November 1969, at her birthplace in Virginia.

Her ownership later passed to the Federal Government – the United States Lines is now a suburban New Jersey-based container firm, in which there is hardly anyone left who was concerned with the superliner. The ship was moved to a disused finger pier in Norfolk and connected to the shore by double lines (she had partially broken away once during a gale). She towers above the sheds in rather forlorn majesty. The occasional liner, perhaps the *Rotterdam* or the *Queen Elizabeth 2*, comes to the Norfolk Cruise Terminal, a few hundred yards away. At night, her form, itself unlit, blots out twinkling harbour lights. A handful of lonely watchmen repel visitors and keep fire watch.

Over the past ten years or so, the *United States* has faced a number of possible futures – as hotel, motel, convention centre, exhibition hall, condominium, museum, missionary church and, of course, the most obvious of all, revival as a cruise liner. There was also a move to sail her into New York Harbour for the Bicentennial's Operation Sail, on 4 July 1976. Her sale price kept coming down until she was finally sold to the Seattle-based United States Cruises Incorporated in November 1978, for $5 million (which was quite close to her estimated scrap value). The new firm hoped to pump new life into the ageing giant by doing her up as a condominium-style cruise ship. Brochures were printed, offices opened, press releases

The Excambion *and her three sisters of American Export Lines' 'Four Aces' were noted to be among the finest combination passenger-cargo liners afloat.*

issued and even a few cabins sold. But, in the end, over $100 million would have been needed to suitably revive the liner. In May 1980, the ship was dry docked at a Norfolk shipyard for the first time in eleven years. She was found to be in surprisingly good condition, but, quickly returned to her lay-up berth. Shortly afterwards, there were rumours that the Government wanted her for use as a hospital ship based in the Middle-East. This time the conversion would cost over $300 million.

During my visit to the *United States* while she lay idle at Norfolk in June 1979, she appeared to be in quite orderly condition. Of course, layers of paint were peeling from her superstructure and the paint on the funnels was badly discoloured. The dehumidification system placed aboard by the Federal Government in 1973 had kept her amazingly free of stale smells and decay. In fact, a copy of the *New York Times* from November 1969 left on a lounge cocktail table remained unfaded. Linens had been stripped from all cabins and the dimly-lit corridors seemed uninviting. In one lounge, rows of vacuum cleaners stood like soldiers at attention. In other areas, chairs were neatly rearranged along the side bulkheads. The wheelhouse was practically bare and the captain's cabin and dayroom were empty. However, in the engine room, we saw the prized control centre, a panel of dials, buttons and electronic gadgetry, which was obviously being well looked after, with shining brass and chromium, and the surroundings swept clean. Over thirty years after that triumphant Blue Ribband summer, the great *United States* is still waiting for her next chapter.

AMERICAN EXPORT LINES

The EXCALIBUR, EXCAMBION, EXETER and EXOCHORDA

This set of ships replaced a very successful and popular group commissioned in the early thirties, of which three had been lost in action. The *Excalibur*, *Excambion*, *Exeter* and *Exochorda*, although designed for American Export passenger-cargo service, were completed near the end of World War II as single-purpose attack transports, which were to participate in the projected sea invasion of Japan. In the Service of the US Navy, they bore the names: USS Duchess (*Excalibur*), USS Queens (*Excambion*), USS Shelby (*Exeter*) and USS Dauphin (*Exochorda*). They were not released to American Export until 1947.

Built by the Bethlehem Steel Company at Sparrows Point, Maryland, the four were converted for commercial service at that firm's shipyard in Hoboken, New Jersey. In their fresh peacetime livery, they were rechristened with their intended American Export names. Fred Sarver, who sailed aboard the 'Four Aces' in their early years and later became the sales manager for American Export, recalled the group as exceptional ships for their time. 'They were the first fully air-conditioned passenger ships in the world. They were also the very first to have convertible cabins: from day-time sitting rooms to night-time bedrooms.' *Excalibur*, the first to be recommissioned, sailed from New York in September 1948. The others followed by the end of the year.

The four liners worked a balanced eight-week schedule, from New York – though they actually sailed from the western shores of the Hudson, at first from Jersey City and later from Hoboken – to Barcelona, Marseilles, Naples, Alexandria, Beirut, the Turkish port of Iskenderun, Latakia, Beirut, Alexandria, Piraeus, Naples, Genoa, Marseilles, Barcelona and then back to New York. In the later years, their exact itinerary often varied. Their passengers often included one-way and inter-port travellers as well as those who treated the round-trip as a cruise. Each had space for 125 passengers, all first class, and all in large, very comfortable staterooms with private facilities. On deck, each ship had a small open-air pool.

Fred Sarver also remembered these ships as important and profitable cargo carriers. 'Each ship could take 6000 tons of general cargo. Westbound to New York, we often carried olive oil, cork, canned fish and oranges.

The Excalibur *nearly sank within the confines of New York Harbour, on 27 June 1950, after colliding with the Danish freighter* Colombia. *The American Export ship was run aground deliberately on the local Gowanus Flats and saved.*

Outbound, the manifests might show as many as 200 crated automobiles per trip. One other important source of business was inter-port cargo within the Mediterranean. As an example, we often would load oranges in Israel for delivery at Genoa or Marseilles, or take apples to Alexandria.'

Unfortunately, although they were widely praised, and popular with passengers, they were losing much of their cargo to faster, larger freighters by the late fifties. Consequently, both the *Excambion* and *Exochorda* were laid

Everett Viez Collection

City docks and an even shorter distance from her former American Export terminal, she was outfitted as the dormitory ship *Stevens*, to ease the institute's accommodation problems. During her conversion in 1967, she was stripped of any further sea-going power, for her propeller and parts of her machinery were removed. For some years afterwards, especially when decorated at night with twinkling fairy lights, the *Stevens* was a prominent fixture in New York Harbour. She looked like some festive cruise ship, about to sail off to the tropics.

When the school's housing situation was finally resolved in 1975, the *Stevens* lost her purpose. She was towed to Chester, Pennsylvania, that August, presumably for scrapping. Then, in March 1979, nearly four years later, she reappeared in New York, a half-dismantled hull minus much of her upperworks. She had obviously been resold and sat for a time at a Jersey City pier until she was taken to the backwaters of nearby Kearny and fully dismantled.

The remaining 'Aces' the *Excalibur* and *Exeter*, sailed for American Export until late 1964. Not long before, the *Excalibur* had suffered a rather serious fire at sea, just hours after leaving New York, which forced her back into port for repairs. Much earlier, on 27 June 1950, she had been rammed by the Danish freighter *Colombia* in Lower New York Bay. Taking on water by the bow, she had been in danger of sinking until grounded deliberately on the local Gowanus Flats.

After their retirement, the *Excalibur* and *Exeter* were returned to the Government and laid up for a time at the Todd shipyard in Hoboken. However, unlike their earlier sisters, they were not sent to the 'mothball fleets', but offered directly for sale, even to foreign interests. Within months, they hoisted the colours of the Orient Overseas Line, part of the growing fleet of Mr C Y Tung, who had bought Cunard's *Queen Elizabeth* several years later. The former American Export sisters were modified only slightly and given new names, *Oriental Jade* and *Oriental Pearl* respectively, for the transpacific run between San Francisco, Yokohama, Kobe, Koahsiung, Keelung and Hong Kong. Like most other Tung-owned passenger ships, they were placed under the Liberian flag. They sailed for the Chinese for nearly a decade. In their final years, they, too, were displaced by a declining passenger trade and, far more so, by the rise in container ships. Both of them were scrapped on Taiwan in 1974.

up in 1959, a mere eleven years after their maiden voyages. Stripped and repainted in anti-corrosive greys, they were sent to the upper Hudson River 'mothball fleet' near Jones Point, New York. Officially, they had been returned to the Government and were being kept for 'emergency military standby'. However, their value was reconsidered some years later, and they were cleared for further civilian service by the mid-sixties. The *Excambion* was handed over to the Texas Aviation & Maritime University at Galveston and refitted as their training ship, *Texas Clipper*. In 1984, she was the sole survivor of the 'Four Aces'.

The *Exochorda* also went to a school, but for non-sailing purposes. Purchased by the Stevens Institute of Technology at Hoboken, just across from the New York

The INDEPENDENCE and CONSTITUTION
'They were years ahead of their time, two fine ships in that last golden era of American ocean liner construction,' according to Fred Sarver. Much like their larger and faster contemporary, the *United States*, both the *Independence* and the *Constitution* were post-war creations, prompted by

liberal Government loans and operating subsidies, and intended both as peacetime money-makers and emergency wartime troopers. More specifically, they were designed to carry the American flag on the Mediterranean, which had long been dominated by the Italians. They were the first big American liners designed for the mid-Atlantic route. Alternatively, since they were fast, exceptionally safe and easily convertible into troop ships, they could have carried upwards of 7500 soldiers each, if they had been called upon to do so.

Designed just after World War II, they were built at the Bethlehem Steel Company's yard in Quincy, Massachusetts, which had built a superb Matson Line trio of liners in the early thirties, the *Lurline, Mariposa* and *Monterey*. As work on the new ships began, American Export was maintaining a rather mismatched passenger fleet consisting of the former troop ship, *La Guardia*, which was an experimental conversion to a commercial passenger ship, and the *Excalibur,* the *Excambion,* the *Exochorda*, each with 125 passenger berths. The firm also acted as temporary agents for the Italian liners *Saturnia* and *Vulcania*. The new ships would run a far better express service, eliminating the *La Guardia* and leaving the 'Four Aces' to a more extended Eastern Mediterranean trade.

The *Independence* was launched on 3 June 1950 and sailed from New York on 11 February, bound for a fifty-three-day Mediterranean cruise as her maiden trip. The *Constitution* followed on 21 June 1951. Both ships were instantly successful, particularly with American and Italian passengers. Much like earlier immigrants to America, Italian travellers chose these American liners for their 'voyage of a lifetime', hoping to ease their entry into the United States. The first-class accommodation was particularly attractive and included a high number of convertible suites and deluxe cabins, combination rooms that could be extended or reduced by means of interconnecting doors. All of the rooms in first and cabin class had private facilities, none did in tourist class. The first and cabin passengers had separate outdoor swimming pools, placed aft on separate decks, adjacent to the cargo hatches.

Along with the *United States*, both the American Export twins became well known, highly publicized ships during that final profitable decade on the Atlantic. Like so many of their competitors, they did not begin to lose passengers until the early sixties. The *Independence* featured prominently in the film, *An Affair To Remember*, with Cary Grant and Deborah Kerr, while the *Constitution* had a

The traditional scene at New York: well wishers at the far end of the dock bid farewell to an outgoing liner. In this instance, the Constitution *is one of six liners, which set a New York Harbour record for departing passengers – 8029 in a single day.*

The Independence *and her sister ship retained their black hull colouring until 1960.*

starring role in one episode of television's *I Love Lucy* with Lucille Ball. Perhaps the best remembered passenger came aboard in the spring of 1956, for a sailing from New York to Cannes. Fred Sarver was concerned with arrangements for the passage of Grace Kelly, the Hollywood actress, for her marriage to Prince Rainier in Monaco. 'Air France was rumoured to be flying Grace Kelly, her family and their party over to Monaco. I was asked by American Export to approach Mrs John Kelly, the mother of the bride, in Philadelphia. While the *Constitution* was already well-booked, we planned to offer about thirty cabins to the group. When I finally met with Mrs Kelly, she readily accepted the idea, but handed me a guest passenger list of six hundred. Fortunately, we were able to compromise considerably and accept about ninety of the family group. Soon afterward, we had some four thousand applications from members of the press, who wanted to cross on the same voyage. The bride-to-be was given a very large, specially-arranged suite and during the crossing, she was quite social and friendly, appearing very often with the other passengers. Ironically, in 1951, when we were commissioning the *Constitution*, during a press trip, we had four young models on board for photographic purposes. One of them was Grace Kelly.'

The *Independence* and the *Constitution* worked a balanced

schedule of three-week voyages, sailing from New York to Algeciras, Cannes, Genoa and Naples, and then home. Frequently, these voyages were offered as round trips, advertised as 'Sunlane Cruises'. Occasionally, there were additional ports of call, such as Casablanca, Palma de Majorca, Palermo and Madeira. Each winter, usually in February, one of the ships began a two-month Mediterranean-Black Sea cruise, which included such ports as Odessa and Yalta in the Soviet Union. Because of their popularity, both ships were sent to the Newport News Shipyards in Virginia early in 1959 for extension of their capacities. The wheelhouse, bridge wings and navigating rooms were moved 21 feet forward and 8½ feet upward, so as to create space for 4 new suites and 52 more cabins. The capacity of each increased by 110, from its original 1000 berths. The *Independence* and the *Constitution* were among the very few large liners to have their annual winter overhauls done within the confines of New York Harbour. Each year, they took turns in the Bethlehem Steel shipyard at 56th Street in Brooklyn. Their only mishap seems to have occurred on 1 March 1959, when the *Constitution* was nearing New York after her major refit at Newport News and collided with the Norwegian tanker *Jalanta*. The liner went directly to the Bethlehem yard in Brooklyn with damage to her bow. The tanker had her bow completely severed, and the two pieces were later towed to Hoboken for rejoining.

Traffic for the two liners began to wane in the jet-dominated sixties. Noel Bonsor recorded in his excellent *North Atlantic Seaway* that the average number of passengers on these ships was 928 per trip in 1962. The average had dropped to 786 by 1967, and to 694 a year later. At first, the ships were laid-up during the winter months, usually at the American Export cargo piers in Hoboken. Only in their last years were they sent on cruises to the Caribbean. In the spring of 1968, with the Mediterranean trade near its end, the *Independence* was given an $8 million refit for future use as a full cruise ship. She was made one-class, and her public rooms were restyled and redecorated. Outside, she was painted with an overpowering psychedelic design in which multi-coloured sunrays surrounded the eyes of Jean Harlow. The effect was intended to attract the 'new generation' of cruise passengers. Time-chartered to Fugazy Travel of New York the ship was supposed to be going to win considerable group bookings from the Ford Motor Company. There was even a new pricing scheme – the passenger fares did not include food. Consequently, a seven-day voyage to San Juan and St Thomas could be

The Constitution *arriving at New York on 26 March 1964, with the* Empress of Canada, Homeric, Queen Elizabeth, Berlin *and* United States *in the background.*

The Constitution *at berth during a Mediterranean crossing.*

offered for as little as $98, against the normal rate of about $200. However, the restaurant costs on board were high and often amounted to more than the additional $100, which annoyed most of the passengers. It was all rather ludicrous. At American Export, Fred Sarver recalled, 'Half of the staff was against the entire idea. We were quite disgusted!' The idea flopped. The ship was shortly afterwards repainted in her original colours, but then rather suddenly laid up (after only two further voyages). By the end of 1968, the *Independence* was ideal at Baltimore and the *Constitution* at Jacksonville (Florida). Neither of them ever sailed again as an American Export liner.

The sisters were the subject of recurrent rumours during the early seventies. There were reports that the Greek Chandris Lines wanted at least one of them for the Australian trade and as a cruise ship, that Italy's Lauro Line had similar ideas, and even that a new American company might be created to sail them. In 1974, they were officially cleared by the US Government for sale abroad to the highest bidder. They went quickly, just like the *Excalibur* and *Exeter*, and later the *Queen Elizabeth*, to the C Y Tung Group, Renamed *Oceanic Independence* and *Oceanic Constitution*, they were placed under Liberian colours and registered to a Tung subsidiary, the Atlantic Far East Lines. The timing could not have been less opportune. Worldwide fuel oil prices had just increased from $35 to $95 a ton and sent the passenger ship business into a universal slump. The former *Constitution* reached Hong Kong in August 1974 and was immediately laid up. The *Independence* was sent to South Africa, where she was

intended to run a series of cruises from Durban, ranging from three-day mini trips to runs to the Far East over forty-six days. Instead, she was chartered to make a single voyage with Angolan refugees to Lisbon, afterwards sailing to Hong Kong, where she joined her sister at anchor.

During 1977, there were further rumours that a South African shipping group wanted to charter the *Constitution* for a revived mailship service between Southampton and Capetown. The Union-Castle Line was then just withdrawing from the passenger business and the opportunity to offer discount fares seemed ideal. The ship was to be renamed *Shannon*, but there were few other developments before the project was abandoned.

In 1980, long after other American cruise firms had withdrawn from the Hawaiian trade, the Tung interests proposed to restore the *Oceanic Independence* as sailing under the American flag, a Government requirement for service between any two domestic ports. With the prospect of jobs for American seamen, the idea was welcome, and the ship was allowed to fly the Stars and Stripes, after considerable improvements and up-grading. She entered the seven-day Hawaiian inter-island service out of Honolulu on 21 June 1980.

The *Oceanic Independence*, which reverted to her original name in 1983, met with some success and prompted American-Hawaii Cruises, the specially-created operating subsidiary, to consider reactivating the *Oceanic Constitution* as well. At first, there were ideas to convert her into a motorliner. Instead, she was thoroughly overhauled, and added to the seven-day Hawaiian cruise service in June 1982. She, too, flies American colours. Just before her re-entry into service, she was rechristened *Constitution* by Princess Grace of Monaco in Taiwan. Mr C Y Tung, the owner of the ship, died suddenly on the following day, and Princess Grace was killed in a car crash only a few months later. A room which was dedicated to Princess Grace in the summer of 1983 aboard the *Constitution* contains a collection of memorabilia loaned by the Grimaldi family of Monaco.

The *Independence* and *Constitution* are again working in tandem, but now as Pacific cruise ships, sailing each weekend from Honolulu. Unlike the larger *United States*, they have been found profitable 'second lives'.

The ATLANTIC

The converted freighter *Atlantic*, the former Mariner-class cargo ship *Badger Mariner*, was taken over by American Export in the autumn of 1959, after two unsuccessful seasons for the short-lived American Banner Lines. Intended more as a tourist liner than a luxurious passenger ship, she was sent to the Sun shipyards at Chester, Pennsylvania for a refit. Among the modifications for her intended service to the Mediterranean was the installation of a swimming pool in place of the aft cargo hatch. At the time, it was the largest outdoor pool afloat.

The *Atlantic* was recommissioned in May 1960 for a more extended American Export passenger run that included Algeciras, Naples, Messina, Piraeus and Haifa. Specifically, she was intended to attract some of the lucrative Greek and Israeli markets, in direct competition with the established Greek and Zim lines, but she did not

become a profitable ship. Fred Sarver later said, 'She was never really successful, mostly because she could not quite compare with our two larger liners or some of the other big Mediterranean ships. Furthermore, the Company became impatient with her. The management was unwilling to wait. We even briefly experimented with a service that included Port Everglades. She was always the odd ship.'

The *Atlantic* was restyled in 1965 as an all tourist-class liner, using some 840 berths. However, it was a brief extension. Two years later, she was withdrawn from service and laid up, first at Brooklyn and later at Baltimore. In 1971, she too joined the C Y Tung fleet, going to yet another subsidiary, Seawise Foundations Inc. She was bought to replace the burnt-out *Queen Elizabeth*, which had been intended as a floating university. Renamed *Universe Campus* (which was shortened to *Universe* in 1976), the ship ran at least two annual educational world or Pacific cruises, one in September for the fall semester and the other in January for the spring term.

The former *Atlantic* continues with her 'floating university cruises', but now sails also as a cruise ship, especially during the summer months, on seven-day voyages from Vancouver along the Alaskan coast. It is rather ironic that the last three American Export liners, the *Independence*, *Constitution* and *Atlantic*, have all gone to the Hong Kong based C Y Tung Group for further sailing.

The maiden outbound voyage of the Atlantic, *in May 1960.*

Peter Lancaric Collection

CHAPTER FOUR

SOME POST-WAR DUTCHMEN

HOLLAND-AMERICA LINE

The VOLENDAM

When Captain Cornelius van Herk joined the Holland-America Line as a young cadet in May 1945, the Netherlands was still devastated after the Nazi occupation. He had to walk from his home outside The Hague to the Rotterdam Docks, as there was no public transport. 'My first ship was the *Volendam*, sailing that June from Rotterdam to Liverpool with 500 Dutch children as passengers. They were being taken to the English countryside for much-needed nourishment. We sailed from the Lekhaven at Rotterdam instead of the usual Company dock at the Wilhelminakade, which was still in ruins.'

Until early 1946, the *Volendam* remained under wartime Cunard-White Star management, with a staff of 350 Dutch and British members, including van Herk. 'From Liverpool, after some long overdue repairs, we took 2500 British troops out to Haifa for the growing turmoil in Palestine. From there, we went empty to Alexandria, and made several trips to Toulon, in the south of France, carrying demobilized British troops being brought in from the Far East. From Toulon, these troops were taken by train to the Channel and then brought across to England by ferry. We also called at Port Said, where we took on Royal Air Force and Royal Navy personnel. We had one special voyage from Port Said to Split in Yugoslavia, loaded with displaced persons. This group was mostly fishermen and their families, originally from the small island of Vis, who had fled Yugoslavia in the early part of the War. The Yugoslav women worked during the voyage and scrubbed the ship thoroughly. She was more spotless than ever.

'Leaving the Mediterranean, we went from Port Said to Glasgow, with more troops, and stopped en route at Malta and Naples. At the Italian port, we loaded some Polish soldiers, who had been fighting in Italy. In compensation for their Allied efforts, they were being given jobs in British coal mines. Once at Glasgow, the ship had a two-month overhaul. Afterward, we made a trip for the United Nations Refugee Association with

Mennonites from Germany, who were being resettled in Argentina.'

In mid-1946, the *Volendam* was returned to Holland-America. She was by then a tired, well-worn ship. Company engineers felt that she was not worth refitting for luxury service. First, she had been so altered during her conversion to a troop ship that her passenger accommodation would have to be built again from scratch. More importantly, her machinery was in decline. She had grown quite 'tender', according to Captain van Herk. 'At times, she could make 14 knots, which was somewhat slow by passenger ship standards and certainly not acceptable for the transatlantic luxury trade, but we often had to work very hard just to do 13½ knots. There was always a competition between the three engine "watches" – shifts from 12 to 4, 4 to 8, and 8 to 12 – to see which could produce the greatest number of propeller revolutions and therefore the greater speed.'

Although the *Volendam* was considered too old to restore for regular commercial service, she was quite adequate for troop transport and immigrant sailings. Consequently, during the late forties, she made a number of voyages out to Indonesia with fresh troops, carrying military personnel and evacuees on her return. She also made several sailings to Australia with Dutch settlers who were seeking a 'new life with greater economic opportunity'. Many of the emigrants had their fares paid under an assistance programme sponsored by the Dutch Government. Returning from Australia, the *Volendam* would either sail direct to Holland, practically empty, or stop in Indonesia to load more returning troops and Dutch nationals.

The *Volendam* made many transatlantic voyages in the years 1947–51. Her accommodation reflected little of her high pre-war standards. In all, she could accommodate 1682 passengers in a single, rather spartan class. She carried thousands of new settlers to North America, at a time when large numbers of immigrants were again making the North Atlantic crossing. Along with other Holland-America liners, and the three sisters of the *Groote*

The Volendam *loading passengers at Rotterdam.*

Beer class, the *Volendam* sailed to New York, Halifax or Quebec City, very often direct from Rotterdam. Many of the immigrant passengers came from the farmlands of eastern Holland, seeking post-war security, freedom or economic opportunity. The ships in which they travelled often returned empty to Holland.

By the early fifties, however, the *Volendam* would not have been able to pass another marine inspection and survey. Even with millions spent on upgrading her, the

ship would still have been thirty years old and in tired condition. She made her last Atlantic crossing in November 1951, and was sold to Rotterdam shipbreakers. Demolition began in the same winter.

The VEENDAM

Holland-America had actually intended to retire the *Veendam* and the *Volendam* in 1940. Captain van Herk recalled that they were not terribly economical ships. 'Each consumed about 120 tons of fuel per day, which was quite high for their relatively small size.' However, when

During a winter cruise voyage, the Veendam *enters Havana harbour.*

the war erupted, there was no further decision on selling the pair. The *Volendam* became a valuable Allied troop carrier, while the *Veendam* fell into enemy hands. In 1945, when Dutch shipping was particularly shorthanded, Holland-America had little choice but to keep these sisters.

Captain van Herk was third mate aboard the restored *Veendam* when she resumed commercial sailings to New York, in January 1947. 'During that first voyage, we had a nine-day stay at Hoboken [the Holland-America terminal, just across from New York City], which was unusually long. The first class on board had been refitted to a pre-war standard: nice, comfortable, quite cosy. The tourist class section became what had been most of the

A night-time view of the beautiful Nieuw Amsterdam.

former second class space.' In her modified, post-war state, the liner seemed to have a rather modest capacity of 586, compared with her pre-war total of 1898. The liner also had a large cargo capacity. In those post-war years, she often carried tulips, caraway seeds, cheeses, beer and agricultural produce from Holland. She took back tin plate and general cargo.

Holland-America revived its cruise operations with the *Veendam* in December 1947 with a two-week trip from New York to Curaçao, La Guaira and St Thomas. For these tropical voyages, a canvas swimming pool was erected on one of the aft decks. The Company is also responsible for popularizing the idea of a 'cruise director', the organizer and co-ordinator of passenger entertainment during a cruise voyage. Some of the earliest cruise directors were employed aboard the *Veendam* and the larger *Nieuw Amsterdam* in the winter of 1947–48.

The *Veendam* was to have been retired at the end of 1952, just as the brand new 'tourist-class sisters' *Ryndam*

69

and *Maasdam* came into service. However, there was some rethinking, prompted in particular by the pressing demand for berths on the Atlantic. The *Veendam* was retained for one further year, her thirtieth, and withdrawn in November 1953. Quite unusually, she was

Gutting and then restoring a public room on board the Nieuw Amsterdam *during her post-war conversion in 1947.*

sold to American scrappers, who rarely bought foreign-flag tonnage. She was handed over to the Bethlehem Steel Company and taken to their Baltimore-Fairfield yard, which had been a very large wartime shipbuilding plant and the producer of the first Liberty ship, but had been converted from a shipbuilding to a shipbreaking yard in the late forties.

The NIEUW AMSTERDAM

The *Nieuw Amsterdam* is still remembered as one of the finest, and most endearing of ocean liners. She was conceived as the national flagship, the biggest liner then built in Holland and something of a triumph in her standards of decoration and modernity. Furthermore, Holland-America Line found itself blessed with a ship that engaged in an immediate and lasting love affair with the travelling public. The *Nieuw Amsterdam* is probably the best known Dutch ship of the twentieth century.

When Nazi Germany collapsed, the *Nieuw Amsterdam* was in the Mediterranean carrying Australian troops bound for home. On her way back, she took part in the evacuation of troubled Indonesia. Captain van Herk,

Vincent Messina Collection

The Nieuw Amsterdam *was repainted with a grey hull during her winter refit of 1957.*

New boilers being lifted into position for installation aboard the aged Nieuw Amsterdam *in the autumn of 1967. The ship is at the Wilton-Fijenoord Shipyards at Schiedam, Holland.*

aboard the *Volendam* at Port Said on Christmas Day 1945, remembers seeing her steaming by in her grey paint, heavily loaded with evacuees from Java. By the time she was released from military duties in the spring of 1946, she had transported 378,361 wartime passengers on forty-four separate voyages, with an average of 8599 per sailing. Her travels were the equivalent of twenty-one times around the world. When she steamed into Rotterdam harbour on 10 April 1946, for the first time since 1939, it was a very special day for the Dutch. To some, it was the most obvious symbol of liberation. A commentator at the time affectionately called her 'the Darling of the Dutch'.

It cost twelve million Dutch guilders to restore the *Nieuw Amsterdam*, only a million less than she cost to build ten years before. The first fifteen weeks were occupied simply with removal of the military fittings: guns, standee (fold-down) berths and hammocks. When the actual refurbishing began, some 2000 tons of original furniture and artwork were brought by freighters from New York and San Francisco. Over 3000 chairs and 500 tables had to be returned to their original makers. All of the ship's electrical wiring was replaced (a huge task in itself), all the wood was planed down to half its original thickness, to

remove the thousands of initials carved by GIs, 12,000 square feet of glass was renewed and the entire brass work reburnished.

When the *Nieuw Amsterdam* resumed commercial sailings in October 1947, she was once again a most magnificent ship. More praise and a loyal relationship with a new generation of post-war travellers came her way. Even in her later years, the ship's popularity did not diminish. On the contrary, it seemed to increase. The liner's sleek Art Deco interiors made her something of a 'floating Grand Hotel'. Many voyagers were nostalgic for pre-war luxury, and the *Nieuw Amsterdam* was often the ship of their choice.

The Dutch flagship sailed between Rotterdam, Le Havre, Southampton and New York, and on cruises to the Caribbean during the winter months. She was often fully booked. Just as in the late thirties, thought was given to the building of a suitable running-mate, a liner of, say, 35,000 tons, but nothing developed, at least for some years. The Company added the 15,000-ton sisters *Ryndam* and *Maasdam* for the tourist-class trade in the early fifties and the 24,000-ton *Statendam*, an improved version of the two earlier ships, in 1957. Only afterwards did they commission a suitable running-mate (in fact a brand new Dutch flagship). The 38,000-ton *Rotterdam* crossed to New York on her maiden trip in the late summer of 1959. After over twenty years, the venerable *Nieuw Amsterdam* had a

Captain Cornelius van Herk and New York's annual Maritime Queen.

companion ship.

Captain van Herk served aboard the *Nieuw Amsterdam* on several occasions during the fifties. 'She was a good sea ship, very solid and strong. However, in heavy weather, we always had to reduce speed very quickly. Once, the bridge windows were smashed in a fierce storm. On another occasion, the window of the chief officer's cabin was torn away. Quickly, his cabin began to flood. However, later during the clean-up, crew men found a huge piece of splintered glass in the chief's bedroom, a full room behind the cabin with the smashed window. We also had to be very careful with the *Nieuw Amsterdam* when going full astern. The trembling was usually very bad. In fact, hundreds of light bulbs would have to be replaced soon afterwards.'

The *Nieuw Amsterdam* also had the occasional mishap. While returning from her annual Christmas Caribbean cruise on 4 January 1965, she collided with an unlighted railway barge in the early-morning mists of Lower New York Bay. She paused briefly, then proceeded to her New York pier. [Holland-America had left their Hoboken, New Jersey terminal after some 90 years in 1963.] Divers inspected the damage to the liner, but found it slight. On 7 January, she sailed on schedule for her next cruise. On another occasion, Captain van Herk was aboard during an overnight stay at Manhattan's Pier 40. 'Suddenly, a tremendous shock rocked the otherwise empty ship. It was soon discovered that a fully loaded railroad carfloat, travelling southward along the Hudson, had lost control and rammed our stern. The barge then swung over to the west berth of the pier. Some stern frames on the *Nieuw Amsterdam* were dented.' On still another occasion, she hit a quayside crane at the Wilhelminakade terminal in Rotterdam. The aft tug used in the docking lacked adequate power, so that the liner shifted in her own wake.

The *Nieuw Amsterdam* was given three major face-lifts to increase her competitiveness and, on at least one occasion, to preserve her life. During the winter of 1956–57, her accommodation was upgraded and improved, full air-conditioning was added and the hull was repainted in dove grey, which was considered more suitable than the original black for her winter tropical cruises. In the 1961–62 overhaul, the liner was restyled as a two-class ship, without the original cabin class. Her revised berthing figures became fairly flexible to fit in with demand: either 691 first class and 583 tourist, or 301 first and 972 tourist. Finally, the most decisive refit came in 1967. In that summer, the *Nieuw Amsterdam* suffered a severe mechanical breakdown which made it necessary for her transatlantic sailings to be cancelled and her passengers transferred to other ships. There were rumours that the 29-year-old 'Dutchman's favourite' would be retired and scrapped. Holland-America directors conferred with shipyard engineers. Captain van Herk remembered this tense period. 'The Company management definitely wanted to save her. The shipyard people agreed that she could be saved, but that new, expensive boilers were needed. Then, the Holland-America Line was suddenly and exceptionally fortunate in being able to buy appropriate second-hand boilers from a retired US Navy cruiser then being scrapped in California. They were put aboard our freighter *Moerdyk* and delivered directly to the Wilton-Fijenoord shipyard at Schiedam, where the *Nieuw Amsterdam* was waiting. The shipyard crews had already cut a huge opening in the side of the liner and removed the worn-out boilers. The "new" boilers were then installed, in fact in record time, and were actually considered improvements. The ship then had one boiler less than before, and the new units were even smaller and lighter. We needed extra ballast afterward. The "transplant" proved to be very efficient, rendering the same service speed [20 knots] as before.'

Several years later, in September 1971, it was the aged, but still much loved *Nieuw Amsterdam* that closed Holland-America Line's transatlantic passenger service. Jet travel had won another battle. Since the late fifties, passenger loads had been declining to such an extent that in the end the staff often outnumbered the customers. The 'grand old

Roger Sherlock

Both the Westerdam *and her near-sister, the* Noordam, *had a low, flattish look.*

lady' was reassigned to year-round service from American ports with the *Rotterdam,* the *Statendam* and other Holland–America liners. The *Nieuw Amsterdam* would never again visit Holland. Her final employment was a series of Caribbean cruises from Port Everglades, Florida.

Two years later, in 1973, as Holland–America lost some $12.5 million on its passenger operations after staggering increases in the cost of fuel oil, the *Nieuw Amsterdam* was the first candidate for disposal. By then, she was thirty-five years old. Captain van Herk felt that she still had another five years or so of life. 'She was not worn out. She was still very well maintained. Instead, her problems were mostly in the engine room. It was pure slavery for those men down below, especially since we were always in the steamy Caribbean. The *Nieuw Amsterdam* did not have a cooling system in her engine room. Furthermore, too many people were needed to keep her sailing. At the time, the Company was anxious to cut all additional expenses. Her crew size was simply too large. Nowadays, aboard the new Scandinavian cruise ships for example, the engine rooms are controlled from air-conditioned glass compartments. They require a small staff and might even be closed down at night and operated completely from the bridge.'

There was much speculation on the fate of the *Nieuw Amsterdam,* from the obvious suggestion that she would go to some Greek company for further trading to ideas that she might be made into a museum or hotel-ship, particularly in her former home port of Rotterdam. However, the most original, and yet least probable, rumour was that the ship would be bought by the City of Rotterdam to become a 'sex centre'. It seemed that the City fathers wanted to centralize the red light district and thought that it might be a clever approach to use a large, out-of-work ocean liner. She could even be berthed at her former pier, the old Wilhelminakade. Holland–America was particularly quiet during this time of rumour and exaggeration. Realistically, the company was simply waiting for the highest bidder.

In the end, she was sold, like so many older liners at the time, to a Taiwanese scrap firm. The scale price was near to thirteen million Dutch guilders, approximately the cost of building her in the late thirties, and of refitting her just after World War II. After her final cruise from Florida in December 1973, she sailed through the Panama Canal and called at Los Angeles to take on fuel and provisions for the slow, final crossing of the Pacific. Under the command of Captain R ten Kate, now the master of a modern containership, the *Nieuw Amsterdam* plodded across to the Far East at a modest 12 knots. She was under the care of a greatly reduced operational staff of sixty.

The liner arrived at Kaohsiung, in pouring rain, on 25 February 1974. Some forty other ships awaited scrapping in the harbour. The Captain and his small crew remained aboard until a berth was available. On 2 March word came to lift anchor and proceed to Berth 57. Two days later, with the ship securely alongside, Captain ten Kate signed the ship over to the Nan Feng Company, the scrappers, and then returned to Amsterdam. Over two months elapsed before the actual dismantling began on 16 May. Another former transatlantic liner, the *Homeric,* was meeting her end at the adjacent berth. The two exiled liners were reduced to scrap within sight of one another. Demolition on the *Nieuw Amsterdam* was completed by early October.

The NOORDAM

When a pair of ships, the *Noordam* and *Zaandam*, were introduced on the North Atlantic in 1938–39, they were notable additions to that trade. Captain van Herk felt that they offered a new concept for their time, all first class travel on the Atlantic. 'As combination passenger-cargo ships, they offered a leisurely, but very comfortable crossing. For this, they appealed especially to a wealthy, older set of passengers, who wanted a quiet sea voyage. The accommodation was excellent, offering a deluxe yet intimate atmosphere. There was very little entertainment, no bands or professional entertainers as we have today aboard cruiseships. A highlight of an evening might be some classical recordings in the lounge.'

The passenger accommodation on both ships was limited to 125 berths, all of them in first class. The level of decor was nothing if not luxurious and superbly modern. The overall style resembled that of the exquisite *Nieuw Amsterdam*, which had been commissioned just four months before the *Noordam*. Obviously, Holland-America directors and designers were following a definite pattern in the styling and decoration of their passenger ships. The Company's ships began to show a decorative link, no matter the differences in size or type of vessel.

After war duties for the Americans, the *Noordam* resumed commercial sailings in July 1946, just a month after Holland-America Line's first post-war crossing with the *Westerdam*. After the torpedoing of the *Zaandam* off Brazil in November 1942, the *Noordam* was paired with the slightly larger *Westerdam*, a ship originally designed for the Europe-North American West Coast run. The two made a team for a revived monthly Rotterdam-New York direct run. Each ship had a monthly departure in each direction, usually at midday on Saturday, and then nine days later, a Monday-morning arrival at the other end. It was a leisurely, gracious crossing of the North Atlantic.

Captain van Herk remembers both the *Noordam* and *Westerdam* as good sea boats. 'They were sturdy, well-built ships. In addition to their passenger roles, both had six large cargo hatches, three forward and three aft. In those busy, hard pressed post-war years, not only were the passengers spaces always booked to capacity, but the freight spaces were as well. Westbound to New York, we often carried large amounts of tulip bulbs, wines, seeds, cheeses, agricultural products and Henniken beer. Homeward to Rotterdam, we took tin plate, grain, machinery and meats. Of course, there were the occasional special cargos, such as the large shipment of Polish hams on one trip and the group of swans on another.'

Passage fares aboard the *Noordam* (and *Westerdam*) were fixed at a price below first class in the larger liners and above cabin or tourist class. Peak summer season rates in 1960 for this pair began at $308. First class on the *Nieuw Amsterdam* began at $362, cabin class at $255 and tourist class at $215.

After the decline in profitability of the late fifties, the *Noordam* was withdrawn from Dutch service in May 1963. Her large appetite for costly diesel oils was a contributing factor. She was sold to Cielomar SA, a Panamanian subsidiary of Italy's Costa Line. The new owners had little intention of operating the ship themselves. Instead, she was chartered to the French Messageries Maritimes and renamed *Océanien*. Her all-first class arrangement was enlarged somewhat, for 202 passengers, divided between

106 in first class and 96 in tourist. She was assigned to an extensive sailing pattern: from Marseilles to Algiers, then across the Atlantic to Guadeloupe and Martinique, followed by Curaçao and passage through the Panama Canal, to French Polynesia, the New Hebrides, New Caledonia, and finally a turn-round at Sydney. The former *Noordam* survived until 1967, when she was retired and scrapped at Split in Yugoslavia.

The WESTERDAM

The combination ship *Westerdam* made the first post-war Holland-America crossing, going direct from Rotterdam to New York, in June 1946. Captain van Herk was aboard for the maiden trip. 'We were given a grand reception along the Hudson – with tugs, fireboats and ferries.' This ship, only partially complete when the war started, was the first to be finished and revive post-war service seven years later.

The *Westerdam* and her sistership *Zuiderdam* were originally designed for Holland-America's North American Pacific Coast service via Panama. The building order for the pair was placed in 1939. Then, shortly after construction began, World War II started. Work continued, but under the watchful eye of the Nazi invaders. Progress was often slowed quite deliberately by hostile Dutch shipyard crews. When the *Westerdam* was first floated in her construction dock, on 27 July 1940, there was little fuss, indeed there was hardly a representative from Holland-America present. A month later, on 27 August, the ship's incomplete hull was hit during an Allied air raid on Schiedam and then sank. The Nazis were quick to order salvage. It was planned to finish the vessel for German war duty, but the scheme was never realized. In September 1944, when it was discovered that the Nazis planned to sink the ship in order to block the harbour entrance at Schiedam, Dutch Resistance forces sank the ship themselves, although in a far less difficult position. The Nazis were furious. They had the ship raised for a second time and planned to resink her as a blockade. The Dutch Resistance again forestalled them by sinking the *Westerdam* for a third time. After the Liberation, she was raised on 13 September 1945 and taken to her builders' yard for completion. The proposed *Zuiderdam* fared less well. Sunk in August 1941 and salvaged a year later, she was sunk in the New Waterway in September 1944. Salvaged in 1946, she was judged too expensive to repair and scrapped two years later in Belgium.

The *Westerdam* had space for 134 passengers, all first class. The accommodation for passengers was arranged on five decks. The Main Lounge was forward on the Promenade Deck, followed by a foyer, small bar, combination writing room-library and Smoking Room, which adjoined a verandah. The restaurant, which seated

The Dining Room onboard the Noordam.

111 passengers at a single seating, was forward on A Deck. All of the cabins except one were outside and all had private bathrooms. William Prins, who later became a vice-president of Holland-America, served aboard the _Westerdam_ in the late forties. The lifestyle aboard the ship, with its one passenger class, struck him as fairly subdued. The passengers amused themselves, reading and lounging in deck chairs during the day, and in the evening watched films projected from the top of a piano in the lounge. He remembers the Captain 'rather discreetly coming down to watch a film, quietly sitting on the piano bench'.

The _Westerdam_ was paired with the _Noordam_, and together they worked a nine-day schedule between Rotterdam and New York. Captain van Herk remembers that both ships went north along the Hudson River to Albany, New York, in the late forties, to load grain. In November 1951, the _Westerdam_ put into Baltimore as an alternative to New York, which was closed by a dockers' strike. During another strike, the _Noordam_ went to Philadelphia to load her passengers and cargo. By the late fifties, just as her passenger loads were declining, the freight that once filled the _Westerdam_'s six holds was being lost to faster, more modern freighters. Older ships like the

Westerdam, with their raked hull designs, were not intended for the new system of pallets, pre-stacked units of goods which exactly fit the holds of newer ships. After the _Noordam_ was withdrawn in the spring of 1963, the _Westerdam_ was paired for a time with the 9300-ton _Prinses Margriet_, which had been bought from another Dutch company, the Oranje Line. Although the _Prinses Margriet_ was a smaller ship, she did have 111 passenger berths and was therefore considered a good partner to the _Westerdam_. In fact, it was only a brief pairing. The _Westerdam_ was withdrawn in the autumn of 1964. Put up for sale, the old ship could not find a buyer. There were reports that she might become a workers' hostel at the steel mills at IJmuiden, but instead she was sold to Spanish breakers in February 1965 and broken up at Alicante.

CHAPTER FIVE

THE MID-ATLANTIC ROUTE

ITALIAN LINE

The SATURNIA and VULCANIA

At the end of World War II, the Italian passenger fleet was in ruins. Four of its illustrious pre-war liners were left, and those only because they had fallen into American hands. The *Rex*, the *Conte di Savoia*, the *Augustus*, the *Roma* and others had been destroyed by bombs, caught fire or sunk. At the home office in Genoa, the Italian Line directorate thought about restoring the company's Atlantic passenger service, using the remaining tonnage. Fortunately, the US Government was to return four converted troopers, the *Saturnia* and her sister ship, *Vulcania, Conte Biancamano* and the *Conte Grande*.

In the summer of 1940, as Italy officially entered the war, both the *Saturnia* and *Vulcania* were caught in home waters and remained there for several years. There were reports that they had been sunk, but both were very much afloat and still seaworthy at the time of the Italian surrender in 1943. Soon afterward, they passed to the Americans, for use as troop ships by the Allies. The *Saturnia* was selected in 1945 to be equipped as a hospital ship and was known for a time as the USS *Frances Y Slanger*. Both completed their military assignments by the end of 1946, and later began the gradual return to Italian flag operations. Initially, however, they were laid-up at New York.

The *Vulcania* made nine voyages to the Mediterranean under American Export Lines' management beginning in March 1946, and was then transferred to the Italian Line. She was subsequently engaged in the repatriation of Italian troops and prisoners from East Africa. The *Frances Y Slanger* reverted to her original name and was returned to the Italians in November 1946. After restoration work, both ships gradually resumed commercial Atlantic service on the express run between Naples, Genoa, Cannes and New York. American Export continued to act as their North American agents, an arrangement which lasted until 1954. Frank O Braynard, the noted American maritime historian, and curator of the Museum of the American Merchant Marine, recalled the revival of the *Saturnia* in January 1947 and the *Vulcania* in the following July. 'It was pure generosity by the Americans to have

returned them to the Italians. They might well have been kept and used as reparations. In some ways, the *Vulcania* was the slightly superior sister. She had one of the finest dining rooms ever to go to sea. Both ships shared another fine feature: a string of elegant first-class suites that include private seaside verandahs. Very few ships could equal such accommodation at the time.'

The *Saturnia* and *Vulcania* were not put back on their original pre-war service until late 1955. They resumed

The first post-war liners to resume Italian Line luxury service on the North Atlantic were the Vulcania *and her near-sistership, the* Saturnia.

sailing out of the Adriatic, from Trieste and Venice, to Halifax (only on the westbound crossing) and New York, via Patras, Messina, Palermo, Naples and Gibraltar. They often called at Boston on the day after New York on the outward journey. Other periodic stopovers included Dubrovnik, Barcelona and Lisbon. In addition to their one-way and inter-port traffic, they were often advertised for round trips, cruises taking upwards of forty days. The two liners led very full lives and were not retired until the spring of 1965 (when they were approaching forty years old), just as the brand new superliners *Michelangelo* and *Raffaello* came into service. At the time of their final sailings, the *New York Times* commented, 'The *Saturnia* and *Vulcania* have carried more Italian immigrants to America than any other ships. There are so many Italian-American children who were either born at sea or near to a voyage in one of these ships that *Saturnia* or *Vulcania* often became their middle names.' Captain Narciso Fossati, who later became the commodore of the Italian Line passenger fleet, recalled these two motorliners as 'very strong, quite superb at sea. They carried tens of thousands of immigrants to America and Canada, especially after the war, and were immensely profitable.'

After being decommissioned, the ships nested together for a time, awaiting their fates. The *Saturnia* was finally sold to the breakers at La Spezia, and demolition began in April 1966. Some of her remains were recycled for a new high-tension wire facility in Italy. The *Vulcania* found new life. Bought by the Grimaldi-Siosa Lines and renamed *Caribia*, she was put on the West Indies trade, sailing mainly from Southampton, or Spanish ports, Emigrants were her principal customers, outward bound from Spain, or travelling from the West Indies to Britain. Later, she sailed more as a cruise ship, on weekly trips around the western Mediterranean from Genoa. Finally laid up at La Spezia in September 1972, she seemed destined for the scrapyard, after forty-four years' work. Instead, her career persisted for two more years. In January 1973, just as she had been sold to Italian shipbreakers, she was resold to Spanish scrappers. She finally reached Barcelona by September, only to be left untouched. She was again resold in February 1974, this time to the ever-hungry Taiwanese. She endured the long tow to Kaohsiung. Unfortunately, once there, she developed serious hull leaks while awaiting a berth and sank in the outer harbour. Another *Caribia*, the former Cunarder *Caronia*, also due at Kaohsiung several weeks later, encountered a tropical storm at Guam during her delivery voyage and became a total loss. She, too, failed to reach her final berth.

The CONTE BIANCAMANO and CONTE GRANDE

The only other large Italian survivors of the War were the near-sisters *Conte Biancamano* and *Conte Grande*, both built in the twenties and occasionally in transatlantic service between the wars. Again, both had come under American control during the World War II. The *Conte Biancamano* sailed as the troopship USS *Hermitage*: the *Conte Grande* as the USS *Monticello*. Afterward, like the *Saturnia* and *Vulcania*, they were returned to Italy in 1947. They were given directly to the Italian Government, then bought by the Società Marittima Finanziaria and subsequently chartered to the Italian Line. In later years, they were bought outright by the Italian Line. Both were given very extensive refits, which included almost complete replacement of the passenger accommodation, a refined exterior look and even some lengthening. Frank Braynard especially remembered the *Conte Biancamano* after her conversion. 'Her restoration was fantastic. From beautiful pre-war Rococo, she went to equally brilliant contemporary, superb modern in fact. Few ships have been transformed as beautifully.'

These ships were to divide their work, sailing in winter to South America and in the peak summer season to New York. However, the *Conte Grande* sailed the North Atlantic for only one summer, in 1956, as a temporary replacement for the *Andrea Doria*. The *Conte Biancamano* started New York summer season sailings in 1950 and

Skyfotos

continued these for a decade. Captain Fossati recalled both ships as 'very solid liners, which had been given good care while with the Americans during the war. On the South American trade, in first class, we carried rich Italians, Argentinians and Brazilians, and the high Catholic clergy, such as cardinals and bishops. Because we were state-owned, we always carried members of the Church. In cabin class, there were more tourist-type passengers. Of course, the officers preferred this section because there was far less formality. In third class, we carried immigrants outbound [to Rio, Santos, Montevideo and Buenos Aires] and then returned with students, budget

The inner port at Genoa in 1954. The brand new Cristoforo Colombo *is in centre position; the* Andrea Doria *is to the right and about to sail. To the left are three other passenger ships: Home Lines'* Homeland, *Argentina's* Salta *and Union-Castle's* Rhodesia Castle.

tourists and reverse immigrants, who were seeking a better life in Europe.' Both ships were retired in 1960. The *Conte Biancamano* went directly to the scrappers at La Spezia, while the *Conte Grande* made a charter voyage out with immigrants to Australia for Lloyd Triestino. She was scrapped in 1961, also at La Spezia.

The ANDREA DORIA and CRISTOFORO COLOMBO
With only four of their liners surviving World War II, the Italians eventually planned a huge rebuilding programme. Rather strangely, however, they chose to build their first new large liners for the South American rather than New York trade. The 27,000-ton liners, *Giulio Cesare* and *Augustus*, were completed in 1951 and 1952 especially for the Latin American route. Then, as attention finally turned to the New York run, a larger, faster team emerged, the 29,100-ton *Andrea Doria* and *Cristoforo Colombo*. Captain Fossati recalled these sisters. 'Both the

Victor Scrivens Collection

Listing badly, the Andrea Doria *as seen in the early morning of 26 July 1956. Within hours, she will be at the bottom.*

Doria and *Colombo* were especially luxurious, built purposely for the high demands of the American trade. We often carried celebrities on board, such as Ambassador Clare Booth Luce, Clark Gable and Elizabeth Taylor. Both liners needed turbines [instead of the preferred diesels] so as to have greater speeds, as much as 24 knots.'

The *Andrea Doria* and *Cristoforo Colombo* were built by the Ansaldo shipyard at Genoa and commissioned in January 1953 and July 1954 respectively. The Italians were aptly proud. Their ships were superb, handsome inside and out – the perfect rivals to American Export's *Independence* and *Constitution*, which had appeared two years earlier. As national flagship, the *Andrea Doria* received the most attention. Not only was she the biggest ship then in the Italian merchant marine (it was long before supertankers), but she was also the fastest, having attained over 26 knots on her trials. The two ships worked the Italian Line's express run, between Genoa, Cannes, Naples, Gibraltar and New York, with a round voyage taking about three weeks. In addition to three passenger classes, each ship could handle four holds of general cargo.

The *Doria* is best remembered because of her fatal collision off the American East Coast in the summer of 1956, early in her fourth year of service. Several books, numerous magazine and newspaper articles, and even some television documentaries have attempted to analyse the disaster. When it occurred, on the night of 25 July, the liner was some sixty miles from Nantucket and just hours from her arrival at New York. In foggy conditions, she was rammed by the Swedish *Stockholm*, which had left her

Sal Scannella Collection

Captain Pietro Calamai and a fellow officer onboard the Andrea Doria *at the time of her maiden voyage, in January 1953. Captain Calamai was master of the ship during her fatal collision in the summer of 1956.*

Sal Scannella Collection

The Cristoforo Colombo *was repainted in white in 1965.*

Manhattan pier that morning. A huge hole ripped in the *Andrea Doria*, just below the starboard bridge, caused an immediate, very severe list. Consequently, none of the portside lifeboats could be lowered. However, there was adequate time for evacuation as the *Doria* lingered for hours, gradually listing further. Finally abandoned, she sank in the early daylight hours of 26 July. The *Stockholm* limped back to New York, her bow smashed. She looked very sad, and to some sinister, as she sailed into New York Harbour late in the afternoon of the same day. In all, there were 52 casualties in the disaster.

The mood at the Italian Line offices on both sides of the Atlantic was grim. The nation had lost a flagship of which it had occasionally been said that her construction made her practically unsinkable. It was a deep blow to Italian pride. Long, very confidential inquiries and hearings followed the tragedy. The compensation amounted to some $48 million, and precise responsibility was never publicly revealed. The final investigations were dropped by mutual consent.

The *Doria*, resting on her starboard side in the cold, shark-infested western Atlantic, gradually became more and more overgrown with marine life. There has been constant speculation concerning her possible salvage. Suggested schemes have included pulling her up from the bottom with cables and chains, dragging her along the sea bed to a shallow shoreline, and even floating her to the surface with ping-pong balls. One plan was directed towards towing the ship, once raised, into New York Harbour, opening her to public view and then cutting up the remains to make souvenir cuff-links, key-rings and bracelets. Many divers have inspected the ship without bringing back hope of her recovery. However a foyer statue of Andrea Doria is among items retrieved and now stands in the lobby of a Florida hotel. The ship's safe has also been recovered, and in January 1982, over twenty-five years after her sinking, a lifeboat washed ashore at Staten Island, New York, not far from the *Doria*'s intended New York City berth. She will probably remain in her underwater grave while stories continue to circulate about her.

With the *Andrea Doria* gone, the slightly less prestigious *Cristoforo Colombo* took over as the Italian flagship. A specially gathered team of relief liners, the *Augustus*, the *Giulio Cesare* and the *Conte Grande*, transferred from the Latin American route to assist her until the *Doria*'s replacement, the larger *Leonardo Da Vinci*, finally joined

the fleet in June 1960. The *Cristoforo Colombo* remained an express ship until the spring of 1965, when the much larger and faster *Michelangelo* and *Raffaello* came into use. The *Colombo* then replaced the veteran *Saturnia* and *Vulcania* on the service out of the Adriatic. The terminal ports were Trieste and Venice, and there were calls at Piraeus, Messina, Palermo, Naples, Halifax (westbound only) and occasionally Boston (eastbound only), Lisbon and Barcelona. In 1966, the liner was repainted to give her an all-white hull, which matched the attractive new Italian superliners.

For some years, the *Colombo* continued to be a popular and in some ways unique ship. Her numerous ports of call made her route one of the most extensive then offered by an Atlantic liner. Michael Cohn was among her passengers at the time. 'On our crossing in 1966, we were making a special stop at Ponta Delgada in the Azores for a group of fishermen and their families. They were travelling with considerable baggage, which included appliances such as refrigerators for their families. During a particularly nasty storm, I shall always recall these fishermen remaining in the lounge and continuing to weave their fishing nets. They were completely unaffected.

'Travelling in tourist class, we also had a large number

Sailing from Naples in 1953, aboard the Andrea Doria. *The imposing Passenger Terminal to the left was built in the late forties, especially for the transatlantic liners, but had the very definite flavour of a 1930s creation.*

Midnight buffet onboard the Cristoforo Colombo.

of Sicilian-Americans, who were returning to the homeland for a visit. I especially remember a fancy dress party one evening. The most beautiful entries were several Chinese girls who were wearing the most fantastic hats, but received only 18 votes. The big rivalry was between the Italian passengers. A contestant from Naples received 82 votes while a Sicilian entry took 84 votes. It had become a domestic rivalry.

'Fares on board the *Colombo* were so devised that they were the best bargain on the Atlantic at the time. The price was even less than a passage in the giant, brand new *Raffaello*. The difference was that the *Colombo* was slower. We were charged for New York to Naples, but were permitted to continue to Venice, and all via Lisbon, Malaga, Naples, Messina, Palermo and Piraeus. When we finally arrived in Venice, it was quite thrilling. You could stand on the upper decks and simply look out over the rooftops.'

Traditional shipboard horse-racing, as seen onboard the Andrea Doria.

Luis Miguel Correia

The Augustus *and her sistership, the* Giulio Cesare, *were the first large brand new Italian liners to be built after the Second World War. The* Augustus *is shown arriving at Lisbon.*

The *Colombo* was rather abruptly reassigned to the South American trade in February 1973, completely abandoning her intended North Atlantic schedule. The *Guilio Cesare* had just been withdrawn from the South Atlantic with machinery troubles and thus prompted a rearrangement of the fleet. Actually, the *Colombo* was completely unprofitable by this time like the other Italian liners. Her continuation in service was upheld by the Italian Government, with urging from the powerful seamen's unions. One of the very last Italian liners, she was finally withdrawn in 1977 and bought, rather oddly, to provide accommodation for workers at a steel plant at Puerto Ordaz, Venezuela. In her temporary role, she soon deteriorated. She was again up for sale in 1981, but with little prospect of further trading. She went to Taiwanese scrappers, who had her towed through the Panama Canal and then across the Pacific. She was a sorry sight at the

Sal Scannella Collection

A three-berth cabin in Cabin Class aboard the Giulio Cesare.

time. She reached Kaohsiung, on 30 June 1981, but then only to have the dismantling delayed. In May 1982, she was towed to Hong Kong and again offered for sale, amid some speculation that she might be reactivated as a cruise ship. Coincidentally, her former fleetmate, the ex-*Augustus*, was laid up nearby. However, the *Colombo* did not secure any further buyers. She returned to Kaohsiung, and scrapping began in October 1982.

The GIULIO CESARE and AUGUSTUS

Built especially for the South American trade, between Naples, Genoa, Lisbon and Rio, Santos, Montevideo and Buenos Aires, these handsome sisters did not sail the North Atlantic until the mid-fifties – the *Giulio Cesare* in June 1956, to help fill increased traffic demands, and the *Augustus* in February 1957, as part of the replacement for the *Andrea Doria*. Although not as luxurious or as spacious as the *Doria* and the *Cristoforo Columbo*, the pair were adequate for service to New York. Ideally, they each carried three classes of passengers. Captain Rossati sailed aboard both of these ships. 'The *Giulio Cesare* and *Augustus*

The first class swimming pool (complete with sliding ramp) and lido area aboard the Giulio Cesare.

Sal Scamella Collection

Sal Scannella Collection

Strikingly modern for her time, the First class Observation Lounge onboard the Guilio Cesare *was done in soothing light colours.*

were unusually big motorliners [over 27,000 tons each]. Having built their diesels, the Fiat company had a very special interest in both of them and inspected each ship following every round voyage. Like the *Conte Biancamano* and to some extent, the *Conte Grande*, these South American ships earned double profits: Latin America in the winter and New York in the summer.' They worked the express run to New York until 1960, by which time the brand new *Leonardo Da Vinci* came into service. Thereafter, they reverted to the South American trade full time. In 1964, they were converted to two-class ships, retaining first class, but losing the cabin class, which merged into tourist. The result was a total of 1000 tourist class berths in each ship.

The South Atlantic service was declining by the early seventies, and when the *Giulio Cesare* developed serious rudder problems during a voyage in December 1972 little effort was made to repair her. Laid up for a short time, she was scrapped at La Spezia in the following summer. The *Augustus* continued, teamed for a while with the *Cristoforo Colombo*, until January 1976, when she was herself withdrawn. A year later, she went to Hong Kong buyers, Great Shipping & Investment Limited. Renamed the *Great Sea*, she was placed under the flag of the Seychelles and sent out to Hong Kong, but then laid up, remaining at a local anchorage for some years. Her registry was subsequently changed to Panamanian, and she passed to other Far Eastern owners in 1980, becoming the *Ocean King*. Soon afterward, she was moved to Manila. It has since been rumoured that she is to become a hotel ship in South Korea. With the larger *Michelangelo* and *Raffaello* now in Iranian hands, the former *Augustus* is the only other survivor of the post-war Italian Line passenger fleet.

HOME LINES

The ATLANTIC
The Home Lines, formed in 1946, was an organization with a Greek president, Swedish investors, Italian staff, Panamanian registry, and links with several other countries. Its purpose was to cash in on the huge South American immigrant trade, and it quickly acquired a notable fleet of second-hand liners. However, it was not until 1949 that the Company turned to the North Atlantic, with the Latin American trade in decline and further complicated by currency problems. Frank Braynard, then a New York maritime reporter, was the journalist who broke the news that the Home Lines was opening a new passenger service to the United States. 'I had quite accidentally come across a friend at the Cosmopolitan Shipping Company, who were just appointed agents for this new liner firm. There was also a strong link between the Home Lines and the Swedish Brostrom Group, who owned the Swedish American Line. In fact, the name Home Lines is derived from the word "holm", the very well-known nomenclature of the Swedish American ships. They also used the golden crown as a funnel decoration in much the same way as the Swedish liners did. This was certainly a very impressive beginning for the Home Lines, a link to the superbly reputed Swedish-American fleet.'

The first transatlantic sailing, between Naples, Genoa and New York, took place in May 1949, using the recently acquired *Atlantic*, formerly the American liner *Matsonia*. American passenger ships have always been desirable once they go on the block. High-quality construction, in association with safety-consciousness, good machinery, and high standards of passenger accommodation (often so spacious that it conveniently allows the increased capacities required for full profitability by overseas buyers), has attracted many buyers who eventually operate the liners under the flags of Greece, Liberia and Panama. When the Matson cruise ship *Matsonia* was first offered for sale in 1948, the Home Lines negotiated a quick purchase. She had become the fourth Home Lines ship within two years.

The *Matsonia*, originally built as the *Malolo* in 1927 and renamed in 1937, had been refitted at the Ansaldo shipyard

Victor Scrivens Collection

Home Lines' Atlantic *later became the* Queen Frederica, *owned by a subsidiary company, the National Hellenic American Line.*

at Genoa. The 700 or so first class berths from her Matson Line days were replaced by a far larger complement of 349 in first class, 203 in cabin and 626 in tourist, which was more appropriate for transatlantic sailing. The Home Lines' initial plan was to place the *Matsonia* on the South American trade, but she started instead on the New York run. The new trade was augmented by a large number of passengers travelling to Rome in 1950, which was a Holy Year.

The *Atlantic* was reassigned in 1952 to a more northerly run, between Southampton and Quebec City. In winter, when the St Lawrence was blocked with ice, she put into Halifax instead. There were also occasional cruises. Then, in late 1954, at the special request of the Greek Government, the liner was transferred to a new Home Lines' subsidiary, the National Hellenic American Line, and renamed *Queen Frederica*.

The ITALIA

As Swedish-American's *Kungsholm*, built in 1928, she was a noted transatlantic liner. Later, beginning in the early thirties, she also developed a good reputation on luxury long-distance cruises. She served with the Americans during World War II, when she was bought outright and used as the transport USS *John Ericsson*, and subsequently worked for the Home Lines under the name *Italia*. One Home Lines official later remarked, 'She was the best ship we ever had. She could do no wrong. She was always profitable and popular.'

In 1947, the former *Kungsholm* had been a battered ship, seriously damaged not long before by a fire at her New York pier while still owned by the US Government. She was suddenly (and surprisingly) sold back to her original owners but then resold before repair to the Home Lines, which was linked financially with Swedish-American. At that time, Home Lines was in almost desperate need of second-hand passenger ships for its service to Latin America. Following full repairs and alterations, the ship was rechristened *Italia* and entered service between Genoa, Rio, Santos, Montevideo and Buenos Aires, in July 1948. However, within a year, because of a sudden decline in immigration to South America, she was moved to the North Atlantic, sailing between Naples, Genoa and New York. In 1952, she was reassigned for operations out of

In the late fifties, the Italia *had both masts stumped so as to clear the bridges along the St Lawrence River and proceed beyond Quebec City to Montreal.*

Hamburg and the Channel ports to Halifax and New York. Her management and operations were then handled by the Hamburg-American Line. Several years later, Quebec City and Montreal became her North American terminal ports. That her high earnings came mainly from westbound immigrants and low-fare tourists was reflected in her berthing plans – 213 in first class and 1106 in tourist. She flew the Panama flag and was staffed by some Italians, but mostly Germans.

The *Italia* was among the earliest withdrawals from transatlantic service as the jets began to establish their dominant position. She finished her last crossing in the autumn of 1960, and was sent to Genoa for a full refit. The improvements included a large, aft-section lido deck with twin pools, greater luxury in cabins and public rooms, and a capacity that was reduced to 680, all in first class. In December 1960, she opened a new Home Lines service: seven-day cruises between New York and Nassau, departing each Saturday afternoon all the year round, with minimum fares of $170. A very successful period followed. The *Italia* developed a fine reputation as one of the forerunners of year-round cruising for such transatlantic firms as the Home Lines. Within five years, the weekly run between New York and Nassau was able to sustain the 39,000-ton *Oceanic*, then the largest liner used throughout the year on cruises, with capacity for 1200 passengers.

The *Italia* was decommissioned in April 1964 and sold for $466,000 to the newly formed Canaveral International Corporation. Her new role was to act as a permanently moored hotel ship at Freeport, Grand Bahama, a tourist spot which was then expanding rapidly. The ship was named the *Imperial Bahama Hotel* and listed as having space for 1400 guests. Unfortunately, the project flopped within a year, despite the $1 million spent on renovation. There were scandals, including reports of embezzlement by the management. The Bahamian Government stepped in, siezing the old liner for auction. The highest bidder, a Spanish scrap firm, offered $265,000. Towed into Bilbao on 8 September 1965, the former *Italia* was scrapped within months.

The BRASIL/HOMELAND
Originally built as the *Virginian* for the Allan Line's service between Liverpool and the St Lawrence, this ship became one of the longest surviving Atlantic liners, of all time. Commissioned in 1905, she ran for fifty years. She and her sister ship *Victorian*, completed by Workman, Clark at Belfast a couple of weeks earlier, ranked as the first transatlantic liner to have direct-action turbines, a successful system that soon spread to almost all subsequent liners. The *Virginian* changed hands in 1920, becoming the Swedish-American Line's *Drottningholm* and remained

Skyfotos

Everett Viez Collection

The Home Lines' flagship, the Homeric, *sailing from New York for a wintertime Caribbean cruise.*

with them until sold to the Home Lines in 1948.

Renamed *Brasil*, the ship began immigrant sailings to South America in July 1948. Two years later, with a large increase in traffic on the Mediterranean run to New York, she was reassigned to the North Atlantic. Proving successful, she was given a major refit in the winter of 1950–51 and her accommodation was styled as 96 in first class and 846 in budget tourist. Soon afterward, she was shifted to Hamburg, sailing across to Halifax and New York via Southampton and Cherbourg. Under the

management of the Hamburg-American Line's passenger department, she was re-christened the *Homeland*, a name that was considered more appropriate.

A year or so later, at the beginning of the 1952 season, the *Atlantic* was transferred to the Canadian service, the *Italia* to the Hamburg service, and the *Homeland* returned to the Mediterranean. Three more successful years followed before the aged ship was retired. She was scrapped at Trieste in the spring of 1955.

The ARGENTINA

The *Argentina* was the first liner in the Home Lines' fleet, having joined in November 1946 and been commissioned two months later. She had been the *Bergensfjord*, the early flagship of the Norwegian America Line which worked the North Atlantic run to New York. Used by the British during World War II, she was not restored for post-war Norwegian service, but instead sold. She was the perfect candidate for the Home Lines' new immigrant service to South America.

As the *Argentina*, she sailed from Genoa to Rio, Santos, Montevideo and Buenos Aires, and later to the Caribbean and La Guaira, Venezuela. She sailed the North Atlantic run for a short time (1951–52), mostly between Naples, Genoa, Lisbon, Halifax and New York. Afterwards, she seemed to fall out of place, without receiving reassignment. Sold to the Zim Lines early in 1953, she became their *Jerusalem*, and the first major passenger ship in the Israeli fleet. She was finally scrapped in 1959, aged forty-six, at La Spezia, Italy.

The HOMERIC

Although she was a fine and well loved transatlantic liner, the *Homeric*, early flagship of the Home Lines, gained her highest acclaim as a winter cruise ship, sailing from New York to the Caribbean. Through a combination of superb maintenance, excellent cuisine and fine service, she became very popular with the cruising public, and there were passengers who travelled aboard her year after year. She was affectionatly known as the 'fun ship'.

The *Homeric* was originally one of a trio of outstanding ships, the Matson liners *Lurline*, *Mariposa* and *Monterey* of the early thirties. Beautifully decorated and handsomely proportioned, they were created by the Bethlehem Steel Company at Quincy, Massachusetts. The *Lurline* was intended for the California–Hawaii trade, while the other two were designed to travel farther, to Australia and the South Seas. By 1941, however, the trio was disbanded, never to sail again as running-mates. All served as wartime troopers, but only the *Lurline* was later restored. Sharp increases in American shipyard costs curtailed any plans for the other two liners, and subsequent evaluations revealed that only one of these ships might be needed by Matson for future service. The *Mariposa* was cleared for sale. She went quickly to the Home Lines. After an extended lay-up after the war at Alameda, California, she had her engines, but little else, refitted and was then taken to Trieste, where she was lavishly rebuilt as the *Homeric*.

Her first subsequent crossing was a midwinter voyage, in January 1955, between Venice and New York. She won instant high praise for her extremely pleasant balance of interior stylings, a blend between the original American and contemporary Mediterranean design. Her accommodation was arranged for easy conversion from 147 first class and 1096 tourist on transatlantic sailings to 730, all first class, for cruises. In the May of her maiden year, she

The hazards of a winter North Atlantic crossing: a frozen, ice-encrusted forward superstructure and bridge section onboard the Italia.

began her intended North Atlantic duties, sailing between Cuxhaven, Le Havre, Southampton, Quebec City and Montreal. For some years, the *Homeric* plied a sensible format as a two-class Atlantic ship between April and October, and as a one-class West Indies cruise ship for the rest of the year.

Home Lines was quite early to recognize the decline of the transatlantic liner trade and suspended these operations in October 1963. The *Homeric* saw out the

Company's Canadian run. She was then placed on the New York cruise trade throughout the year, making longer trips in winter and weekly runs from New York to Nassau for the rest of the time.

Even after forty years, the *Homeric* might have survived a little longer, but she was seriously damaged by a galley fire some ninety miles off the New Jersey coast on 1 July 1973. She was forced to return to New York and offload her passengers. She was taken to Genoa for further inspection and then promptly laid-up. While the actual fire damage was limited and might have been repaired, the accommodation reeked of smoke, and large financial investment would have been needed to restore her. Economically, she was beyond repair. Sold to Taiwanese breakers, she reached Kaohsiung in January 1974 and was scrapped. On the other hand, her two former Matson sisters survive. The former *Lurline* (now the Chandris *Ellinis*) is laid-up in Perama Bay, near Piraeus, while the original *Monterey* is still sailing, also for Chandris, as the American-based cruise ship *Britanis*.

GREEK LINE

The NEA HELLAS/NEW YORK

The Greek Line, owned by the very large Goulandris Group, was created to provide Greek-flag (or Greek-owned) passenger service across the Atlantic and to offer inexpensive accommodation wherever there was a demand. The Company's first ship, the 16,991-ton *Nea Hellas*, joined the fleet in the spring of 1939, just months before the outbreak of World War II. Previously, she had been the *Tuscania* of the Anchor Line, a roving ship that plied the Glasgow-New York trade, sailed on runs to India, on cruises and was, for a time, under charter to Cunard. She spent the worst period of the Depression laid up, and served as a floating grandstand for the launching of the *Queen Mary* at Clydebank in September 1934. She was returned to the British for wartime troop transport, when she was referred to as the 'Nelly Wallace'.

After a suitable refit, the *Nea Hellas* resumed Atlantic service in August 1947, trading between Piraeus, Malta, Naples, Lisbon, Halifax (westbound only) and New York. Her accommodation was divided between 179 in first class, 404 in cabin and 1399 in tourist. It was a boom period, especially for emigrants, refugees and displaced persons, and the liner was often booked to capacity.

Early in 1955, the Greek Line transferred the new flagship, *Olympia*, to the Mediterranean route and put the *Nea Hellas* on the busy Northern run, primarily between Bremerhaven, the Channel ports and New York. She was again refitted. Her name was changed to *New York*, and her accommodation became 70 in first class and 1300 in tourist. The *New York* was retired in the autumn of 1959,

The Greek Line's New York *made occasional calls at Boston (usually the day following New York) on her eastbound Mediterranean crossings. She is seen sailing from the Massachusetts port in the late fifties.*

at the age of thirty-seven. Her final Greek Line crossing was, in fact, an unusual voyage, from Quebec City to the Mediterranean, with calls as far east as Odessa. Soon afterward, she was laid-up at Piraeus. She sailed out to Onomichi, Japan, two years later to be broken up.

The NEPTUNIA

Frank Braynard, a New York maritime reporter in the late forties and fifties, enthusiastically recalled the Greek Line's passenger fleet. 'They were a fascinating company that took old ships, rebuilt them, operated them well, made them look interesting – and all to make lots of money.' At the end of 1948, the Company was preparing for its fourth ship, the former *Johan de Witt* of the Nederland Line, which had worked the colonial East Indies trade out of Amsterdam. The Greek Line had just bought two Australian coastal passenger ships, the 9400-ton *Katoomba*, which became the *Columbia*, and the 7700-ton *Canberra*, which retained the same name. Both of these

ships had been reworked for the North Atlantic as well.

The former *Johan de Witt* was given the most extensive Greek Line refit to date. Her second funnel and mainmast were removed, and the accommodation was increased to 787 berths, compared with her earlier figure of just over 350. Renamed *Neptunia*, she was registered to the Company's Panamanian subsidiary, Compania Maritima del Este. Her first assignment was the Mediterranean-New York trade. She moved in 1951 to a service from Bremerhaven and the Channel ports to New York and, finally, in 1955 went on the Canadian run to Quebec City and Montreal. During a Canadian crossing, the *Neptunia* became the Company's first loss. After striking Daunts Rock, near Cóbh, Ireland, and suffering serious hull damage, she was considered beyond repair. Some months later, in March 1958, she was freed and then towed to Rotterdam for scrapping.

The OLYMPIA

The *Olympia* was the first brand new liner to be built for Greek interests. Considering the nation's long and colourful maritime heritage, it is ironic that no tonnage had been built before 1953. Instead, the Greeks made do with second-hand passenger ships. It was hoped that the arrival of the new *Olympia* would start a fresh chapter of

A view of the Olympia *in the early seventies, with her mainmast removed.*

Victor Scrivens Collection

Luis Miguel Correia

The rebuilt Arkadia, *a former three-stacker, had the rather eccentric feature of a smoke-dispensing dipod mast in addition to an operative funnel. She is seen docked at Boston, in preparation for a series of Caribbean cruises.*

Greek-flag passenger shipping. However, just before her completion there were complications. As the Greeks, like several other western European nations, were unable to build a 22,000-ton ship in home waters, they looked overseas to Alexander Stephen & Sons Limited, Glasgow. During completion of the ship, the Greek Government became increasingly dissatisfied with the plans for her operation. First, the Greek Line wanted to staff the hotel department with 258 German stewards, all formerly with North German Lloyd. It had been decided that the ship would initially sail between Bremerhaven, the Channel ports and New York, rather than out of the Mediterranean. The early fifties were a period of great activity on the North European run, particularly in the transport of German immigrants. The additional German crew therefore seemed essential. However, Greek maritime law insisted that Greek-flag ships must have all-Greek crews. Secondly, the new liner had a foreign mortgage, which was again forbidden for a Greek-flag vessel. All the plans seemed disrupted. Even the proposal that the ship should be named *Frederica* in honour of the reigning Queen of the Hellenes was abandoned. On 16 April 1953, the vessel slipped into the River Clyde as 'Yard Number 636', the biggest ship ever launched without a name.

Just before her maiden voyage, in October 1953, she was finally named *Olympia* and registered to the Transatlantic Shipping Corporation of Monrovia on behalf of the Greek Line. Although her owners were the Goulandris family, she was to fly the Liberian flag. Following an introductory mini-cruise in the Irish Sea, she sailed from Glasgow, on 15 October, bound for Halifax and New York via Belfast, Liverpool, Southampton, Cherbourg and Cóbh. On her return crossing, she continued to her new terminal port of Bremerhaven. For the next two years, she worked on the North Atlantic and, for about three months each winter, went cruising to the Caribbean. Initially, the *Olympia* was not without her problems. She ran aground at Southampton in December 1953, when just two months old. In the following March, she developed turbine troubles during a Caribbean cruise. Days behind schedule, she limped back to New York, where specialists from the General Electric Company eventually made the necessary repairs.

In March 1955, the *Olympia* was re-routed to the Mediterranean and replaced on the North European service by another Company liner, the *Nea Hellas*. The *Olympia* was then based at Piraeus. She sailed from New York on the western end and often called at Boston a day later. Her general routing was to Ponta Delgada in the Azores and then on to Lisbon, Naples, Messina and finally Greece. In later years, this service was extended to include Limassol on Cyprus and Haifa in Israel. However, the *Olympia*, like so many other Atlantic liners, turned more and more to cruising by the late sixties. Week-long runs to Bermuda and Nassau, and even three day weekend jaunts out to sea, the popular 'cruises to nowhere', were her mainstay. While she was docked at New York's Pier 97 on 27 September 1968, with that early dispute long forgotten, the *Olympia* finally hoisted the Greek colours. At last, she was a Greek ship in all respects.

In 1970, she was given a major facelift at Genoa and refitted as a full-time cruise ship. The two original classes were replaced by 1037 one-class berths. A new lido section was built in the stern and all cabins were given private bathrooms. The liner resumed New York cruises for a time, but was scheduled for weekly voyages from Piraeus to the Greek islands, Turkey and Israel in 1974. However, the initial bookings for this new venture were light, and a sudden, very sharp increase in transatlantic airfares further reduced the *Olympia*'s intended American market. There was also a sudden price-increase in fuel oils, which jumped from $35 to $95 per ton. The new cruise programme was hastily cancelled, and the ship laid up at an anchorage at Perama, near Piraeus. She would never sail again for the Greeks.

The entire Greek Line passenger operation collapsed a year later, in January 1975. The *Olympia* was claimed for debts by the Greek Government and then sat out the following years forgotten and neglected. Although she was generally thought to be destined for the scrapheap, she was the subject of several rumours. Among others, the Carnival Cruise, Costa, Home and Lauro lines had a look

over her. Her fate was decided in 1982, when she was bought by the Sally Line of Finland for their American subsidiary, Commodore Cruises of Miami. After a thorough refit and refacing (the original funnel and mast are now gone), she has been renamed *Caribe I* and was introduced on the Caribbean cruise trade in August 1983, flying the Panamanian flag.

The ARKADIA

The *Arkadia* was one of the Atlantic's more interesting, almost eccentric passenger ships. A long single-stacker, rather flat in appearance, she had a special bipod mast which was also a funnel, and was often seen under way with smoke pouring from both stack and mast!

Commissioned originally in 1931, she was the first of an illustrious and very popular pair, Furness-Bermuda Line's *Monarch of Bermuda* and her sister, the *Queen of Bermuda*. Both were among the earliest luxury cruise ships aimed particularly at the short-sea market with six-day cruises between New York and Bermuda. Later, both were used as troop ships during World War II and survived unharmed. However, during her post-war conversion at Newcastle, the *Monarch of Bermuda* was badly damaged by

The last passenger ship in the Greek Line fleet, the Queen Anna Maria, *which sailed for a decade, from 1965 until 1975.*

Alex Duncan

fire. Since Furness lost interest in her, she was taken to the Firth of Forth for lay-up and eventual disposal. The British Government was at that time in rather urgent need of additional passenger tonnage to serve the fare-assisted passage scheme for emigrants to Australia. The *Monarch's* damaged hulk was suitable for conversion, which was carried out at the Thornycroft yard at Southampton. She was totally rebuilt as the austerity liner, *New Australia*, with accommodation for 1600 tourist-class passengers. Managed by the Shaw Savill Line's passenger department, she sailed the Australian run out of Southampton and via Suez.

Passing into Greek Line hands early in 1958, she was again the perfect candidate, with some slight modifications and improvements, for the transatlantic Canadian immigrant and tourist trade. The Greek owners wanted to replace their older, smaller passenger ships on this run, and the larger *New Australia* was modified to carry 150 in first class and 1150 in tourist (later changed to 50 first and 1337 tourist). Placed under the Greek flag, she was renamed *Arkadia*. She was routed between Bremerhaven, Amsterdam, London, Le Havre, Cóbh, Quebec City and Montreal. In winters, she cruised, first from New York, then Boston, but mainly on the 'sunshine route' from Southampton to ports like Tenerife, Las Palmas, Madeira, Casablanca, Gibraltar and Lisbon.

By 1966, however, the Canadian trade had slumped. The *Arkadia* was consequently taken off the North Atlantic that November. As her British cruise service had been taken over by a newer vessel, the chartered Norwegian *Oslofjord*, the older ship was out of work. Considering her rather tired thirty-five years, only the scrappers seemed interested. She arrived at Valencia, Spain, on 18 December to be broken up. Ironically, the *Queen of Bermuda*, was also being broken up at the same time, at Faslane in Scotland.

The QUEEN ANNA MARIA

In 1964, the eight-year-old *Empress of Britain* was up for sale. She had outlived her transatlantic use for Canadian Pacific and then worked as an unprofitable cruise ship. She was another perfect candidate for the Greek serivce to North America.

Liner services between the Mediterranean and New York were still fairly healthy in the mid-sixties. On the other hand, the Northern runs were dwindling far more rapidly in their contest with jet travel. The Mediterranean

lines were still supported by considerably numbers of emigrants, particularly from Italy and Greece, who sought to settle in America. Passenger ships offered competitive prices, and space for cases, crates and trunks. Furthermore, the Italians and Greeks were particularly sea-minded – they looked to the sea as their ancestors had done long before, and were generally slow in changing over to air travel.

The former *Empress* needed to be brought up to date.

A classic gathering of Atlantic liners at New York (dated 11 July 1957), which includes the Greek Olympia. *From top to bottom are the* Britannic, Queen Elizabeth, Mauretania, Liberté Olympia *and* United States.

She needed more colour, to be turned into an outdoor, rather than an indoor, ship. A large lido deck was built in the stern area and fitted with no less than four pools and rows of multi-coloured chairs. Below, the public rooms were enlarged and refitted, and a stern lounge was added. All of the cabins, both first and tourist class, were fitted with private toilet facilities, which would increase the liner's usefulness as a cruise ship in the future. Her capacity was increased to 109 in first class and 1145 in tourist. When her refit was complete in the spring of 1965, the liner left Genoa for her official renaming by Her Majesty Queen Anne Marie of Greece at Piraeus. The ship then left via Messina, Naples and Lisbon for Halifax and New York as the *Queen Anna Maria*. The Mayor, John Lindsay, proclaimed 'Queen Anna Maria Day' on her arrival at Manhattan.

The *Queen Anna Maria*'s work was a blend of transatlantic crossings (often extended to include Haifa

Port Authority of New York & New Jersey

and Limassol) and cruises to Bermuda, Nassau and the Caribbean. The Greek Line also became particularly well known for weekend jaunts to 'nowhere', sensible sailings that left the New York City piers at about 6.30 on a Friday evening and returned early enough on the following Monday for passengers to reach their offices by 9 a.m. In the late sixties, minimum cabin fares were $85.

Exactly when and why the Greek Line began to fall on hard times is not certain. Financial problems began to show in the early seventies. Soon after the *Queen Anna Maria*'s only remaining fleet mate, the *Olympia*, had started service as a cruise ship, her sailings were abruptly cancelled, and the ship was laid up. A year later, in January 1975, the entire pasenger division collapsed. Creditors, including New York's Chase Manhatten Bank, wanted to seize the *Queen Anna Maria* for debts. She landed her last passengers quickly at her Manhattan berth and then fled to the safety of home waters.

I once met an elderly English gentleman, an experienced traveller who had worked as an accountant for the Goulandris-Greek Line, during a crossing on the *Stefan Batory* in September 1981. It was one of those cordial but fleeting encounters – we both wanted to chat further, but never did. He mentioned that the company's passenger

operation never fully recovered after the death of Basil Goulandris, owner and chairman of the Greek Line, in the late sixties. Working in London, from a suite in Claridge's, Goulandris had guided the firm through a series of aged, second-hand liners, mainly serving emigrant passengers, and in the process the Greek Line made millions. (The Goulandris Group also had considerable holdings in tramp cargo and tanker shipping.) In my conversation on board the *Stefan Batory*, I learned that Goulandris's successors had lacked his business skills. Poor operational decisions, mismanagement, and financial losses due to the increases in the price of fuel oil in 1973 brought about the end of the company.

In late 1975, the *Queen Anna Maria* joined the Carnival Cruise Lines of Miami and, after a suitable refit at the Newport News Shipyards in Virginia, entered service on weekly Caribbean cruises as the *Carnivale*. With a consistent occupancy rate above a hundred per cent, the ship – now in her third life – might well be in her most profitable days.

ZIM LINES

The SHALOM

Israel's largest shipping company, the Zim Lines, first began deep-sea transatlantic operations in the spring of 1953, with the forty-year-old *Jerusalem* formerly the

The Shalom *of 1964 was the largest and last of the Zim Lines' passenger ships.*

Zim Lines

The Santa Maria *sailing from Port Everglades, Florida.*

Bergensfjord of Norwegian-America, and later to work as the *Argentina* for the Home Lines). A West German reparations pact made possible the addition of two sleek combination liners, the 9800-ton sisterships, *Israel* and *Zion* soon afterwards. Atlantic service was further augmented by the 9900-ton *Jerusalem*, also financed and built in West Germany in 1957.

With the full support and encouragement of the Israeli Government, the Zim Lines also sought a big liner for both Atlantic service and lucrative American cruises. Although there were frequent reports that she, too, would be paid for out of a West German reparations account, she was financed completely with national funds. With designs (very much in the style of Holland's new and highly acclaimed *Rotterdam*) finally in hand, the order went to Chantiers de L'Atlantique at St Nazaire, builders of many notable liners, particularly for the French themselves.

It was initially thought to name the new ship *King Solomon*, then *King David*, but *Shalom* was the final choice. Mrs David Ben-Gurion officiated at the christening, on 10 November 1962. As flagship of the Israeli Merchant Marine, and assuredly the largest ship then under Israeli colours, she crossed to New York on her maiden run in April 1964. I recall her fireboat and tug reception, and the procession of regularly scheduled outbound liners, such as *America*, *Bergensfjord*, *Independence*, *Santa Magdalena* and *Statendam*, that sailed past in salute. Representatives of the Zim Lines joyously welcomed the press and interested public, and hinted of bigger and better days ahead. Realistically, the *Shalom*'s appearance could not have come at a less appropriate time. She was to have barely three seasons on the Atlantic before turning completely to cruises and then a fairly rapid sale.

Of course, the growth of air travel was an enormous hindrance, and running alone the *Shalom* made her line's voyages seem infrequent as far as potential travellers were concerned. High Israeli labour costs were another drain on the ship's projected revenue. Lastly, but by no means least, only Kosher food was served on the trips to and from Haifa, by special order of religious leaders in Israel, and unfortunately the menu deterred many American passengers. Running well below capacity, the *Shalom* barely earned her expenses.

The ship made unfavourable headline news on 27 November 1964, after ramming the Norwegian tanker *Stolt Dagali* the night before in thick fog outside New York Harbour. The tanker was cut in half, and nineteen lives were lost. Among other embarrassments, it was found that the *Shalom* had been going too fast. Her smashed bow had to be repaired at a Brooklyn shipyard.

In 1967, the *Shalom*'s last season with the Zim Lines, she sailed mostly to Montreal on special Expo 67 Cruises in a last-ditch effort to make her profitable. She was sold to the German Atlantic Line in November that year and became the *Hanseatic*. Soon afterward, Zim ended its passenger services completely.

COMPANHIA COLONIAL

The VERA CRUZ and SANTA MARIA

Portugal's Companhia Colonial was primarily interested in passenger-cargo trades to Angola and Mozambique, then part of Portuguese Africa, and across the South Atlantic to Brazil, but their two largest liners, the 21,000-ton sisters *Santa Maria* and *Vera Cruz*, were experimentally

97

Companhia Colonial

The Cabin Class restaurant and salon onboard the Santa Maria.

detoured to a mid-Atlantic service to Port Everglades, Florida, in 1956–57. Based in Lisbon, they made intermediate calls at Madeira, Tenerife, La Guaira, Curaçao and Havana (later changed to San Juan). The *Vera Cruz* lasted only two seasons (1957–58) before returning to her original run, the Brazilian trade. The *Santa Maria*, however, remained in Florida service throughout the year until the end of her career in 1973. The most noteworthy event of her rather unusual service is surely the hijacking on 22 January 1961. While in the Caribbean, an armed band of Portuguese political insurgents, travelling as passengers, took command of the ship for eleven days. There was a huge air-sea search for the liner, which was eventually surrendered without any loss of life or damage to the ship and docked at Recife, Brazil. The terrorists were promptly arrested.

In April 1973, the *Santa Maria* was abruptly laid up with engine trouble. Her Atlantic schedule was cancelled. Repairs would have been fairly costly in view of the ship's age and, even more so, her dwindling trade. That summer, she sailed to Taiwan for scrapping within months of the *Vera Cruz*.

SPANISH LINE

The COVADONGA and GUADALUPE

Like the Portuguese, the Spanish did not invest in big ships for a passenger link to North America. Instead, they relied on smaller, often older ships. At the end of World War II, the Spanish Line or, more formally, the Compañía Trasatlántica Española, ran three pre-war ships on the New York trade: the *Habana, Magallanes* and *Marques de Comillas*. In 1952, to bolster and improve its North American operations, the Spanish Line brought two cargo ships, the *Monasterio de la Rabida* and the *Monasterio de Guadalupe*, then being fitted out for the Empresa Nacional Elcano. After conversion, they became the *Covadonga* and *Guadalupe* respectively. Their cargo areas were reworked, and accommodation for 349 passengers in two classes was added. The ships were commissioned in 1953, and replaced all earlier Spanish tonnage on the New York run. In fact, they were the last Spanish Line passenger ships. The Spanish Government refused to finance a project in the late fifties, to build twin 20,000-tonners, to be named *Samos* and *Silos*, which would have offered a far greater passenger capacity of 60 in first class and 800 in tourist. They gave increasing competition from aircraft as their grounds for refusal.

The *Covadonga* and *Guadalupe* ran a rather extensive service from Bilbao, Santander, Gijon, Vigo and Lisbon across to New York, then southward to Havana (or San Juan) and Vera Cruz. Julio Del Valle recalled the ships as

fairly pleasant and profitable. 'They were different in decor – the *Covadonga* being very Spanish in style whereas the *Guadalupe* was more European-modern. They served excellent continental cuisine in their first class restaurants and ethnic menus in tourist class. Among their more noted passengers, they carried the last groups of Catholic priests and nuns out of Communist Cuba in 1962–63.

'Each ship had space for 6000 tons of cargo as well. To America, they carried mail, tinned fish, squid, octopus, wine, mercury, cork, lead, Spanish canned goods, olives and olive oil. Homeward, they took coffee and tobacco from Mexico, then sugar and more tobacco from Cuba and finally machinery, tin plate, steel and agricultural machinery from New York.'

By the early seventies, the Spanish sisters had become unprofitable. Their routing had been altered somewhat to include calls at Norfolk and Miami, and the passenger spaces reduced to approximately seventy-five in first class only. The *Covadonga* was retired in December 1972 and quickly sold off to breakers at Castellon, Spain. The *Guadalupe*, at first thought to have been sold for conversion as an Indian Ocean pilgrim ship, followed three months later. She ended the North Atlantic passenger services for the Spanish Line.

Spain's Covadonga *and her sistership, the* Gualalupe, *had the balanced arrangement of about 350 passenger berths and five holds for cargo.*

Victor Scrivens Collection

—NATIONAL HELLENIC AMERICAN LINE—

The QUEEN FREDERICA

On 23 December 1954, following the special request of the Greek Government and in the presence of Her Majesty Queen Frederika of Greece, the Home Lines *Atlantic* was rechristened the *Queen Frederica*. The ceremony was held at Piraeus for the new Home Lines subsidiary, the National Hellenic American Line. The Panamanian flag was replaced by Greek colours. On 29 January the ship set out on her first crossing from Piraeus via Naples, Palermo and Gibraltar for Halifax and New York as the largest Greek-flag liner (the Greek Line *Olympia* of 1953 was then under the Liberian flag).

The new *Queen* did very well and was a particular favourite with Greek sea travellers. She was then part of a four-liner marketing programme for the Home Lines with the *Homeric, Italia* and Hamburg-Atlantic's *Hanseatic*. She had a major refit at Genoa in the winter of 1960–61, when her accommodation was changed from 132 first class, 116 cabin and 931 tourist to 174 in first and 1005 in tourist. About three-quarters of her cabins were given private toilet facilities.

On one Saturday, in 1962, the *Queen Frederica* was forced to anchor in the mid-Hudson, off West 79th Street in Manhattan, well beyond the normal docking area; very unusually, the appropriate City piers were completely occupied by the *Homerica, Italia, Hanseatic, Queen of Bermuda, Ocean Monarch* and even on a special visit the giant *Canberra*.

The *Queen Frederica* was sold to the Themistocles Navigation Company, a member of the expanding Chandris Group (see below), in November 1965, when Chandris acquired the National Hellenic American Line (the ship's operating company).

—————CHANDRIS LINES—————

The QUEEN FREDERICA

When the National Hellenic American Line's *Queen Frederica* passed into Chandris ownership, little changed except that the twin funnels were repainted black and blue, with large white X's.

Hereafter, the ship divided her time between taking emigrants from Southampton to Australia and New Zealand, full round-the-world voyages, and only periodic transatlantic crossings between the Mediterranean and New York. She even made occasional cruises. I was aboard her for a long holiday weekend in September 1967, on a five-day run to Bermuda and back, with a full day at anchor at Hamilton. I had a minimum-priced room, inside on B Deck, with a private shower and lavatory, for $150.

Under new safety standards that became effective in

Vincent Messina Collection

One one of her last visits to New York, the aged Queen Frederica *appeared in Chandris Lines' colours.*

the United States during 1967–68, the ageing *Queen* needed several million dollars worth of improvements, which to Chandris accountants would have been far too extreme. Instead, she was placed on the Australian run full time. In 1970, she was chartered out to Sovereign Cruises, a British air-sea holiday firm, for seven-day summer trips out of Palma de Majorca and Cannes to ports around the western Mediterranean. Sovereign logos were painted on her stacks. As if exhaustion was finally setting-in, she was laid up at an anchorage at Perama, Greece, in 1973, with other assorted, elderly tonnage. There were rumours in 1976 that she was to reactivated for use as a tourist hotel on the Suez Canal and then again, a year later for use as a floating prop in a film about the *Titanic*. Neither of the suggestions ever came to pass. Instead, men with acetylene torches went aboard and began to break her, bit by bit, until, on 1 February 1978, as if in angry desperation, she burst into flames and burned down to a mass of tangled steel.

JUGOLINIJA

The VISEVICA, KLEK, TUHOBIC and ZVIR
Yugoslavia's Jugolinija began transatlantic passenger service in the autumn of 1949, using the 7900-ton *Hrvatska*, with space for sixty passengers, and the 6600-ton *Srbija*, carrying forty-four. It was a passenger-cargo service that traded mostly between Rijeka, Trieste, Naples and Casablanca, and then across to New York, Baltimore and Philadelphia. These early ships remained in service until the mid-sixties.

In 1964–65, Jugolinija added four nationally-built combination liners, the *Visevica, Klek, Tuhobic* and *Zvir*, for their transatlantic operations. The accommodation was positioned farther aft than that on most similar ships and provided room for twenty in first class and thirty in tourist. First class tended to be used by Americans, who travelled in these ships mostly for round-trip voyages of approximately sixty days. The tourist section generally appealed to Yugoslavians, some of them returning to the homeland for a visit with American-made household appliances as part of their baggage. Such ships had space for passengers' freight that would have been impractical and uneconomic on aircraft. In later years, as interest in informally scheduled freighter-type voyages began to surge, the popularity of these four ships actually began to increase. In the end, by the late seventies, they were the last ships apart from twelve passenger freighters to offer regular passenger service to the Mediterranean from North America.

By 1980, however, the shift to containerized cargo shipping spelled the end for such conventionally designed vessels. A year later, they were abruptly withdrawn. They were sold to Egyptian buyers, the newly created Rashid Shipping Company. The *Visevica* became the *Abu Hosna*, the *Klek* changed to *Abu Alia*, the *Tuhobic* to *Abu Rashid* and the *Zvir* to *Abu Yussuf I*. The intention was to have a coordinated operation in Egypt and Yugoslavia, with an operational base at Alexandria. The ships were to continue carrying passengers. Unfortunately, the new venture suffered several problems, notably financial ones, and ceased after only a few sailings. The former Yugoslavian quartet no longer sail as passenger ships.

CHAPTER SIX

FROM NORTHERN WATERS

NORTH GERMAN LLOYD

The BERLIN

In the thirties, the North German Lloyd had one of the largest passenger fleets afloat, which included two of the world's largest liners, the speed queens *Bremen* and *Europa*. In the spring of 1945, the German owners had nothing but a few coastal and harbour craft left. Larger survivors were seized as war prizes or reparations, the most notable being the big *Europa*, which went first to the Americans and then became the French *Liberté*. It was nearly ten years before the Lloyd could even think of reopening their transatlantic liner service. In 1954, they and the Swedish American Line agreed to form a temporary operating company, the Bremen-America Line, that would resume German passenger service. The Swedish Line provided the ship, the 19,100-ton *Gripsholm* of 1925, which was to work a season on the Bremerhaven-New York route, and then transfer to the Lloyd, change to West German colours and become the first national passenger ship since 1939. Renamed *Berlin* in January 1955, the ship and her new operation had an immediate, strong following of Germans who wanted to travel in a national ship. A new, highly profitable career started for the thirty-year-old liner. Westbound on her nine-day crossings to New York (which were sometimes via Halifax), she was often booked to capacity with emigrants from Germany. Eastbound, she often carried German-Americans, many of whom who had not been to the homeland since the thirties.

It became almost immediately apparent that the Lloyd could use an even faster, larger and more luxurious liner.

When North German Lloyd's Berlin *first crossed to New York in early 1955, she was the first German-flag liner on the North Atlantic since 1939.*

Roger Sherlock

Company agents began to search for available second-hand tonnage, appropriately, since finances were still inadequate for a brand-new vessel. When this additional ship, the *Bremen* of 1959, joined the Company, the veteran *Berlin*, certainly one of the *grande dames* of the North Atlantic, was relieved for some variations in her scheduling. She began to call regularly at Southampton, made an annual, late-year crossing to Montreal and even ran some cruises – from New York to Bermuda, the Caribbean and Eastern Canada, and from Bremerhaven to the Baltic, the Norwegian Fjords, the Canaries and the Mediterranean. Although she was hardly a modern liner, her heavily wood-panelled, almost sombre interiors gave her a rare charm. She seemed to have come from a lost era. The *Berlin* sailed from New York for the last time in September 1966 and, after some final cruises, sailed to La Spezia, Italy for scrapping. By then, she was forty-one years old.

The BREMEN

France's Compagnie Sud-Atlantique hoped to make their brand new *Pasteur* the fastest and most luxurious liner on the Europe-South America service. A flood of descriptive literature heralded the new 'queen', which was actually a long-awaited replacement for the 42,000-ton *L'Atlantique*, destroyed by fire when only two years old in 1933. If the *Pasteur* was somewhat smaller, at 30,000 tons, she was equally interesting and well appointed. Her maiden trip from Bordeaux to Rio, Montevideo and Buenos Aires was set for early September 1939. Then, events further east, in Poland, changed everything. At the beginning of the war, the freshly completed liner was sent to Brest for temporary safety, without ever having had her formal maiden voyage.

The *Pasteur* finally returned to sea eleven months later, in August 1940, when the French Government sent her to Halifax with a large shipment of gold from the National Reserves bound for wartime storage in Canada. As France was then invaded, she quickly passed to Cunard-White Star, which managed her on behalf of the British Government. Her subsequent role was as a troop ship, mainly on the North Atlantic and often in company with the illustrious *Île de France*. Although brief thought was given to restoration, the *Pasteur* was rerouted to Indo-China in the summer of 1945, to provide something of a relay service for the troubled Asian colonies with French troops and evacuees. As the situation became more tense, the possibility of a return to commercial service became less likely. The 'world's largest peacetime troop ship' was not decommissioned until January 1957. Again, she was considered for use as a full luxury liner, specifically for the French Line, as a replacement for the *Île de France* on the North Atlantic. However, the 66,000-ton *France* was

In an exceptional refit, the French troop ship Pasteur *was converted to the German* Bremen. *The funnel remained far forward in position.*

already under construction as a large, single-ship replacement for the *Île* and the 51,000-ton *Liberté*. There was really no place for the *Pasteur* under the tricolour.

The ship's next owner, the North German Lloyd, finally beginning a strong recovery from its wartime devastation, took delivery in September 1957 and had her moved to Bremen for thorough modernization and upgrading. The ship was completely stripped. New turbines capable of producing 23 knots (or the equivalent of 2000 Volkswagen beetles operating simultaneously) were installed together with improved wiring and plumbing, and passenger accommodation that was as handsome and comprehensive as that in any other Atlantic liner of the day. She was called *Bremen* – long considered Germany's most distinguished sea name – and set course for New York from Bremerhaven via the Channel ports in the summer of 1959. She quickly showed herself to be a superb vessel. In the winter months, she travelled south to the Caribbean for single-class cruising. Overall, she

seemed successful in the fierce competition with jet travel.

The Lloyd eventually merged with the Hamburg American Line to create Hapag-Lloyd, certainly one of the world's mightiest shipping firms. It was a union of economies in the ever-growing competitiveness of the maritime industry. An early decision was to discontinue the transatlantic liner run in 1971 and concentrate on the more lucrative cruise trades, both from New York and Bremerhaven. However, soon after, the mechanics of the *Bremen* began to play havoc with her schedules. Engine failures delayed or cancelled sailings, which did little to maintain Hapag-Lloyd's impeccable image. Costly repairs were the only obvious answer. Accountants at Hapag-Lloyd looked at the ship as a weak investment, discounting any form of nationalistic or nostalgic indulgence. The *Bremen* was sold to the Greek-flag Chandris Cruises and became their *Regina Magna*, not to be confused with the smaller *Regina* (formerly *President Hoover* and, before that, *Panama*), which was renamed *Regina Prima* to avoid confusion.

Beginning in the summer of 1972, the *Regina Magna* was sent on cruises from Amsterdam and London to Scandinavia, and then from Genoa to West Africa and the Mediterranean. Still later, there were Caribbean trips out of Curaçao and San Juan. However, the ship's machinery

When Sweden's Kungsholm *of 1953 became Germany's* Europa *in 1965, she was repainted with a black hull and two mustard-coloured stacks.*

continued to prove troublesome and costly, even to the methodical Chandris Company. A mere two summers later, she was laid-up at Perama, near Piraeus, with an assortment of other ships, mostly unwanted and nearing their end. The *Regina Magna* had little hope of survival, but managed, through some form of good fortune, to find one further buyer, The Philippine Singapore Ports Corporation, in 1977, and left Piraeus for Jeddah, Saudi Arabia, on 6 October for use as a permanently moored accommodation centre. Under the Philippine flag and the name *Saudi Phil I*, she was part of a major construction project for 3600 workers. She changed her name once more, in March 1978, to *Filipinas Saudi I*. When her work assignment ended in 1980, her only prospect, since she was forty-one, in bad condition, and had those faulty engines, was the scrapyard. She was put under tow, destined for Kaohsiung, Taiwan, but heeled over and sank at sea on 6 June, making for a quick end to her long life.

The EUROPA

The North German Lloyd could not have found a better acquisition than Swedish American's smart *Kungsholm* of 1953. She went on the sales lists in the autumn of 1965, just as the Swedes were preparing for their newest (and last) liner, the fourth *Kungsholm*, completed in spring 1966.

The earlier *Kungsholm* was a dream ship – beautiful looking, mechanically sound, finely maintained, supremely well thought of, and all with the perfect ability, because of her compact size, to work either the two-class North Atlantic or single-class luxury cruises. The Germans had little to do when they took delivery of the ship and rechristened her the *Europa*. Certainly, the accommodation was pure delight. The liner offered a pre-war ambience of glistening veneers and soft lighting, with everything polished to perfection. She was inviting and comfortable, much like some well-established old hotel. The *Europa* first crossed to New York in January 1966 and then went directly into winter Caribbean cruising. By the late sixties, she was, in fact, expected to assist on the Atlantic run only in the peak summer periods. However, along with the larger *Bremen*, she faced increased operational costs and a declining passenger trade. In 1970, when the Lloyd and the Hamburg America Line merged, there were some adjustments within the fleet. After over a century, the Atlantic service was dropped in the autumn of 1971. The fuel-hungry, mechanically dubious *Bremen* was sold off, leaving only the *Europa*, but specifically as a European-based cruiseship. Again, her wonderful interiors proved popular, especially with a multitude of older travellers, who longed for an idealized notion of time gone by. The *Europa* sailed either from Bremerhaven or Genoa (with which there was a special German air link) on luxury trips which ranged from seven days in the Baltic

to seventeen days to West Africa, or a hundred days to the Middle East and the South Pacific. There was even another appearance at New York, in September 1978, as part of a long North American-Caribbean cruise.

The *Europa* continued in German service until the autumn of 1981, when she was replaced by a new, far larger *Europa*. The older ship was sold off to the Italian Costa Line for further cruising as the *Columbus C*, a name which was selected as a tribute to a pre-war Lloyd liner. During the summers, Costa chartered the ship to other German travel interests, and a link with earlier German-flag sea travel was therefore an important marketing advantage. In winter the ship shifted to the South American trade, sailing mostly from Buenos Aires and Rio. Early in 1984, there was a Costa fleet reorganization, in which the ship's name was modified to *Costa Columbus*. Unfortunately, this ship rammed the breakwater at Cadiz in Spain in July 1984. Badly holed, she made her pier just in

time and safely landed all passengers and crew, but then capsized. She was damaged beyond economic repair.

NORWEGIAN AMERICA LINE

The STAVANGERFJORD

As World War II ended, the Norwegians were left with one Atlantic liner, which was fortunate not to have been harmed during the Nazi retreat. (One other, the *Bergensfjord* of 1913, had in fact survived as well, but was considered too old to be brought back into service.) After duty as a troop ship for the British, she was sold to the Home Lines and became their *Argentina*. The sole survivor, the *Stavangerfjord*, was immediately made ready for service to New York. She crossed the Atlantic in August 1945,

Norwegian-America Line's stately Stavangerfjord *made the first post-war commercial crossing, in August 1945.*

becoming the first commercial ship to resume service.

The *Stavangerfjord* had been built at the Cammell Laird yard at Birkenhead, near Liverpool, in 1918, just as World War I was nearing its end. However, there was some last-minute concern about the ship's safety and accordingly she was moved to New York. Not having previously visited home waters, she is the only European liner to have had an eastbound maiden voyage from New York to her home port. She continued in Atlantic service without interruption until December 1939. At first, the *Stavangerfjord* was laid up at Oslo for safety, but she fell into enemy hands soon after the Nazi invasion and was used as a troop depot ship. She did not sail during the war and needed only a fresh coat of paint and some cleaning before she was ready to resume service.

The *Stavangerfjord* was one of those dependable, sturdy ships that had a loyal national following and worked the Atlantic year after year. Even the loss of her rudder during an Atlantic storm in December 1953 delayed her arrival by only a few days. Her crew worked in teams with such determination to navigate the ship that they reached home in time for Christmas. In all, some 14,000 messages passed between bridge and engine room to guide the rudderless liner.

Although the *Stavangerfjord* was to have been retired and replaced by the new *Bergensfjord* in 1956, her strong appeal to Norwegian passengers earned her a few more years. She was finally withdrawn in December 1963, at the age of forty-five, just at the right time for a final Christmas sailing to Norway. There were moves to preserve her as a hotel, museum or moored training ship, but the highest bid came from Hong Kong scrappers. She completed her last and longest voyage in February 1965.

The OSLOFJORD

When the Norwegian America Line decided to build their first North Atlantic passenger ship after World War II, they selected a rather sensible, conservative design – a 16,000-ton motor liner with a two-class capacity of less than seven hundred berths and five holds for cargo. Unable to build this new ship in home waters, the Company turned to the Netherlands Shipbuilding Company of Amsterdam. Named *Oslofjord*, she had a royal christening by Her Royal Highness Crown Princess Martha of Norway, on 2 April 1949. Six months later, in November, the ship first crossed to New York. For about nine months of each year, she sailed between Oslo and New York, via Copenhagen, Kristiansand, Stavanger and Bergen. In winter, with her capacity reduced to 360 in first class only, she cruised to the Caribbean and on special long cruises to the Mediterranean, Africa and South America.

In the mid-sixties, with the Atlantic trade in rapid

Vincent Messina Collection

decline, the *Oslofjord*'s future seemed uncertain. In 1966 it was reported that the Finnlines wanted to buy her for their entry into the cruise trade. Instead her Norwegian owners sent her to Amsterdam that winter for an extensive three-month refit, after which she would be better suited for cruising and would sail the Atlantic only on rare occasions. However, less than a year of Norwegian service followed. In December 1967, the *Oslofjord* began a charter to the Greek Line for cruises from Southampton which varied from a three-day mini trip to Amsterdam to thirty-five days to the West Indies. It seemed rather successful, but an even more lucrative charter was offered in October 1968. The Italian Costa Line wanted her for their Caribbean service out of San Juan in the winter and on runs from Genoa to the Mediterranean and West Africa for the rest of the year. Sailing as the *Fulvia*, the ship then carried a mainly Italian staff. This was to be her final career change. On 20 July 1970, she caught fire off Tenerife while on a cruise to the Canary Islands, had to be abandoned and then sank.

The BERGENSFJORD

When the Norwegian America Line decided to add a third Atlantic liner in the mid-fifties, she was meant as an improved *Oslofjord*. With an extended superstructure and less cargo space, the ship was designed to provide greater passenger accommodation (878 berths compared with her predecessor's 640). Launched by Her Royal Highness Princess Astrid as the *Bergensfjord*, she came from the Swann, Hunter yard at Wallsend. She entered service in May 1956 as the flagship of the Norwegian merchant marine. The *Bergensfjord* plied the Atlantic in summer and then was sent on extensive cruising, from two weeks in the Caribbean to 'around the world in eighty days'. For the luxury voyages, her capacity was reduced to 420, all first class.

By the late sixties, the *Bergensfjord*, like so many of her Atlantic fleetmates, spent more and more of her year on cruises. There were even some summer trips out of Oslo to the Fjords, North Cape and Spitzbergen. She was to have been withdrawn in early 1973, just as the brand new *Vistafjord* came into service, but left the Norwegian America Line two years earlier than expected. Since their *Antilles* had been lost by fire in the Caribbean in January 1971, the French Line was in rather desperate need of a replacement ship. The *Bergensfjord* was ideal, and the French offered more money than the Norwegians could possibly refuse. The *Bergensfjord*'s schedule was scrapped and the ship raised the tricolour. With the new name, *De Grasse*, she was assigned to the Le Havre-West Indies trade in addition to cruises. Unfortunately, she was not the success the French had hoped, and their difficulties were made worse by increases in the cost of fuel oil during 1973.

Rather similar externally the Oslofjord *of 1949 (lower berth) and the* Bergensfjord *of 1956 are seen berthed at New York's Pier 42.*

In that November, the ship was resold to the Norwegian firm, Thoresen & Company Limited, for their new Singapore-registered cruise division. Renamed *Rasa Sayang*, the ship was refitted for special fly-sail cruises out of Singapore to the Indonesian islands and Far Eastern ports. The new operation prospered for a time, but suffered a hard blow when the ship was damaged by fire and abandoned at sea on 2 June 1977. The press reports were particularly scathing. Later towed to Singapore and repaired, the *Rasa Sayang* lasted only another year before being laid up and offered for sale in June 1978.

Like so many exiled passenger ships, she was sold to Greek owners, who rechristened her the *Golden Moon* and registered her to a Cypriot-based holding company, Sunlit Cruises Limited. It was not very clear what the new owners intended for the ship. I saw her anchored at Perama in February 1979, among a large, silent fleet of once notable passenger ships which included the former *America*, the Chandris *Ellinis* and the Greek Line's *Olympia*. Despite rumours the following May that she would be chartered to a Dutch travel firm for summer Scandinavian cruises as the *Prins van Oranje*, she remained in Perama Bay. In July 1980, the ship was sold to other Greek owners, who

Norwegian America Line

Port of Le Havre Authority

During a West European cruise, the Sagafjord *is seen berthed at Le Havre. The Port Tower stands immediately behind the ship.*

planned to charter her to the Soviet-owned CTC Lines for cruises from Sydney to the South Pacific. In preparation, the ship reverted to her earlier name *Rasa Sayang*. Again, however, the project failed to develop. On 27 August, during her refit, the ship burned out. She had to be towed to nearby Kynosoura and deliberately sunk in shallow water. About a fifth of her port side can still be seen, twisted and charred above the harbour waters.

The SAGAFJORD

When she was commissioned in the autumn of 1965, the *Sagafjord* (which was briefly reported to be called *Norway*) was intended to spend a part of her year, no matter how brief, on the North Atlantic run between Oslo, Copenhagen, Bergen and New York. In reality, she rarely made such trips, but has been used mainly for cruises, particularly deluxe, expensive voyages. In the early eighties, with her reputation as strong as ever, she is regarded as one of the very finest vessels afloat. In an annual cruise ship survey, she came in first place over fifty or so other liners for two consecutive years (1982 and 1983).

The VISTAFJORD

As an even more refined version of the elegant *Sagafjord's* design, the *Vistafjord* of 1973 was intended from the start to be a high-standard, luxury cruise ship. She is included here, not because of any intended transatlantic trips to Oslo, but because of her annual 'positioning' voyages, usually between Port Everglades and either Genoa or Hamburg. In winter, she cruises in the Caribbean, and in summer in European waters.

While a planned merger with the Royal Viking Line in 1980 failed, the Company, afterwards restyled as Norwegian America Cruises, was taken over by the British-based Trafalgar House Limited, parent of the present-day Cunard Line, in the autumn of 1983. Both the *Sagafjord* and *Vistafjord* now bear Cunard funnel colours and sail under the Bahamian flag. Rumour has it that they may even become the *Cunard Saga* and *Cunard Vista*.

─────SWEDISH-AMERICAN LINE─────

The DROTTNINGHOLM

At the end of the World War II, the Swedish-American Line had two surviving passenger ships, the *Drottningholm*, the oldest passenger ship on the Atlantic, and the *Gripsholm* of 1925, the Atlantic's first motor liner. Two successive ships of the late thirties, both named *Stockholm*, had been lost, and the *Kungsholm*, dating from 1928, was in American hands as the troop ship USS *John Ericsson*.

The veteran *Drottningholm* was retained only because of the apparent shortage of suitable tonnage within the 'White Viking Fleet', as it was known. She had been commissioned in April 1905 for Britain's Allan Line, as the *Virginian*. She worked the Canadian trade out of Liverpool until World War I and then served as an auxiliary cruiser and troop ship. Made redundant when the Allan Line was absorbed by Canadian Pacific soon after the war, she was sold to her Swedish owners and remained an important, popular passenger vessel. Between 1940 and 1945, she sailed for the International Red Cross as a neutral exchange ship, exempt from attack. Consequently, she was readily restored in 1945 and made the first post-war Swedish-American sailing in the following spring. She was sold in 1946 to the Home Lines, but had two further years of Swedish transatlantic service during which her sailings were often booked to capacity. The ship reached the rather remarkable age of fifty. Details of her last years, when she worked under the names *Brasil* and *Homeland*, have been listed in the Home Lines section.

The GRIPSHOLM (1925)

The Swedes were rather bold in the design of their new flagship (and first brand new liner) in the early twenties. They selected diesel propulsion, which was then still experimental, and their noted success prompted similar use by several other Atlantic liner companies. This ship, the first *Gripsholm*, completed in the autumn of 1925, was not only a popular transatlantic liner, but developed a superb reputation as a cruise ship, especially in the early thirties. More so than most other Atlantic firms, the Swedish-American Line was to maintain its reputation in two areas, one regular crossings and the other cruises.

Like the *Drottningholm*, the *Gripsholm* was used by the International Red Cross during World War II as a neutral exchange ship. She too, came out of the hostilities

When completed in 1925, the Swedish Gripsholm *was the North Atlantic's first motorliner. During the War, she was exempted from troopship duties and instead served as a diplomatic exchange ship.*

Luis Miguel Correia

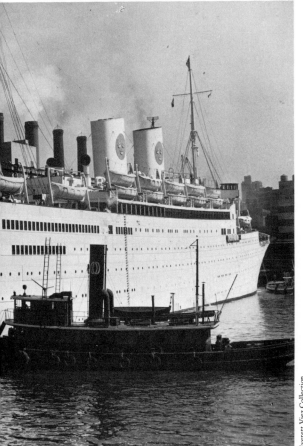

Everett Viez Collection

The first new transatlantic liner to be ordered following World War II, Sweden's Stockholm *is seen in her second career, as the East German trade union cruise ship* Volkerfreundschaft. *She is shown arriving at Lisbon.*

practically unchanged and was therefore able to resume the Gothenburg–New York service quickly in March 1946. Three years later, over the winter of 1949–50, she was sent to a Kiel shipyard for modernization. She was fitted with new, wider funnels and a new bow, which increased her overall length from 573 to 590 feet. Her capacity was reduced from 1557 to 920. In all, she seemed more in line with contemporary styling.

Early in 1954, the Swedish-American Line entered into an agreement with the North German Lloyd, which was keen to revive a national service on the North Atlantic, despite the loss of all its passenger ships. Together, the two companies formed the Bremen-America Line, a temporary operating company. The *Gripsholm* was to continue under her Swedish name, and retain her white hull, though her stacks were to be painted in North German Lloyd's mustard yellow. A year later, as had been planned, she was purchased outright by the Lloyd and became the *Berlin*. She was the first German-flag liner on the Atlantic since 1939.

The STOCKHOLM

In retrospect, it seems odd that the Swedes should have opted for a smallish, almost combination-style liner when they decided to build new passenger tonnage after the war. They may have been early in noticing the potential

Swedish American's Gripsholm *of 1957 shown at a night-time cruise anchorage.*

supremacy of air travel and therefore have felt that only passenger ships of moderate size would be profitable. (A few years later, however, they planned a larger, more suitable ship, the 21,100-ton *Kungsholm* of 1953.) This first post-war passenger ship was launched on 9 September 1946 as the *Stockholm*. She was the first Atlantic liner to be sent down the ways since before the war, and was also notable as the largest passenger ship yet built in Sweden. She first crossed to New York in February 1948. Along with five holds for cargo, the sleek-looking *Stockholm* had handsome, yet rather limited, accommodation for 395 passengers – 113 in first class and 282 in tourist. In 1952, during a special refit, this was increased to 86 first and 584 tourist. In another alteration three years later, the first class was reduced to 24 berths.

The *Stockholm* worked the North Atlantic for most of the year, sailing between Gothenburg, Copenhagen and New York, with occasional calls at Bremerhaven, Aarhus (in Denmark) and Halifax. In 1955, there were rumours of a sale to the new Denmark-America Line, for a direct Copenhagen-New York service, but it never came about.

A year later, the *Stockholm* gained maritime notoriety. On 25 July 1956, while outbound for Gothenburg, she fatally rammed the Italian *Andrea Doria* in thick fog off Nantucket. The Swedish ship lost most of her bow while the *Doria* was pierced just below the starboard bridge and sank the next day. After standing by for survivors, the

Stockholm limped back to New York for inspection and repairs. Frank Braynard was at the Italian Line offices in Lower Manhattan, on the afternoon of 26 July, as the little liner crept past. 'The Italians stood silently at their harbourview windows, just staring at the Swedish ship. They had "daggers" in their eyes. To them, she was the villain.' In point of fact, the inquiry was later settled out of court and the blame never publicly announced. The *Stockholm* was sent to the Bethlehem Steel Shipyards at 56th Street in Brooklyn and given a new bow. She did not return to service until December 1956, over four months after the collision.

Like so many smaller passenger ships, the *Stockholm* was an early victim of the competition with aircraft. She finished her Swedish service at the end of 1959 and was sold to Deutsche Seereederi, East Germany's national shipping company. Renamed *Volkerfreundschaft* ('International Friendship'), she was refitted as the world's first trade union holiday ship, for cruises with workers and their families. She has served in this capacity ever since.

The KUNGSHOLM (1953)

She was one of the loveliest passenger ships ever to sail the Atlantic, and her serene, classical exterior was balanced by superbly decorated accommodation. This third *Kungsholm* was always a very popular ship. Built by the Dutch, at the De Schelde yard at Flushing, she was named by Her Royal Highness Princess Sybilla of Sweden, on 18 April 1952 and came into service at the end of the following year. She had two distinctive features. She was the first transatlantic liner to have only outside cabins, and

Swedish American Line

cruise ship. With her capacity reduced to 425 berths, she was acclaimed for her long, expensive voyages – six weeks to Scandinavia, Africa and South America, eight weeks to the Mediterranean, fourteen weeks around the world or in the Pacific. She had a loyal following, passengers who sailed in her year after year.

In the early seventies, ships such as the *Gripsholm* encountered serious financial difficulties with increasing expenditure on labour, maintenance and fuel. One former Swedish-American staff captain remarked 'More and more, ships like the *Gripsholm* became prestige symbols. They were increasingly unprofitable.' After careful consideration of their options, the Swedish-American managers might have transferred their liners to the Panamanian flag and used less costly 'mixed' crews, though possibly at the expense of their extremely high standards, but their final decision, a sad one, was to end passenger service completely and sell off their remaining liners.

The *Gripsholm* was retired in the late summer of 1975, briefly laid up, and then sold to Greek buyers, Karageorgis Cruises. Renamed *Navarino*, she was used for year-round cruising from Venice and Piraeus to the eastern Mediterranean, from Capetown and Durban on South Atlantic runs or, later, from Rio de Janeiro or Buenos Aires for South American coastal trips. Even in this role, she earned enthusiastic praise for her fine accommodation and level of service.

In 1981, however, the Karageorgis interests decided on reorganization and planned to sell the ship to the Finnish-owned, Miami-based Commodore Cruise Lines, who wanted to augment their seven-day Caribbean cruise service. The sale never quite went through. On 26 November, just hours before the final transfer of ownership, the ship partially capsized and sank while resting in a drydock at Skaramanga, Greece. Her accommodation and machinery suffered damage from flooding, the sale was promptly cancelled, and the liner was declared a total loss. She was re-examined later and righted in March of the following year. After some preliminary repairs, she was acquired by Italian buyers, who renamed her the *Samantha* and plan to use the liner as a condominium-style cruiseship. Restoration is under way.

the first to have a private bathroom adjoining every stateroom. Her schedule was divided between nine months or so on the North Atlantic and the rest spent on cruises. In January 1955, she made Swedish-American's first round-the-world cruise, a fourteen-week trip that proved highly popular and became an annual event during over a decade of Swedish service. The *Kungsholm* was replaced in 1965 by a more modern liner bearing the same name. Then, much like the *Gripsholm* in 1955, she appeared an ideal ship to the North German Lloyd, and was purchased for further, highly successful service as their *Europa*.

The GRIPSHOLM (1957)
The *Gripsholm* of 1957 was close relative, a first cousin, if you like, to the *Kungsholm* of 1953. Externally, the ships were very similar in appearance, characterized especially by their twin raked stacks, and both bearing the blue discs and golden crowns of the Swedish-American Line. Even the *Kungsholm*'s internal beatuty was repeated in the newer ship. The *Gripsholm* received very high praise.

She was built at the Ansaldo yard at Genoa. Ironically, she was under construction when the *Stockholm* rammed and sank the Italian flagship *Andrea Doria*, which had been built at the same yard, and the feelings of the Italian work crews are easy to imagine. The *Gripsholm* was launched on 8 April 1956 by Her Royal Highness Princess Margaretha of Sweden, and reached New York for a fireboat welcome in May 1957.

The *Gripsholm* spent less and less time on the North Atlantic and perhaps became best known as a luxury

The KUNGSHOLM (1966)
To build what was to be their last passenger liner, the Swedish-American Line turned to Scotland's John Brown shipyards, builders of the three Cunard *Queens*, among others. The result was a startlingly beautiful twin-stacker (one of the very last with this type of design) that was equally well decorated internally. This fourth *Kungsholm* entered service in the spring of 1966. Although capable of

The Kungsholm *of 1966 was the last of the Swedish-American liners. Her forward funnel was a dummy and it was removed in 1978, when she was rebuilt by the P&O Lines.*

two-class North Atlantic operations, she rarely made regular crossings. Her transatlantic runs were 'positioning' trips for annual overhauls or crew changes between cruises from New York. Assuredly, she is best remembered as a luxury cruise liner. Her one-time staff captain recalled, 'She was an exceptionally handsome ship, but never quite had the operational perfection of the earlier *Gripsholm*. Among other problems, the *Kungsholm* always had air-conditioning trouble.'

When Swedish-American decided to abandon passenger services in 1975, the *Kungsholm* was sold to a new firm, Flagship Cruises, which hoped to capitalize on the ship's impeccable reputation by retaining her Swedish name. She was then Norwegian owned, Liberian registered and staffed by a 'mixed' crew. The former sparkle was somehow missing, and Swedish-American loyalists were not invariably satisfied. The ship ran a schedule of both long and short cruises in an attempt to cater both to rich, elderly passengers, and a middle-aged, professional group. The decisive blow came, however, in January 1978, during a Caribbean cruise. The ship went aground in Fort de France Bay on Martinique and remained locked in position for five days. Frank Braynard was aboard on that trip. 'This unfortunate incident killed Flagship Cruises. The salvage fees, the delays, the disruption to the schedules, the repairs needed and then all of it compounded when the world-cruise passengers [scheduled for the next sailing] had to be flown to Florida with their luggage to meet the ship. The costs were enormous.'

Months later, in September, the *Kungsholm* was sold to Britain's P&O Cruises and rebuilt (with a rather ungainly single stack) as the *Sea Princess*. First used on a Sydney-South Pacific cruise service, she was reassigned to Southampton in spring 1982. She remains in P&O service.

POLISH OCEAN LINES

The BATORY

The Poles so much wanted two new liners in the otherwise impoverished thirties that they arranged to make payments in coal for the building of ships in Italy. The sister ships *Pilsudski* and *Batory* were completed in 1935–36. The *Pilsudski* became one of the first casualties of World War II, when she was sunk in the autumn of 1939.

The *Batory* was handed over to the British and used as a troop ship. She was returned to Poland in 1946. This handsome, twin-stack liner resumed Atlantic service in April 1947, sailing between Gdynia, Copenhagen,

Polish Ocean Lines

Southampton and New York. It was a happy return and one that might have enabled her owners to provide her with a new running-mate, but then a single event changed everything. A convicted spy named Gerhard Eisler escaped from American authorities aboard the *Batory* with the knowledge of the captain and some officers. In an era of strong anti-communist feeling it became an unpleasant affair. Stevedores eventually refused to handle the ship, repair crews would not accept her, and harbour authorities insisted that she arrive and sail only in daylight, always under escort. When docked, she remained under police guard. In January 1951, the Poles sensibly withdrew their flagship, had her refitted and placed her on an alternative service from Gdynia and Southampton to Karachi and Bombay via the Mediterranean and Suez. Six years later, she returned to the North Atlantic, but to Quebec City and Montreal, since she was still banned from American ports.

On this route, the *Batory* became one of the most popular passenger ships on the Atlantic. Seemingly unattracted by air travel, Polish passengers, whether emigrants or visitors, preferred ships, with their capacity to transport such items as household appliances, motorcycles and even foodstuffs. The *Batory* sailed mainly betwen Gdynia, Copenhagen, and Southampton or London before crossing to Eastern Canada. Occasionally, she would put into additional ports, such as Leningrad, Helsinki, Bremerhaven and Le Havre. In the mid-sixties, with earlier political difficulties mostly forgotten, she began to make an annual late-season crossing to Boston. In deep winter, she cruised, usually from London to the Atlantic Isles and West Africa, but periodically to the West Indies, South America and Florida.

In the sixties, the Poles were often said to be ready to order a new transatlantic liner, a 20,000-tonner which would be named *Polonia*. Instead, they bought the Holland-America liner *Maasdam* in 1968 and had her refitted as the *Stefan Batory*. As she came into service in the spring of 1969, the *Batory* was retired. She was sold to the city of Gdynia for preservation as a floating hotel, but the project was hardly successful. She was sold to Hong Kong and broken up in the summer of 1971.

The SOBIESKI

In the late thirties, the Polish Ocean Lines added two 11,000-ton liners to serve emigrants leaving for South America. They were the British-built *Chrobry* and *Sobieski*. Only the *Sobieski* survived the war, during which she had served as an Allied troop ship.

As the *Sobieski* was being refitted in 1946, it was decided to use her in Mediterranean service, between Naples,

Poland's highly popular Batory *sailing from Gdynia.*

Genoa, Cannes, Lisbon and New York. The timing seemed right, especially as the Italian fleet was greatly diminished, the Americans had not yet added large tonnage, and all the while the passenger traffic was high. The chief purser of the latter-day *Stefan Batory* recalled, 'On the *Sobieski* in those years, we carried endless immigrants and refugees to America, but we also had a strong first-class following. On one voyage, we had Ernest Hemingway. Frequently we had members of the diplomatic corps. We ran a three-class liner service that filled a void in those years.'

Whether or not the Poles would have continued in the Mediterranean trade remains uncertain. In 1950, while replenishing their own fleet, the Soviet Union claimed the *Sobieski* and had the ship recommissioned as the *Gruzia*. There was no compensation to the Poles. Under Soviet colours, the vessel sailed mainly along the Black Sea, usually out of Odessa, but occasionally made trips across the Atlantic to Cuba with troops, technicians and students. She was retired and then scrapped at La Spezia, Italy in 1975.

One of the more amazing conversions of a passenger liner: the three-funnel design of Canadian Pacific's Empress of Scotland *into the sleek look of the twin-stack* Hanseatic *for the Hamburg-Atlantic Line. The transformation took place in 1958.*

HAMBURG-ATLANTIC LINE

The HANSEATIC (1930)

Not only was the North German Lloyd interested in reopening a luxury national-flag service across the Atlantic to New York, but several investors joined forces to create the Hamburg-Atlantic Line in the mid-fifties. There was even a link with the successful Home Lines, which would act as the North American agents for the new firm. While unable to build a brand new liner, the Company searched for available second-hand tonnage that might be suitable for modernization. Almost at the same time, Canadian Pacific's *Empress of Scotland*, their three-funnel former transatlantic flagship and one time speed champion on the Pacific run, was put up for sale. To the Germans, she seemed the perfect candidate for a huge transformation. Bought for £1 million, she was provisionally renamed *Scotland* and then taken to the Howaldtswerke yard at Hamburg. After a face-lift which cost a further £1.4 million, the ship was barely recognizable. Her three stacks had been replaced by two of more modern shape, the superstructure had been rebuilt, a new bow fitted (increasing the length from 666 to 672 feet) and the passenger quarters largely reshaped and updated. Rechristened the *Hanseatic*, she was a very fine addition to the Atlantic run. Generally, she worked

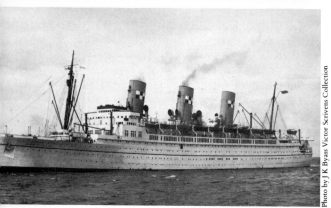

the traditional route, between Cuxhaven, Southampton, Cherbourg and New York from April to October. For the rest of the year, she cruised from New York and later Port Everglades to the Caribbean, and from Cuxhaven to Scandinavia and the eastern Atlantic. In November 1961, I was aboard her for a three-day holiday cruise out to sea. It was the first such 'nowhere' cruise to be offered from New York after 1939. The fares began at $75.

On 7 September 1966, only hours before her departure for Europe, the *Hanseatic* caught fire at New York's Pier 84 at the foot of West 44th Street. Smoke poured from the liner as the fire brigade cautiously avoided pouring too much water on the blaze. They certainly did not want to repeat the capsizing of the *Normandie*. The liner was later towed to a Brooklyn shipyard for a thorough inspection. The fire damage could have been repaired, but the smell of smoke had permeated so much of the ship that she was not worth the extensive repairs needed. She was sold for scrapping and towed across the Atlantic, reaching Hamburg on 10 October. She was then handed over to local shipbreakers.

The Soviet liner Mikhail Lermontov *briefly reopened a transatlantic service between New York and Leningrad in 1973. The ship was converted into a white-hulled cruise liner in 1982.*

Luis Miguel Correia

THE SOVIETS

The ALEXANDR PUSHKIN and MIKHAIL LERMONTOV
Many details of the early Soviet passenger ship fleet remain a mystery. There are limited records of their transatlantic operations in the late forties, just after World War II and before the worst period of the Cold War. Soviet passenger services in those years were indeed rather haphazard. There seemed to be no intention of creating a regular liner link between Odessa or Leningrad and New York.

Almost all of the ships which crossed the Atlantic for the Soviet Union at that time were former Germans. The most notable and the largest was the 17,700-ton *Rossia*, formerly the *Patria* of the Hamburg-America Line. She made about seven voyages to New York, sailing from Leningrad, Odessa, or Batumi. On her Mediterranean trips, she occasionally called at ports, such as Piraeus. Among her passengers was the operatic star Maria Callas. The *Rossia*'s final crossing seems to have been direct from New York to Odessa in February 1948. Thereafter, the ship was assigned to the local Black Sea run out of Odessa. Other Soviet-flag passenger liners, which made one or two Atlantic crossings to New York included the *Pobeda*, the former Hamburg-America *Magdalena* of 1928; the *Illich*, formerly the *Caribia* of Hamburg-America; and the *General Chernakhovsky*, formerly *Bochum*, also ex-Hamburg-America.

Soviet transatlantic services were not resumed until April 1966, when the new *Alexandr Pushkin* was assigned to sail from Leningrad, Bremerhaven, London, and Le Havre, to Quebec City and Montreal between April and October. Rather surprisingly it outlived all the traditional liner services on the Canadian run, with the exception of the Polish Ocean Lines. With the earlier fear of the Soviet Union replaced by a sense of curiosity, the ship and her sailings prospered. Particular support came from passengers who disliked air travel. The service was finally discontinued in 1981, and the ship reassigned to European cruising.

An occasional, mainly peak-season, New York service opened in May 1973, with the *Mikhail Lermontov*. She sailed between Leningrad, Bremerhaven, London, Le Havre and New York. There were also periodic cruises to Eastern Canada, Bermuda and the Caribbean. Again, the service was rather well supported by travellers who wanted the advantage of leisure time at sea or who had large luggage requirements. However, it, too, was discontinued by 1981. Shortly afterwards, the *Lermontov* was rebuilt as a cruise ship.

CHAPTER SEVEN

SHIPS TO THE ST. LAWRENCE

CUNARD LINE

The AQUITANIA

To many, she was the most handsome of the great four-stackers, that series of early superliners built before World War I. Even to this day, her magical-sounding name (after the Roman Province that is now France) conveys the image of a mighty ocean liner. She was, indeed, one of the great floating palaces. The *Aquitania* was long and slender, with four evenly balanced stacks (all of which actually worked, unlike those of many other three and four funnelled ships). Her sharp, no-nonsense bow was offset by an attractive counter stern. She lived up to her nickname 'the Ship Beautiful'.

The *Aquitania* came back to North Atlantic service just after World War II, her second international conflict, for a two-year austerity service between Southampton and Halifax. Even in the late forties, she must have seemed historic, certainly a distinctive member of the world's passenger fleet. At the end of her career, she achieved yet another Cunard distinction as the last ship with four funnels. (Twenty years or so later, Cunard's *Queen Mary*

The long, slender and well-proportioned lines of the Aquitania *are evident in this photograph, taken as the ship sailed from New York in the late thirties.*

Photo by Pat Laing Havers

A poetic, misty photograph of the outbound Aquitania *taken at Southampton in 1946. The ship is still painted in military grey, but her four funnels have the Cunard colours.*

Richard K Morse Collection

ranked as the last three-stacker.)

In 1945, the *Aquitania* was the only giant ship still surviving from before 1914. Even after her post-war decommissioning, her long task was unfinished. Cunard had her repainted in civilian colours, but did little else in the way of restoration. She was placed on an 'austerity service' with immigrants, displaced persons, some regular passengers, some of the few remaining troops, but mostly GI brides and their children. Sailings between Southampton and Halifax hardly brought back the grand old luxury ,days. Among her passengers at the time was the designer and photographer, Cecil Beaton, who rather briefly recorded his *Aquitania* voyage in his diaries: 'A bleak and awful winter crossing on a troop ship filled with GI brides and their seasick children. Dreadful food with potatoes still in their jackets!' The *Aquitania* made twelve such voyages in 1948 and a further thirteen in 1949. She might have continued, except that some serious structural problems emerged, certainly as a result of her long, very busy life. Captain Eric Ashton-Irvine was aboard in her final days. 'She was rotting everywhere. The funnels were crumbling, except that they were kept in place by layers and layers of paint. You could push your fingers through some of the bulkheads. She seemed quite a relic by this time. Alone, we had ten tons of brasswork on the bridge.' In the autumn of 1949, the *Aquitania*'s operating certificate was not renewed.

The liner reached Southampton for the last time on 1 December, finishing thirty-five years of continuous service, three million steaming miles and 443 voyages. Apart from being the last four-stacker, she was one of the most famous and successful passenger ships of all time. On 21 February she docked at Faslane in Scotland and was broken up by the British Iron & Steel Corporation.

The SCYTHIA, SAMARIA, FRANCONIA and ASCANIA

Cunard lost none of its major liners during World War II, but did suffer casualties among its medium-sized passenger fleet. Only four survivors from that group were able to reopen the Company's Canadian trade in the late forties. They were the Cunard 'single stackers', more functional than beautiful.

The *Scythia* and *Samaria* were the only sister ships, the *Franconia* came from a separate pre-war pair and the smallest, the *Ascania*, came from yet another group. The

Scythia and *Samaria* dated from the years following World War I. The *Scythia* was laid down soon after the Armistice, in 1919. Both were designed for the Liverpool-New York trade. A third sister, the *Laconia*, became a war casualty in 1942. The others served as troop ships, although the *Scythia* was nearly lost during the bombings of Algiers on 23 November 1942. She was towed to Gibraltar for patching of her damage and then crossed to New York for full repairs.

The *Franconia* and her original sister, the *Carinthia*, made a celebrated and extremely popular pair of cruise ships before the Second War. They were, in fact, Cunard's inspiration for the larger *Caronia* of the late forties. Both of the earlier ships were specially painted in white for their long, mostly tropical voyages. Their single-class accommodation, with overall capacities reduced from a transatlantic scale of 1650 to 400, became a byword of

One of a long series of rather similar ships, the Samaria *survived the Second War and continued in commercial service until the late fifties.*

Victor Scrivens Collection

The Ascania *of 1925 was the smallest and slowest of Cunard's post-war Canadian liners.*

thirties ocean travel. Their voyages varied from nine-day runs out of New York to Nassau and Havana for $60, to fortnights around the Caribbean for $120. Then, of course, there were the very luxurious longer trips to the Mediterranean and Scandinavia, around continental Africa and South America, and annual world cruises. These latter trips, sometimes lasting as long as 180 days, frequently left New York in January and returned in June. Fares started at $1900. These ships had a devoted following, which included such personalities as Noel Coward, Cole Porter and the last Empress of Austria.

The *Carinthia* was lost in 1940, but the *Franconia* survived some hardships to give heroic service. She was in a serious collision in the Mediterranean on 5 October 1939, with the Royal Mail liner *Alcantara*. Then, in the following summer, she was damaged in a Nazi air raid off France on 16 June. In both instances, she was promptly repaired and returned to her vital war duties. Steward Len Houghton was with the *Franconia* early in the war. 'We were at St Nazaire, for the evacuation of France, and moored across from another Cunarder, the *Lancastria*. Soon afterward, that latter ship took a bomb down her funnel, exploded and then quickly sank with the loss of over 3000 souls. On board the *Franconia*, we later took part in the landings on Norway, Madagascar and Sicily.' Toward the end of the war, Mr Houghton rejoined the ship just in time to serve her most famous passenger. 'Winston Churchill used the liner as his headquarters for the Yalta Conference, in

February 1945. He lived and worked from a refurbished suite on board. Some of his favourite and most personal effects had been brought down from London. He spent long hours in his cabin – writing, dictating, preparing – often from a special shelf desk fitted across the bathtub. Churchill soaked in the tub for hours.'

The only other post-war survivor, the *Ascania* of 1925, came from the largest pre-war class, which also included the *Andania, Antonia, Aurania* and *Alaunia*. The *Andania* was, however, the only wartime loss. The others seemed to have caught the eye of the Admiralty, for they were bought outright from Cunard and converted into military fleet repair ships. The *Ausonia* survived the longest, until 1965. The *Ascania* was returned to Cunard in 1947, and the *Scythia*, the *Samaria* and the *Franconia* soon followed.

The *Franconia* was renovated and resumed commercial sailings in June 1949, the *Ascania* in April 1950. The *Scythia* and *Samaria* had been assigned to British Government 'austerity service' in the late forties and often carried refugees, displaced persons and troops, sailing not only from London and Southampton, but often from Hamburg as well. Their restorations were the last in the post-war Cunard fleet. The *Scythia* returned to regular Cunard Canadian service in August 1950, and the *Samaria* in June 1951. All four ships were nevertheless intended only for temporary service. The Cunard Company was well aware that new, larger tonnage was needed to keep up their St Lawrence passenger run. Captain Ashton-Irvine remembered this group as being 'worn out'. They were all nearing thirty and had given long service, with particularly strenuous duty in the war. They had even developed mechanical faults. Captain Robin Woodall sailed in the *Franconia* in the mid-fifties. 'She was a tired old girl where one engine was faster than the other and so we always had to allow for a twist.' Captain Ashton-Irvine recalled the *Ascania*. 'She was quite troublesome in those final years. She was no longer very stable.'

The *Scythia* and *Samaria* sailed between London or Southampton, Le Havre and Quebec City. In the icy winters on the St Lawrence, they went instead to Halifax. The *Franconia* and *Ascania* sailed alternately between Liverpool and Quebec City from April to December, and to Halifax in the winter. Of course, there were occasional alterations in these patterns. All of the ships periodically went to New York, or took some detours, such as a series of sailings between Greenock and Quebec City by the *Franconia* in 1954. In their Canadian service, they had occasional problems. The *Franconia* went aground off Orleans Island, near Quebec City, in 1950, and the *Scythia* sheered 32 feet off the steamer *Wabana* in a collision in June 1952. The Cunarder had to put into the local Lauzon shipyard before recrossing to Southampton for more lasting repairs. The *Samaria*, however, was selected for the honour of representing Cunard at the Coronation Fleet Review off Spithead, on 15 June 1953.

The passenger accommodation on these four ships was greatly reduced from their pre-war standards. The *Ascania* had the biggest cut of all, from an original 1700 to a post-war 696 berths. Only first and tourist class passengers were carried. One Cunard officer, who served aboard these ships, especially remembered. 'I seem to recall only GI brides, their infants and immigrants on board.' Captain Woodall was aboard the *Franconia* in 1955 and later noted, 'We were doing some special voyages, running NATO troops from Quebec to Rotterdam. Homeward, we carried more troops as well as exchange personnel. She was then still a magnificent old ship – with a grand interior, splendid food and lots of young girls aboard' [so unlike the earlier Company freighters in which Woodall had served previously].

The arrival of the first of the new *Saxonia* class meant that this aged pre-war foursome could be retired. The *Samaria* went first, in November 1955, and sailed to Inverkeithing to be scrapped. The *Franconia* and *Asconia* followed at the end of 1956. The *Franconia* also went to Inverkeithing while the *Ascania*, following a final charter voyage to Cyprus for the British Government, finished her days at Newport, Monmouthshire. The *Scythia* was decommissioned in December 1957. A BBC-TV crew

met her at she reached Inverkeithing, recording the end of her thirty-eight years.

The SAXONIA/CARMANIA, IVERNIA/FRANCONIA, CARINTHIA and SYLVANIA

Rather sensibly, Cunard turned to an old friend, the John Brown Company at Clydebank, for the construction of four new Canadian service liners, in fact the largest Cunard ships yet for that trade. The 22,000-ton ships had

The first of four new Canadian liners, the Saxonia, *and her sisters were rerouted to New York and Halifax in the deep winter. The* Saxonia *is shown arriving at New York for the first time, in December 1954.*

balanced passenger and cargo capacities, a single domed stack, a short mast placed above the bridge and a considerable number of freight-handling kingposts and booms. In retrospect, Cunard (and John Brown's) used little foresight in planning these four ships. Among other disadvantages, there was not a single provision in their overall design scheme for the possibility of winter cruise service, which was becoming a very profitable off-season alternative for transatlantic liners in the mid-fifties.

Cunard Line

Captain Ashton-Irvine felt that they were impractical designs in general. 'Each had seven hatches for ten thousand tons of cargo, a fact which severely limited their passenger deck spaces. Furthermore, since we operated a basic passenger ship schedule, which often had us "in" on Thursdays on "out" again on Saturdays, we often missed much lucrative freight.'

Captain Woodall agreed that there were drawbacks with the newest Cunarders. 'The *Saxonia* class was not as wildly successful as we had hoped. To Canada, our cargo was usually very light, generally high-priced, small quantity goods. Homewards, we went light as well, often with just grain and timber. For passengers, we carried many westbound immigrants. But those winters on the diabolical, awful North Atlantic were quite sparse. I recall a crossing on the *Sylvania* in February 1961, to Halifax and New York, with only 311 passengers [her total capacity was 868]. Unfortunately, these four ships were not designed for the alternative of cruising. In fact, they were quite out of touch.'

As the first of the series, the *Saxonia* was launched by Lady Churchill, on 17 February 1954. The ship entered service in the following September. The *Ivernia* followed in July 1955. This first pair – with accommodation divided between 125 in first class and some 800 in tourist – sailed between Southampton, Le Havre, Quebec City and Montreal. In the winter, they took in London and sailed to Halifax and New York. The second identical pair were the *Carinthia* and *Sylvania*, which entered Cunard service in June 1956 and June 1957 respectively. They sailed between Liverpool, Greenock, Quebec City and Montreal, and then via Cóbh to Halifax and New York in winter. Their accommodation was slightly different, with 154 in first class and approximately 725 in tourist.

The ships were scheduled as a team, making weekly sailings from Montreal, with a round trip each month. Although they were intended to be fairly alike, they had undergone some modifications during construction. According to Captain Ashton-Irvine, 'The *Saxonia* and *Ivernia* were quite flashy in decor and lacked what many passengers felt was a Cunard standard of decoration. Consequently, the *Carinthia* and *Sylvania* were revised and were superior in taste and styling. In fact, there were even some historic touches: the chairs in the first class restaurant on the *Carinthia* were actually brought from storage after having been on the *Aquitania* of 1914.'

The four ships did not have many profitable years with Cunard, at least as North Atlantic liners. Captain Woodall was serving aboard the *Carinthia* in 1963–64. 'In October 1963, I recall taking a mere two hundred passengers westbound and then returning empty because of a Canadian labour dispute. We were beginning to sweat. Then, in January, we sailed out to New York via

The third of the new Canadian class, the Carinthia, *is seen approaching Montreal for the first time, in July 1956.*

Bermuda with 260 passengers and 1800 tons of cargo, and then returned from New York with 480 passengers and 250 tons of freight. Considering that ship such as the *Carinthia* could carry 868 passengers and 10,000 tons of cargo, the situation was quite gloomy.'

Cunard selected the *Saxonia* and *Ivernia* for thorough refits in the winter of 1962–63. They went back to their builder's yard on the Clyde and were altered for cruising. (Thereafter they would spend only the peak summer months on the Atlantic, with a route that was to be extended to include Rotterdam and therefore pick up more European passengers as well.) Private plumbing was installed throughout the ships, new and restyled public rooms appeared with some experimental features on trial for the big, new transatlantic Cunarder then planned, and the overall berthing figures were adjusted to 119 in first class and over 750 in a vastly improved tourist class. In place of the aft cargo hatches, there was a large lido deck with a kidney-shaped swimming pool. The ships were even given fresh names: the *Saxonia* became the *Carmania* while the *Ivernia* changed to *Franconia*. Cunard also decided to repaint the ships in their so-called 'cruising green', a colour scheme inspired by the *Caronia* of 1949 and applied not long beforehand to the *Mauretania*. In 1963, with four liners still in their black hull colours and four in shades of green, Cunard seemed to be turning more and more to lucrative cruising.

The *Sylvania* left the Canadian route in the spring of 1961, replacing the veteran *Britannic* on the Liverpool trade

Heavy seas encountered by the westbound Saxonia.

Luis Miguel Correia

The Sylvania *was repainted in white in 1966 and sent on cruises. She survived a mere two years longer.*

Eric Ashton-Irvine Collection

to New York. Six seasons later, in November 1966, this service finished. Thereafter, Cunard would sail only from Southampton. The Liverpool passenger business was gone completely, the cargo trade left to fast freighters. The *Sylvania* was repainted in white (the green colouring was then being abandoned) during her annual overhaul in December 1966, and afterwards used mostly for British cruising, often out of Gibraltar on Mediterranean fly-and-sail trips. The *Carinthia*, too, was painted white soon afterwards.

In October 1967, the *Carinthia* terminated the Cunard Canadian passenger service entirely. The New York operation had just had its final season with the two *Queens*. The Company's losses were already into the millions through competition from the airlines, greatly increased British labour costs and an aged, less competitive fleet. For Cunard, a careful examination of the Company's operation was needed, and for the original Canadian foursome, there were more alterations to come. The *Carmania* cruised throughout the year – from Southampton between late spring and early autumn and from Port Everglades in Florida, for the remainder. The *Franconia* took over the seven-day New York-Bermuda cruise trade from the defunct Furness-Bermuda Line. The *Carinthia*, left without any lucrative work, went to lay-up, and the *Sylvania* continued as a cruise ship until May 1968, when she too was withdrawn.

The *Carmania* continued cruising until December 1971. However, her popularity was dwindling, especially in the face of newer, smarter ships, and her overheads were mounting. She also had frequent misfortunes – aground in

the Bahamas in January 1969, a collision with a Soviet
tanker off Gibraltar in the following May, and some
underwater damage in the Caribbean in 1970. The
Franconia finished trading at the end of a four year contract
stint on the New York-Bermuda run. Nevertheless,
Cunard was interested in continuing with Bermuda
cruises and at first wanted to charter the Greek *Atlantis* of
Chandris Cruises to replace the *Franconia*. The proposal
was never carried out. The Company briefly resumed
Bermuda sailings in 1973, with the *Cunard Ambassador*, and
again during 1977, with the *Cunard Princess*.

The fate of the *Carmania* and *Franconia*, which later
rested alone together in Cornwall's River Fal was the
subject of many rumours. First, there was a suggestion
that the Greek Chandris Group wanted them for their
Australian immigrant service. Then the Japanese Toyo
Yusen K K came forward with a plan to make them
Pacific cruise ships. Others who were said to have
approached Cunard included the Italian Costa and Lauro
lines, more Greek shippers, and Arab financiers.
However, the sale eventually went (in 1973) to the Nikreis
Maritime Corporation of Liberia, who were in fact agents
for the Odessa-based Black Sea Steamship Company. The
Carmania and *Franconia* were to fly the Soviet colours. As
the *Leonid Sobinov* and *Feodor Shalyapin* respectively, they
have since served on a varied pattern of line voyages and
cruises – Southampton to Australian ports and cruises,
Soviet and Eastern Bloc workers' cruises, Australian and
Far Eastern cruises, and even carrying troops for the
Cubans to East Africa and the Middle East. At the time of
writing, they are still at work, although the exact details
are difficult to obtain.

Also resting together, the *Carinthia* and *Sylvania* became
fixtures along the Southampton Docks for nearly two
years. Soon after their withdrawal by Cunard, they were
sold to the Monte Carlo-based Sitmar Line, in spring 1968,
for conversion into high-standard luxury cruise ships. The
Carinthia became the *Fairland*, a choice that was soon
changed to *Fairsea*, while the *Sylvania* became the *Fairwind*.
Their projected conversions were at first delayed, but in
January 1970 they were moved to Trieste. The resulting
ships were hardly recognizable. With all the right
touches, lido decks, new public rooms, rebuilt cabins and
even vastly changed exterior profiles, they had turned into
contemporary cruise liners. One was to be based in
California, the other in Australia. However, the
Australian route was later dropped and both ships went to
America. The *Fairsea* cruises mostly from San Francisco
and Los Angeles, and the *Fairwind* from Port Everglades.
Having established very popular and profitable new lives,
they are probably the most effectively modified
Cunarders.

———CANADIAN PACIFIC STEAMSHIPS———

The EMPRESS OF FRANCE and EMPRESS OF CANADA

The great Canadian Pacific Company, the largest transportation network in the world for some years, was left rather short of liner tonnage at the end of World War II. All that remained were two medium-sized former transatlantic ships, the *Duchess of Bedford* and the *Duchess of Richmond*, and one larger liner, the *Empress of Scotland*, which had been the fastest ship on the Pacific before the war. Fortunately, the Company decided to concentrate on the North Atlantic. The earlier Vancouver-Far East run was not reopened. On the route between Liverpool, Greenock, Quebec and Montreal (to Saint John, New Brunswick, in deepest winter), they were the arch rival to Cunard. Both firms vied for the superior position to the St Lawrence.

The transatlantic *Empress* liners were famed. Consequently, it was decided to restore the twin *Duchess* ships with similar nomenclature. The *Bedford* became the *Empress of France*, and the *Richmond*, *Empress of Canada*. After strenuous war duties, they reappeared on the Canadian run in September 1948 and July 1947 respectively.

The *Empress of Canada*'s revival was rather brief, however. On 25 Janury 1953, she caught fire and later capsized while at her berth in the Liverpool docks. It was a particularly severe loss, as the spring-summer season was expected to boom because of the Coronation in London in June 1953. Rather desperate, Canadian Pacific searched for a replacement and were fortunate to find the *De Grasse* (see *Empress of Australia*). Over a year later, on 6 March 1954, the blackened and buckled remains of the *Empress of Canada* were refloated, certainly beyond repair. In September she was towed to La Spezia, for final dismantling.

The *Empress of France* had a better run. In the autumn of 1951, she received her most distinguished passengers Princess Elizabeth and the Duke of Edinburgh, who were bound for a goodwill tour of North America. She worked the Atlantic throughout the year and, unlike most of the other *Empress* liners, never cruised in the winter months. Rather late, she was given an extensive refit in the winter of 1959, one which included the modernization of her twin funnels. Two seasons later, in December 1960, she was sold to the breakers, at Newport in Monmouthshire.

The EMPRESS OF SCOTLAND

In the pre-war years, she was the 'Queen of the Pacific', the fastest liner on the Far Eastern run. She achieved her best record, Yokohama to Victoria, British Columbia, in

Everett Viez Collection

The Empress of Canada *of 1928 outbound from Montreal.*

The Empress of Scotland *approaching the famed Landing Stage at Liverpool.*

just under eight days sailing as the *Empress of Japan*. She was called up for troop duty soon after the war began and then, in 1942, because of Japan's enemy position, she was renamed *Empress of Scotland*. Not released from military duty until 1948, she took nearly two years to restore and modify for the Atlantic trade. She made her first crossing in May 1950. At first, however, because of her towering masts, she turned around at Quebec City, unable to clear the bridges at the entrance to Montreal. These masts were finally reduced in height in 1952 and her sailings were then extended. In these early years she, too, carried Princess Elizabeth and the Duke of Edinburgh, who were on this occasion returning from a North American tour. The *Empress of Scotland* divided her work between the North Atlantic for nine months of the year and Caribbean cruises from New York for the winter. In December 1957, she was the last surviving three-stacker apart from the *Queen Mary*. She might have gone for scrap after twenty-seven years, but the West German Hamburg-Atlantic Line wanted to rebuild a large liner for a revived Hamburg-New York service. The *Empress* changed hands for £1 million, was temporarily renamed *Scotland* and then became the *Hanseatic*.

The EMPRESS OF AUSTRALIA

Having spent nearly thirty years as the French Line's *De Grasse*, this ship was bought by Canadian Pacific purely as a temporary measure. She was their immediate replacement for the fire-gutted *Empress of Canada*, which had been heavily booked for the spring season of 1953, Coronation year in Britain. As the *Empress of Australia*, she was retained for three seasons, until January 1956, when

the new *Empress of Britain* was about to come into service. She found further employment as the immigrant ship *Venezuela* for the Italian Grimaldi-Siosa Lines. Mostly, she sailed to the West Indies until she was stranded near Cannes in March 1962. Damaged beyond economic repair, she went to the breakers at nearby La Spezia.

The EMPRESS OF BRITAIN and EMPRESS OF ENGLAND

Canadian Pacific ordered two new liners in the mid-fifties that would pose a serious challenge to the Cunard Canadian liners. To at least one observer, they were superior ships to the four new Cunarders of the *Saxonia* class, particularly because the *Empress* ships had less space for cargo and therefore more for passengers, and also because they were intended to cruise profitably in the winter months.

The first of this pair, the *Empress of Britain* was launched, in June 1955, by Her Majesty Queen Elizabeth II – Canadian Pacific is, after all, a British firm and not Canadian as many people wrongly assume. The new ship was, at least for a few years, the Company's flagship, and their first new Atlantic liner since the earlier *Empress of Britain*, a legendary three-stacker commissioned in 1931. That *Empress* was, in fact, launched by the Queen's uncle, then the Prince of Wales. She also carried the Queen's parents, King George VI and Queen Elizabeth, now the Queen Mother, in the summer of 1939.

The new *Empress of Britain* – and her twin sister, the *Empress of England*, which appeared a year later, in 1957 – were created for the pre-jet trade on the North Atlantic. For most of the year, the *Empress of Britain* would travel between Liverpool, Greenock and then across in six days to Quebec City and Montreal, before turning round and reversing the process. Her accommodation conformed with what was then prescribed format, a mere 160 in

Canadian Pacific Steamships

upper-deck first class and the remaining 860 in the less expensive tourist class. All of the first class staterooms had private toilet facilities, most of those in tourist did not. Fares for a peak summertime one-way passage in the late fifties started at $337 in first class, $217 in tourist. Her accommodation, while pleasant enough, was hardly startling. She had a much-appreciated indoor pool for those frequently cold, wet or foggy Atlantic crossings, and a series of spacious but rather bland public rooms. There

The Empress of England *and her sistership, the* Empress of Britain, *were Canadian Pacific's response to the four new sisters of the* Saxonia *class owned by their rival Cunard.*

Formerly the French De Grasse, *the* Empress of Australia *served as temporary relief within the Canadian Pacific transatlantic fleet following the loss of the* Empress of Canada.

was one further distinction: she was Britain's first fully air-conditioned liner. In winters, when the trip to Quebec and Montreal was made impossible by ice in the St Lawrence, the two *Empresses* could sail to Saint John, New Brunswick, where the passengers used train connections (also part of the enormous Canadian Pacific transport system) for inland destinations. Otherwise, the ships might spend three or four months (December to April) at New York for a series of two to three week cruises to the

Vincent Messina Collection

Caribbean. For these, the accommodation was adjusted to 650 berths, all first class.

However, like so many post-war liners, the *Empresses* began to lose clientele and therefore revenue by the early sixties. In a space of five years or so they might just have paid for themselves. As an alternative, Canadian Pacific sent them on more and more cruises – from Liverpool as well as Southampton. At about the same time, they were frequently chartered to the short-lived Travel Savings Association (TSA) in a sea-travelling scheme invented by Mr Max Wilson, a South African entrepreneur who anticipated a profitable development for cheap, no-frills voyaging. Among other marketing plans, Mr Wilson saw prospective passengers 'banking' their travel funds with TSA and taking an annual cruise in place of interest. The *Empresses* and other fading liners were sent on a varied pattern of sailings, from Britain to the Canaries, West Africa, Spain and Portugal, into the Mediterranean and even across to the Caribbean for four to five weeks. There were also some cruises from Capetown in an effort to lure South Africans on board for westward jaunts to South America or more locally to the Seychelles and East Africa. However, Mr Wilson's TSA was foundering by 1964. Bargain cruises with special offers on the fares seem to survive only briefly in the business. Passengers always want a certain degree of luxury, at least a basic level of comfort. Ocean liners have always offered this. When Canadian Pacific put the eight-year-old *Empress of Britain* up for sale, she was snapped up by the Goulandris Group

The Empress of Canada – *seen sailing from Montreal – was the last of the* Empress *liners and closed out Canadian Pacific's Atlantic service in late 1971.*

for their Greek Line operation to North America. In the spring of 1965, she was rechristened by Her Majesty Queen Anne Marie of Greece as the *Queen Anna Maria*.

The *Empress of England* remained until early 1970, when she was sold to another dwindling British passenger firm, the Shaw Savill Line. A long, expensive refit followed, costing over £4 million and intended to make the ship more suitable for one-class cruising. Unfortunately, as the *Ocean Monarch*, she was a dismal flop, suffering variously from too few passengers, a loss of reputation, and mechanical troubles. She was sold for scrapping on Taiwan in 1975.

The EMPRESS OF CANADA (1961)

This was Canadian Pacific's largest post-war liner and proved to be the Company's last Atlantic passenger ship. When her keel was laid in January 1959, there was a suggestion that the company were to break with tradition by calling her the *White Empress*, but she was eventually named the *Empress of Canada*. Introduced in April 1961, although somewhat late for an already declining Canadian run and in fact the very last liner to be purpose-built for that service, she fairly soon displaced the two previous *Empress* liners, the models for her design. The *Empress of Canada* made more frequent off-season cruises from New

York, mostly to the Caribbean, but also on some annual nine-week Mediterranean trips. By the late sixties, however, she was suffering from a variety of ills – lost trade, high British labour costs, and the general difficulties of a single-ship operation. Early rumours were that she would be sold to the Shaw Savill Line and become their *Dominion Monarch* for Australian service and cruising. Instead, after being laid up in November 1971 and thereby closing Canadian Pacific's liner trade, she was sold to the Miami-based Carnival Cruise Lines. Becoming the *Mardi Gras* and hoisting the Panama flag, she was refitted as a Caribbean cruise ship, with much of this work being done during her early cruises.

—————DONALDSON LINE—————

The LAURENTIA and LISMORIA

After World War II, many American transport-freighters seemed ripe for conversion, particularly for passenger service. A number of this very vast group (America built over six thousand merchant ships during the War) were, in fact, declared surplus after the war and quickly passed into foreign hands. Some remained as freighters, with several carrying the customary dozen or so passengers. Others went to shipyards for rebuilding and alterations that included the extension of passenger space. Two such ships were the sisters *Laurentia* and *Lismoria*, restyled for the Atlantic service of Britain's Donaldson Line.

Both ships were built as standardized Victory Class freighters with added troop accommodation. The *Lismoria* (formerly *Taos Victory*) came first, in January 1945, from the now long-defunct California Shipbuilding Yard at Los Angeles. The *Laurentia* was delivered two months later, as the *Medina Victory*, by the Permanente Shipyard at Richmond, also in California and also long since closed. They were only two of a large class of ships (over five hundred Victory freighters were built), but the *Medina Victory* was distinctive as the first American merchant ship to be fitted with radar. The two ships went on the surplus lists in 1946 and soon passed to the British Ministry of Transport. Shortly thereafter, they were transferred to Donaldson's, no doubt in reparation for war losses. The first ship lost in World War II, the liner *Athenia*, was a Donaldson vessel.

These ships seem to have retained their American names until they went to the Barclay Curle yard at Glasgow in 1948 for thorough refitting. The process included extension of the superstructures and the creation of fifty-five first class berths in each vessel. The passenger spaces were arranged on two decks. The Promenade Deck consisted of cabins and a forward lounge which overlooked the bow area and had smallish twin verandahs along each side. Below, on the Main Deck, there were

The passenger accommodations on board Donaldson's Laurentia *and her sister, the* Lismoria, *consisted of an extended superstructure on a standard Victory Ship hull.*

Fred Hawks

Oranje Line's Prinses Irene *took part in the opening ceremonies of the St Lawrence Seaway in June 1959.*

more cabins, the dining room and a hairdresser's shop. All of the cabins were outside, all were single or double, and yet only two had private bathrooms. It was a different era with different demands. Captain Harvey Smith, who served aboard the *Lismoria* before joining the Cunard Line, recalled, 'There were tartans everywhere. It was the first time I'd seen tartan rugs.'

The former *Taos Victory* came into service in October 1948 as the *Lismoria* (although the name *Cabotia* had originally been considered). The former *Medina Victory* followed the next May as the *Laurentia*. Between April and November, the pair worked in direct service between Glasgow and Montreal, taking nine to ten days in each direction. For the remainder of the year, they sailed a long-haul service between Britain and the American West Coast (as far as Vancouver) via the Panama Canal. Not until 1955 was the winter schedule altered and replaced with a shorter Atlantic run to Saint John, New Brunswick and Halifax. Revenues came from both passengers and freight. Captain Smith recalled, 'Aside from our first class passenger business, we carried considerable cargo in five holds. Outwards to Canada, we took general cargo including whiskies and cars. Homebound, we carried wheat, timber and apples.'

The pair were sturdy and dependable, two little noticed 'hard workers' in their line's operation. Then, as passenger figures began to decline, the fifty-five berths were closed off during the winter voyages from 1961. At the end of 1966, Donaldson voted to discontinue its North Atlantic passenger-cargo run altogether. Both ships finished out

the year's schedules and then went on the sales lists. The *Lismoria* actually finished her Donaldson service by making several charter trips for Cunard as a freighter to such ports as Boston, New York, Baltimore and Philadelphia. She was then purchased by the Greek-flag Astroguarda Compania Navigation, a small firm that specialized in buying older ships just prior to their last voyages to the scrapheap. Such was certainly the case with the *Lismoria*. She was renamed *Neon*, loaded with a cargo of scrap metal and sailed outward to Kaohsiung, Taiwan. Her demise came in May 1967. The *Laurentia*, like her sister, an elderly and hardly competitive freight carrier in the fast approaching container age, also went to scrap. She was broken at Valencia, Spain, also in 1967. Shortly

The Prinses Margriet *sailed for three successive Dutch steamship firms: the Oranje Line, Holland-America and Royal Netherlands. She was the last combination passenger-cargo liner to sail from North European waters to North America.*

thereafter, the entire Donaldson Company went into liquidation.

FURNESS-WARREN LINE

The NEWFOUNDLAND and NOVA SCOTIA

The Furness-Warren Line, an obvious division of the giant Furness Withy Group, ran two pre-war combination liners, the 6700-ton *Newfoundland* and *Nova Scotia*, on the North Atlantic between Liverpool, the Canadian Maritime Provinces and Boston. Both lost in World War II, they were replaced in the late forties by a new team, also named *Newfoundland* and *Nova Scotia*, built in the Vickers-Armstrong yard at Newcastle, where the liners *Monarch of Bermuda* and *Queen of Bermuda* had been built in the early thirties for another Furness Withy subsidiary, the Furness-Bermuda Line. At a mere 7400 tons each, they were moderately sized vessels with room for 154 passengers in the customary transatlantic class divisions (62 in first and 92 in tourist). They had conservative interiors and service speeds of a rather modest 15 knots. Because they were expected to sail the North Atlantic throughout the year, they were fitted with special ice-strengthened hulls.

The *Nova Scotia* first crossed, in September 1947, the *Newfoundland* in February 1948. The ships maintained a monthly timetable, going from Liverpool to St John's, Newfoundland, then to Halifax and finally a turn-round at Boston. There seemed to be little interruption in their working balance. In their four holds, the ships carried general cargo (especially cars) to Canada, and mostly grain and timber eastbound.

The *Nova Scotia* seems to have made the pair's only detour, when she was briefly substituted on the New York-Bermuda trade in the winter of 1961. On the other hand, when the Furness-Bermuda liners, the 22,500-ton *Queen of Bermuda* and 13,500-ton *Ocean Monarch*, crossed to Britain for their annual overhauls, they often carried transatlantic passengers. I remember at least two occasions when the *Ocean Monarch* returned to New York from drydocking at Newcastle with passengers on board. However, since they were mostly midwinter crossings, the figures tended to be quite light. On one of these voyages, the *Ocean Monarch* delivered a mere twenty passengers to New York.

In December 1961, the *Nova Scotia* and the *Newfoundland* were downgraded to twelve-passenger freighters. Their trade had declined to such an extent that Furness could reduce their passenger staffs (including the necessary doctor for ships carrying more than a dozen passengers) and be less concerned about maintaining a 'tight' passenger schedule. Eventually, the two ships were used only as freighters. A year or so later, in 1962, they were

Roger Sherlock

both sold to the Australian-based Dominion Far East Line, which used Bahamian registry. They were refitted, altered to carry 130 first-class passengers, and repainted with light grey hulls. The *Nova Scotia* became the *Francis Drake*; the *Newfoundland* changed to *George Anson*. Their new schedules were extensive. From Melbourne, Sydney, Brisbane and Cairns, they went to Hong Kong and Keelung, then to Kobe and Yokohama, before returning southbound to Australia via Guam and Rabaul. Along with freight, they also offered 63-day round trip cruises. The service lasted almost a full decade, until the eventual change to containers for the carriage of cargo deprived this small pair of port of its use. Both were scrapped on Taiwan in the spring of 1971.

ORANGE LINE

The PRINS WILLEM VAN ORANJE, PRINSES IRENE and PRINSES MARGRIET

Holland's Oranje Line began running freighter service (often with limited passenger space as well) to Eastern Canada in the late thirties. However, it was not until they created their largest ship yet in the early fifties, that they considered increased Atlantic passenger service. When the 7300-ton *Prins Willem Van Oranje* was commissioned in the late summer of 1953, she had sixty first class berths. She traded between Rotterdam, Southampton and Montreal (to Halifax and St John, New Brunswick, in the winter). Then, once the St Lawrence Seaway had been opened in 1959, the Company was able to consider extending its services to the Lakes. In fact, it was an Oranje Line freighter, the *Prins Willem Oranje Frederik*, that became the first overseas commercial vessel to use the Seaway. There were other developments as well at that time. The Oranje Line merged with the Fjell Line and afterwards traded as the Fjell-Oranje Line, although the passenger division was always thought of simply as the Oranje Line. Secondly, the Oranje Line itself was sold to a Dutch partnership, the Holland-America Line and the Koninklijke Paketvaart Maatschappij. Finally and perhaps most important, the Oranje directors saw the new Seaway as a prime opportunity to extend their passenger and cargo business into the Great Lakes. For that purpose, they added two new combination liners, the near-sisters *Prinses Irene* and *Prinses Margriet*. The *Prinses Irene*, which had been christened by Princess Irene of the Netherlands, entered service in April 1959. Two months later, she participated in the official opening of the Seaway and was thereafter able to go on to Chicago and other Great Lakes ports. The *Prinses Margriet*, also given a royal christening by the Princess whose name she bore, was commissioned two years later, in July 1961. Both ships were single-class and had extremely high standards of accommodation. Every

passenger cabin had private toilet facilities.

The three ships maintained a transatlantic service out of Rotterdam and Southampton. Mini-cruises were also offered on the sections between Chicago and Montreal, with cargo stopovers in the Lakes. In winter, the ships went to Halifax and St John, New Brunswick, although the *Prinses Irene* also made several trips to the Gulf of Mexico, with turn-rounds at Vera Cruz and Tampico. However, the Oranje passenger business was not wildly successful, in fact quite disappointing. Furthermore, even the cargo trading did not provide enough of an alternative. In 1962, the *Prins Willem Van Oranje* became a twelve-passenger freighter. Shortly afterwards, in the spring of 1963, the comparatively new *Prinses Margriet* was chartered to Holland-America for their Rotterdam-New York direct service (replacing their *Noordam* and paired with the *Westerdam*). The *Prinses Irene* finished at the end of the summer season in 1963. She was then chartered to Cunard for a year as a cargo ship on their 'whisky run' between Glasgow and New York. The *Margriet* was finally bought outright by Holland-America in December 1964. At the same time, with her Cunard charter concluded, the *Irene* was sold to the Dutch Verolme Shipyards and then shortly afterwards to the Djakarta Lloyd of Indonesia. She was rebuilt with some nine hundred berths for the Moslem pilgrim trade, mostly across the Indian Ocean to Jeddah, and became the *Tjut Njak Dhien*. She has remained in Indonesian hands ever since. The last former Oranje passenger ship (although then reduced to twelve berths), the *Prins Willem Van Oranje*, also left the fleet. In February 1965, she was sold to the East German Government and became the *Ferdinand Freiligrath*. A decade or so later, in the mid-seventies, she went to Panamanian owners for general tramp services and became in succession the *Freijo*, the *Universal Honolulu* and finally the *August 8th*. Laid-up at Singapore in October 1977, she was scrapped two years later on Taiwan. The *Prinses Margriet* finished her Holland-America North Atlantic service in late 1967 and then went to another Dutch firm, the Royal Netherlands Steamship Company, for a series of twelve-day cruises from New York to the Caribbean. Holland-America continued to serve as her passenger agents. However, it was a very late use of a combination ship in such a highly competitive cruise run. She was sold in 1970 to the Government of the Republic of Nauru, a phosphate-rich island in the western Pacific. Renamed *Enna G*, she sailed on passenger-cargo cruises from San Francisco to Honolulu, Majuro, Ponape, Truk and Saipan. The round trip took six weeks. She was withdrawn and laid up in early 1984. As for the Oranje Line itself, after giving-up passenger service, its operations slumped even further. The Company ceased trading altogether at the end of 1969.

CHAPTER EIGHT

THE TOURIST AND IMMIGRANT SHIPS

HOLLAND-AMERICA LINE

The RYNDAM

In the late forties, just as its North Atlantic passenger service to New York had been firmly re-established, the Holland-America Line turned its attention to the North American Pacific Coast service via Panama. The plans called for two combined passenger-cargo ships, with sixty first class berths each, that would be known as the *Dinteldyk* and *Diemerdyk*. The keel plates for the first ship were put in place in December 1949, at the Wilton-Fijenoord yards at Schiedam. Then, quite suddenly, Company thinking changed.

The transatlantic trade was beginning again to boom. Liners were often filled to capacity and calculations

The Maasdam *docked at Southampton, with the inbound* Queen Mary *in the background.*

Pat Laing Havers

Victor Scrivens Collection

The Maasdam *sailing from Willemstad, Curaçao during a winter Caribbean cruise.*

suggested that more passenger ships would be needed. However, there was a major difference from earlier predictions. The need would now be for far more tourist class space, less expensive accommodation that could be used, not only by the new wave of westbound emigrants seeking passage to North America, but by students, budget tourists and a new generation of European-bound travellers who had been increasing in numbers since the end of World War II. Therefore, just as the combination ship *Dinteldyk* was beginning to take some initial shape, she was redesigned totally as an Atlantic liner. The fresh plans would make her nothing short of revolutionary in design, however. For the first time, the tourist class accommodation would occupy some ninety per cent of the ship's spaces. The first class quarters would be extremely small, in fact a mere gesture to the transatlantic liner agreements concerning two-class ships.

The intended 11,000 tons of the *Dinteldyk* became the 15,000 tons of the *Ryndam* (a name derived from the River Rhine). Replacing the six cargo holds originally intended were seven passenger decks – Sun, Navigating Bridge, Boat, Promenade, Main, A and B. The thirty-nine berths in first class were contained entirely on the Boat Deck, in what was often described as the 'penthouse' section of the ship. First class had a small, separate dining room, combined lounge and smoking room, and partially

enclosed promenade deck. All of the first class cabins had private bathrooms.

The tourist class spaces occupied the major portion of the *Ryndam*, using the Boat, Promenade, Main, A and B decks. The cabins were located on the Main, A, and B Decks, and some 63 per cent were doubles (overall, there were 6 singles, 270 doubles, 28 triples and 56 four-berth). Very few of these rooms had private bathrooms. Instead, passengers shared lavatories, showers and bathrooms that were conveniently located on each deck.

The concept of giving such a large proportion of the passenger spaces over to the tourist class certainly represented a stark change in thinking by the Holland-America Line. Commissioned almost fifteen years before, the *Nieuw Amsterdam* was arranged in such a way that one-third of the passengers (first class) occupied two-thirds of the available space. By the fifties, however, it was becoming more and more apparent that both first and cabin class were declining (cabin class sections were actually disappearing completely) while the need more comfortable, yet still economical, tourist class quarters was expanding. The idea spread rapidly. When Canadian Pacific and Cunard built new liners in the mid-fifties, they catered for only a hundred or so passengers in first class and eight hundred or more in tourist.

The *Ryndam* was launched on 19 December 1950. Her intended sistership, the *Diemerdyk*, was also redesigned and became the *Maasdam*, also for North Atlantic tourist service. The *Ryndam* first crossed in July 1951, and was

van Herk Collection

The Tourist Class Smoking Room on board the Maasdam *of 1952.*

instantly acclaimed as an outstanding, novel ship, where passengers could enjoy comforts in tourist class for as little as $20 per day, or $160 for the eight-day passage between New York and Southampton. The *Ryndam* and *Maasdam* quickly became known as 'the economy twins'. The sisters had two further distinctions, the unique colouring of their dove-grey hulls and a most unusual funnel design. Holland-America had originally intended that both ships would be painted in the traditional black, but made use of the superior heat-reflecting quality of light colours, since they meant that the ships should cruise in the Caribbean during the winter season. The light grey surface assisted the air-conditioning system by reducing the interior temperature as much as ten degrees. It soon proved so successful that it was adopted during the major refit of the *Nieuw Amsterdam* in 1956–57, as well as on the new *Statendam* in 1957 and, finally, the *Rotterdam* in 1959.

The design of the single funnels for these sister ships was the result of considerable testing. Preliminary sketches showed rather conventional, slightly raked stacks, but liner companies (and their designers) have been bothered for decades with the shedding of smoke and smuts on after decks and the passengers themselves. The funnels of some liners were made taller in the hope of reducing this problem. New stacks, designed in France, were intended to improve this difficulty in the *Ryndam* and *Maasdam*. The

Herbert G Frank, Jr Collection

Tourist class deck space on the westbound Ryndam.

new funnels, known as Strombus Aerofoils, appeared wide when seen broadside, but looked almost wafer thin from the bow or stern. The tops were tapered, narrowing from top to bottom in the aft portion. The shape was meant to direct smoke well away from the open aft decks of the ships, and was to some degree successful. Captain Cornelius van Herk recollected a rumour which circulated during the construction of these twin liners that they would, in fact, have the world's first movable stacks, units that could actually turn in the direction of the wind and therefore blow smoke away from the ship itself. However, one obvious problem was that they would require heavy-duty machinery arranged along the upper

The Tourist Class Restaurant aboard the Maasdam.

A pleasant setting for younger passengers: the Children's Playroom on board the Maasdam.

decks. As the extra weight might seriously have jeopardized the balance of the ships, the idea was abandoned.

The *Ryndam* and *Maasdam* sailed between Rotterdam, Le Havre, Southampton (occasionally this was limited to tender service from Cowes), Cóbh or Galway, in Ireland, and then across to New York. On some sailings, they also called at Halifax to land Canadian-bound immigrants. During the slack winter season, they were sent to Bermuda and the Caribbean, each carrying about six hundred single-class passengers. Holland-America was indeed right to invest hope in these small, tourist-oriented liners. In a matter of a few years, both ships had paid for themselves and earned large profits for their Dutch owners. Nevertheless, their design was modified in the *Statendam* of 1957, which was even more luxurious and had far more private plumbing in her passenger cabins. The *Ryndam* and *Maasdam* were not without their problems, however. Neither was a good sea vessel. Because they were short (only 503 feet overall) and fairly high in their superstructure, they pitched tremendously at sea. Seasickness was common among the passengers. In 1954,

136

van Herk Collection

At Holland-America's Wilhelminakade Terminal at Rotterdam: a view from the deck of the outbound Nieuw Amsterdam *to the* Statendam *and the* Ryndam *farther along.*

Soon afterwards, the Ryndam found yet another role, as a floating college in the winter months. Chartered to an American university, she became known as 'the World Campus Afloat' and made two annual world voyages, for the autumn and spring terms, which teachers, guest lecturers and about five hundred students. Subjects and topics were linked to the ports of call. This cruise concept continues to date, most recently using the liner *Universe*, the former American Export *Atlantic*.

In November 1964, the *Ryndam* was used for another experiment, a Holland-America service to Australia and New Zealand, sailing out via the Suez and homeward via Panama. Unfortunately, after only a few trips, the service proved totally unprofitable. The 15,000-ton, 16-knot *Ryndam* could hardly be expected to compete with more established liners, particularly Britain's big P&O fleet. By the mid-sixties, her life was changing frequently. In 1966, she was replaced on the St Lawrence run by her sister, the *Maasdam*. That September, the *Ryndam* was transferred to the Europe-Canada Line, a Holland-America subsidiary company that had West German registry, for two reasons: the wages of German crew members were then at least 20 per cent less than those on Dutch ships, and it was thought that Europe-Canada Lines's strong reputation in Germany might give the ship an important competitive edge. In fact, the change was fairly brief. Among other problems, the new West German crew accidentally ruined one of the *Ryndam*'s three boilers. The Holland-America Line was hardly pleased. Consequently, in October 1967, the ship rehoisted the Dutch colours and joined another firm that was closely linked to Holland-America, the Trans-Ocean Steamship Company of The Hague. Trans-Ocean had been created in 1960 for budget transatlantic service and had initially used the three 'Constellation sisters', the *Groote Beer*, *Waterman* and *Zuiderkruis*.

In May 1968, while berthed at New York's Pier 40, the *Ryndam* was renamed *Waterman*, expressly for a series of summertime student crossings. She reverted to her original name in the following October and shifted back to direct Holland-America operations. More low-fare student, immigrant and university sailings followed. At twenty years old, the *Ryndam* was withdrawn from Dutch service and laid-up at Rotterdam, in 1971. She was offered for sale and, it was rumoured, would go to the Cypriot-registered Sovereign Cruises, for bargain Mediterranean trips with British fly-sail tourists. Instead, she was actually idle for some time before going in the summer of 1972 to the Epirotiki Lines of Greece. She changed hands for $2.5 million. When she resumed sailing in May 1973, she was hardly the same ship. Her name had been changed to *Atlas* and her exterior thoroughly, modernized with a novel funnel device added. Her superstructure was raked rather severely, giving the overall effect of a far newer ship. A

the Royal Netherlands Navy invented a special hemispherical device that was attached to the bow of the *Ryndam*. It was intended to reduce the pitching, and did so to some extent. However, it also had the effect of making ship's stern section swing rather furiously. On her first trip out with the hemispherical attachment, the *Ryndam* swung frantically enough for her engineers to fear that she might crack in half or that her pipes might break and cause tremendous flooding, possibly even sink her. The home office at Rotterdam ordered the ship to return immediately to Southampton, where the device was removed in dry dock. Later, both ships were fitted with fin stabilizers, which in some measure reduced their motion problems.

When the new flagship *Rotterdam* came into service in the late summer of 1959, the *Ryndam* was released from the New York run. Beginning in the following April, she opened a new Holland-America route to Quebec City and Montreal. The ship suddenly had a renewed popularity.

large lido and swimming pool area had been made in the stern. All of her public rooms and staterooms were rebuilt and decorated in modern style. All her cabins were fitted with private facilities. Carrying 731 passengers, all first class, she was placed on the ever-popular Aegean islands trade, with weekly departures from Piraeus. In later years, she has cruised also to the Norwegian fjords, in the Baltic, the western Mediterranean and the Caribbean, and even from Rio de Janeiro to lower South America. In September 1980, she was to have been sold to Mexican interests, who wanted to run her as the condominium-style cruise ship *Royal Prince*. The project never quite materialized and the ship remains in Greek hands at the time of writing.

The MAASDAM

The *Maasdam* was a duplicate of her sistership *Ryndam*. Her measurements were practically identical, as were her accommodation and decoration. The ships even suffered the same disadvantage, serious pitching at sea.

After years on the Rotterdam service, the *Maasdam* was selected to inaugurate an extended Company transatlantic run to Bremerhaven in 1963. It was a bid to attract additional customers, namely German travellers, on the declining North Atlantic. Holland-America promoted the new service, but could not have realized the publicity that would come on the ship's first call to the German port.

Her arrival was scheduled for February 1963. The Royal Netherlands Marine Band was on board to add some formality to the occasion. Then, just as the ship entered the River Weser, she collided with the wreck of a sunken Soviet ship. The damage was serious, and the ship took a noticeable list. As a precaution, the captain ordered all passengers ashore, some in the local pilot boat and others in the liner's lifeboats. It was all rather dramatic. Newspapers on both sides of the Atlantic featured bold headlines: 'Near sinking of the *Maasdam*' and 'Passengers Take To The Boats in Great Tragedy'. Although the *Maasdam* was damaged, she was repaired immediately and had never been in danger of sinking. A subsequent investigation proved that the harbour buoys had been moved by ice floes and had misled the liner's navigating officers.

The *Maasdam* replaced the *Ryndam* on the Montreal service in 1966. However, the overall trade, both to the United States and Canada, was shrinking rapidly. Two years later, in October 1968, the *Maasdam* was sold to the Polish Ocean Lines as a replacement for their aged flagship, the *Batory*. Completely refitted and modernised, she resumed service in the following spring as the *Stefan*

A dramatic photograph of the brand new Statendam *made by a camera attached to a kite.*

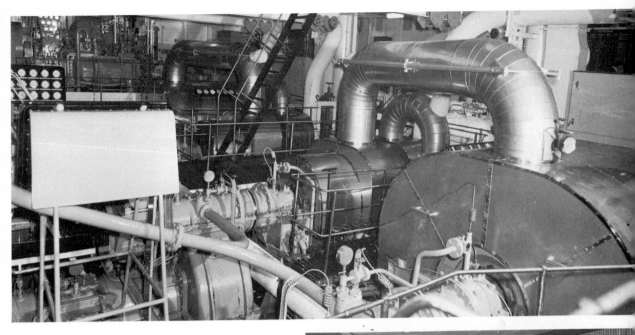

Part of the engine room aboard the Statendam.

Batory. During my own voyage in that ship, in September 1981, I noticed a small model ship on the captain's desk. It was the *Maasdam*.

The STATENDAM

The *Ryndam* and *Maasdam* were such a great success in the fifties with their predominantly tourist-class accommodation that it prompted the Company to think of an even larger, more improved version of these ships. The design of this new liner was begun in 1954 and the contract placed a year later, again at the Wilton-Fijenoord yard at Schiedam. The new ship would be the *Statendam*, the fourth to bear that name. This new 24,000-tonner, although larger than the *Ryndam* and *Maasdam*, was not as large as the *Nieuw Amsterdam* at 36,000 tons. A liner of similar large proportions was to come in 1959, in the form of the new national flagship *Rotterdam*. The medium size of the *Statendam* represented, once again, the Company's restrained, almost cautious approach to passenger shipping on the North Atlantic. There was simply no need for a bigger ship that was in fact being purposely designed for the tourist trade. The improvements aboard the *Statendam*, were based mostly on experience with the earlier *Ryndam* and *Maasdam*. Some ninety per cent of the tourist class cabins were fitted with private shower and toilet, a higher speed (19 knots) was used so that she could run alongside the *Nieuw Amsterdam*, and there was greater adaptability for luxury cruising (which required, among other features, larger staterooms, greater open-deck

van Herk Collection

The Tourist Class Verandah on the Statendam.

spaces and a large pool).

Holland–America was proud to announce that the new *Statendam* was paid for directly by the Company itself. There were no Government loans or subsidies. Most unusually, the 642-foot liner was floated out of her construction dock, on 12 June 1956, rather than being given the more customary launching. Water was admitted to the dry dock through valves until it reached the required level and five tugs towed her through the dock gate (which was only 18 inches wider than the liner). This difficult operation passed without mishap, and the ship was then taken to a fitting-out dock. Even her christening ceremony was unusual. On 23 January 1957, during the liner's trial runs, Her Royal Highness Crown Princess Beatrix poured a glass of champagne over the ship's bell, which weighed three hundred pounds and was positioned in the flower-decorated dining room for the occasion.

Despite some brief problems with her reduction gears during the trial voyages, the *Statendam* proved to be another well designed, strongly built liner. She crossed to New York, in February 1957, to make her first arrival just at the time of a tugboat strike. Only a small flotilla greeted the new ship. Furthermore, she was forced to dock under her own power, with guidance coming from crewmen who had been lowered in some of the ship's own lifeboats to the chilly waters of the Hudson. The *Statendam* was skilfully docked, eventually, on the north side of the Company's 5th Street Pier in Hoboken (the *Nieuw Amsterdam* was at dock on the south side of the same pier).

Practised judges of ships considered the *Statendam* one of the finest looking liners of her time, with her shortish radar mast above the bridge, her tapered funnel and her heavily-flared bow, which was designed to reduce striking water during heavy weather. Her interiors were equally handsome. She carried 84 in first class and 868 in tourist. Again, the first class section occupied a penthouse section of the liner's upper decks, whereas the tourist class had the great majority of the passenger area. In the modern decorative scheme, woods such as Bleached Ash, Rio Rosewood and Bubinga from the African Cameroons, were again used, as in all the Company's liners.

Following her initial summer season on the Atlantic, between Rotterdam, Le Havre, Southampton and New York, the *Statendam* turned to luxury winter cruising, with accommodation reduced to 650, all first class. Her first voyages were to the Caribbean. However, Captain van Herk was then helping to prepare for the ship's grand world cruise, planned for the winter and spring of 1958. 'We scheduled a 110-day voyage, from 7 January until 7 May. From New York, she went to Dakar, Freetown, Pointe Leone, Luanda, Walvis Bay, Capetown, Durban, Zanzibar and Mombasa. We then went across to India, to Bombay, and then on to Colombo, Penang, Singapore, Bangkok and to Bali. Because of troubles with the then President Sukarno, none of the Dutch crew was permitted ashore at Bali. Only the American passengers were allowed. From Indonesia, we sailed northward to Manila, Hong Kong, Keelung, Okinawa, Kobe, Yokohama and then across the Pacific to Honolulu, San Francisco and Acapulco. We passed through the Panama Canal and then steamed homeward to Hoboken.'

Beginning in 1960, the *Statendam*, the *Nieuw Amsterdam* and the new *Rotterdam* formed 'The Big Three' sailing from New York each Friday at noon, from April to the end of October, bound for the Channel ports and then to Rotterdam. Passengers could choose the basically tourist atmosphere of the *Statendam*, the 'old world' charms of the *Nieuw Amsterdam* or the prestige of the two-class *Rotterdam*. It was a perfect arrangement, one that lasted several more years.

The *Statendam* was the first of the three to fall victim to the competition from jet travel. She was transferred to permanent cruise service in 1966, sailing initially from the California ports of San Francisco and Los Angeles. This was a new step for the Company and succeeded in attracting a luxury market for rather long voyages to the South Seas, Australia, the Orient, Hawaii, Mexico and even journeys through the Panama Canal to the Caribbean. Later, when the *Statendam* was replaced by the even more luxurious *Hamburg* of the German-Atlantic Line (another firm affiliated with Holland-America), the Dutch liner made long cruises from New York to the Mediterranean and Scandinavia, and subsequently shorter trips to Bermuda and the Caribbean.

In the winter of 1971–72, *Statendam* was given a major refit costing nearly $5,000,000, that transformed her into a permanent cruise ship. Her public rooms were redecorated in a more modern style, and her total capacity was adjusted to 740, all first class. In 1973, as with all of the Holland-America liners, her registry was changed to Willemstad, Curaçao in the Netherlands Antilles. High taxes and other expenses in Holland no longer made registry at Rotterdam, however patriotic, a viable proposition. A year later, the ship began regular week-long cruises from New York to Bermuda, departing from Manhattan each Saturday afternoon and then spending four days docked at Hamilton. In the new generation of cruise services, she was paired with the *Rotterdam*, which also plied a seven-day pattern, but to Nassau as well as Bermuda. During the winter months, the *Statendam* shifted to Florida for longer voyages to the Caribbean.

After a rearrangement of the fleet in 1981, the *Statendam* was sent to Vancouver for a series of summer sailings to Alaska, which had fast become one of the most popular and profitable cruising areas in the world. However, the twenty-four-year-old liner, like some of her predecessors, was growing 'tired'. Her machinery had become tender and often faulty, and she required frequent dry docking and emergency repairs. Put up for sale a year later, in 1982, she was sold to Paquet Cruises, a French-based company that uses Bahamian registry and a multi-national crew. Now renamed *Rhapsody*, the former Dutch liner

Victor Scrivens Collection

sails from Miami to the Caribbean during the winter months and from Vancouver to Alaska in the summers.

A converted Victory Ship transport, the Groote Beer *and her two sisters were rebuilt by the Dutch in the early fifties for low-fare passengers. They were the last Atlantic passenger ships to use the early style Quadrant lifeboat davits.*

NETHERLANDS GOVERNMENT

The GROOTE BEER, WATERMAN and ZUIDERKRUIS
During World War II, the United States built some 6000 merchant ships in the largest shipbuilding effort the world has ever seen. Most of these ships belonged to specialized classes, the largest of these being the 2700 of the Liberty Ship type. These Liberty ships were mostly pre-fabricated vessels designed to be successful even if they made only a single wartime voyage with supplies, munitions or personnel. Then, as the Allied victory came closer to reality, a new type of improved, larger cargo vessels was created for later use in commercial service as well. Some five hundred of this group were known as Victory Ships. When the War ended, the US Government cleared nearly a hundred of these ships – among many others – for sale to foreign owners, to revitalize depleted fleets and also to create new ones. Three Victory ships were sold to the Dutch Government in 1947, particularly for peacetime use as troop ships to politically troubled Indonesia. (Others which went to Holland were used as freighters). The three troopers were quickly given Dutch names: the *Cranston Victory* became the *Zuiderkruis* (Southern Cross), the *Costa Rica Victory* was changed to *Groote Beer* (Great Bear) and the *La Grande Victory* to *Waterman* (Aquarius). They were known, in due course, as the 'Three Constellations'. As troop ships, they had most spartan accommodation, used by both troops and evacuees.

When their more pressing military duties were completed (by 1951), each of the three was sent to a Dutch shipyard for refitting as a passenger ship. However, from the start, there was no intention of using them as regular liners. Instead, they were redesigned with improved, yet still rather austere, accommodation for sailings with immigrants, students, low-fare tourists, workers, and even more troops, should the occasion arise. The new arrangement of passengers was listed as 900 in one class to each ship. The three ships were practically identical in size and each was powered by steam turbines linked to a single screw that provided a service speed of 16 knots. The passenger spaces were arranged on six decks, A, B, C, D, E and F. There were cabins with three, four, five, six, eight and ten berths and dormitories to sleep fifty-five. Every cabin contained a wardrobe and at least one or two wash basins. Public lavatories and showers were located on each accommodation deck. The public rooms included twin lounges, a reading-writing room, a theatre, children's playroom and a dining room. In ship design annals, they were the last vessels to have the rather old-fashioned quadrant lifeboat davits with double boats in position.

Although still owned by the Dutch Government (the Netherlands Ministry of Transport and the Directorate General of Shipping), the ships were managed by the country's three largest national steamship companies, the *Groote Beer* by Holland-America, the *Waterman* by Royal Rotterdam Lloyd, and the *Zuiderkruis* by the Nederland Line. It was a convenient arrangement, but the ships carried their own funnel markings and operated on schedules that were independent from those regularly associated with their managers. Their purpose was to provide low-fare passage, mostly for Dutch nationals and Dutch-related passengers. During most summers, they crossed the North Atlantic between Rotterdam and North

V H Young

The Waterman *finished her life as a Greek-flag pilgrim ship, taking Moslems to Jeddah.*

America, either to New York (sometimes via Halifax) or to Quebec City. Occasionally, they would call at Le Havre and Southampton. At each port of call, particularly Rotterdam and New York, they used Holland-America pier facilities and technical assistance, and local staffing. For the remainder of the year, the three sailed according to inducement – to Australia or South Africa with immigrants, to Indonesia, to the Far East, to the Caribbean with workers and, on occasions, with Dutch troops. In 1964, the *Groote Beer* brought home members of the Dutch Air Force, who had been studying missiles in Texas. As sea-going ships, they were, for most of their lives, rather notorious 'rollers' at sea.

In 1960, the ships were transferred to the ownership of the Trans-Ocean Steamship Company, a creation of the Dutch Government and also linked to the Holland-America Line. The accommodation on board the three ships was somewhat improved. A new lounge was added, the number of dormitories was reduced – some of them replaced by more two-berth cabins – and an outdoor pool was installed. Since Trans-Ocean was not a member of the established Trans-Atlantic Passenger Steamship Conference which, among other activities, formulated guidelines for passenger rates, it could offer low fares. As always, the ships remained popular with both students and immigrants. The three ships were particularly active with the American Field Service and MBBS (the Netherlands Society for Foreign Student Relations), under whose auspices students were able to spend a year abroad as part of their studies. Sample fares in 1963 amounted to $197 per person in cabins for six or less, $180 in rooms for eight to

ten, and $170 in the dormitories. However, the three ships were sold in a rather abrupt move during that year. The *Groote Beer* and *Waterman* were bought by the John S Latsis Line, a Greek operation, and were renamed *Marianna IV* and *Margarita* respectively. Their new purpose was mostly as 'pilgrim ships', transporting Moslems to Arabia from ports in North and West Africa. The former *Groote Beer* was often so overcrowded, with as many as 2200 on board, that many passengers slept on deck using their own mattresses. (Another Latsis ship in similar service at the time was the former P&O liner *Stratheden*. Renamed *Henrietta Latsi*, she was reported to have carried as many as 4000 pilgrims per voyage, compared with her original P&O capacity of 1200.)

During the summers of 1965 and 1966, the *Marianna IV* was chartered to Holland-America, at one time her partial owner, to cater for a sudden peak in Atlantic student travel. Although she retained her Greek registry and flag, she resumed the name *Groote Beer*. Captain van Herk served for a time as the Holland-America liaison officer and advisor. 'Latsis ran a very tight ship. Everything had to be accurately accounted for. Detailed explanations for every expense had to be given. We were under the command of a Captain Metropolis and had Greek officers, engineers and deck staff. The catering department was mixed, although there were many Dutch.'

The year 1966 proved to be the *Groote Beer*'s final phase of service. On 12 July she had a serious collision off England's Needles Lighthouse with the sand dredger *Pen Avon*. Given temporary repairs, she lasted only two months more. In September, she was laid up in Greece – first at Piraeus and then in the backwaters of Perama, an area noted for its vast assortment of idle tonnage awaiting the scrap-heap. The *Groote Beer* had by then reverted to her Greek name of *Mrianna IV*. After her retirement in 1963, the *Zuiderkruis* passed to the Dutch Navy for use as a permanently moored hotel and stores ship at the naval base at Den Helder. She was officially classified as a member of the Royal Dutch Navy, under the pennant number A 853. The former 'Three Constellations' were scrapped within months of one another, although in quite different areas. The *Zuiderkruis* was towed to Bilbao, Spain, in November 1969. The former *Groote Beer* and *Waterman* both went in 1970, at Eleusis, Greece, and Onomichi, Japan, respectively.

----------AROSA LINE----------

The AROSA KULM

The Arosa Line, whose ships flew the Panamanian flag, was created by the booming immigrant and low-fare trade on the North Atlantic in the fifties. The Swiss-owned Company was the brainchild of a businessman, Nicolo Rizzi, who lived in the shadow of Mount Arosa. Working under the name of Compania Internacional Transportation, Mr Rizzi purchased his first ship, the *Protea*, from Panamanian owners in 1951. He had the 8900-ton ship fitted to carry some 46 in first class and 919 in tourist class dormitories. Renamed *Arosa Kulm*, she was the beginning of the Arosa Line fleet. Peter Eisele, editor of the journal *Steamboat Bill*, later wrote. 'The old ship was not meant to be luxurious; instead, she was designed to

move large numbers of passengers at reasonable fares.' This was the Arosa concept. The *Arosa Kulm* entered service in March 1952, sailing between Bremerhaven, Zeebrugge and Southampton to either Montreal or Halifax. As in all subsequent Arosa operations, the ports of call were frequently changed from then on. Fares ranged from $150 in a tourist dormitory to $165 in a first class cabin. The passengers were mostly immigrants and students, and in fact the ship was often chartered to New York's Council on Student Travel.

The *Arosa Kulm* had been built as a standardized Hog Island-type passenger freighter, 'the Hog Islanders', as they were often known, just after World War I. King Albert of Belgium, who was visiting the United States at the time, accepted the invitation to christen her at the American International Shipbuilding Yards at Hog Island, Pennsylvania. Named *Cantigny*, the ship was commissioned as a commercial freighter. In 1924, she was sold to the United States Lines, renamed *American Banker* and rebuilt to carry sixty-five (and later eighty-five) first class passengers for the New York-London trade. After the outbreak of World War II, she was passed to the Belgian-flag Antwerp Navigation Company in order to have neutral sailing rights. Renamed *Ville d'Anvers*, she survived the war intact. Afterwards, starting in 1946, she

The little Arosa Kulm *was the Arosa Line's first passenger ship. Initially, she had a white hull, but this was later changed to black, matching the Company's other liners.*

went through a succession of owners and changes after a brief return to the United States Lines. She was first sold to the Luckenbach Line and placed under the Honduran flag, and then to the Sociedad Naviera Transatlantica of Panama, who used her as the *City of Athens* on the Piraeus-New York immigrant run. On the bankruptcy of her owners, she passed in 1947 to the Panamanian Lines to become the *Protea*, and finally to the Compania de Operaziones Maritima, also Panamanian, in 1949. She mainly ran immigrant or refugee sailings, often to Australia, but reappeared on the North Atlantic briefly in 1951, running on three charter voyages between Antwerp, Plymouth and Montreal for the Incres Line. Arosa bought her shortly afterwards. Despite her small size, the *Aroza Kulm* was an initial success. She underwent several refits, which included the creation of more and more cabins in tourist class to satisfy an increasing demand. By 1953, her accommodation had been changed to 30 in first class and 802 tourist. Staffed by German and Italian personnel she was advertised as offering such amenities as a beer garden, children's playroom, two dining rooms and a 350-seat lounge. There was even a small outdoor pool forward.

By 1957–58, with three other Arosa liners then in service, the aged, often creeping *Arosa Kulm* spent more time under charter first to the Canadian Government for the transport of troops to Germany, then for immigrant service to the Caribbean and even for an $88 eight-day cruise from New York to Bermuda (which was cancelled at the last minute). When the Arosa Line went bankrupt with debts of $8.5 million in December 1958, the *Arosa Kulm* was in England. She was seized by local authorities at Plymouth and later put up for auction. She went to Belgian scrappers for a scant $150,000, arriving at Bruges under tow on 7 May 1959, at the end of her thirty-nine-year career.

The AROSA STAR

In 1953, the Arosa Line paid a rather meagre $500,000 for the laid-up American cruise ship *Puerto Rico*. She, too, was to be refitted for the booming Atlantic tourist service. She was sent directly to Bremerhaven for a $1 million conversion and became the *Arosa Star*, the Company's second passenger ship.

Another small liner, she had been built in 1931 at the Bethlehem Steel shipyard at Quincy, Massachusetts, for the New York & Porto Rico Steamship Company as the *Borinquen*. She ran weekly cruises between New York and San Juan until December 1941, just as America officially entered the War. After military trooping, spent mostly on the North Atlantic, she was returned to the Agwilines, the parent company of the original owners. She went back to Caribbean service until 1949, when she was sold to

another American steamer firm, the Bull Line. They had her refitted with a mere two hundred first class berths for eleven-day cruises between New York, San Juan and Ciudad Trujillo (in the Dominican Republic.) She lasted another four years before becoming a victim of aircraft competition and rising American labour costs. Then, for nearly a year, she sat idle alongside the Brooklyn waterfront.

As the *Arosa Star*, she was lengthened with a new raked bow and greatly enlarged to carry 806 passengers – 38 in first class and 768 in tourist. Without dormitories, she carried her passengers in cabins for two, three, four or six. Beginning in May 1954, she was assigned to the Canadian run, sailing between Bremerhaven, Zeebrugge or the Hook of Holland, London or Southampton, and across to Quebec City. In winter, she went to Halifax.

The *Arosa Star* was later used for a rather full programme of cruises, which included numerous three and four day trips between Miami, Nassau and Havana. Her most unusual trip was in September 1958, when she sailed on an eight-day jaunt from New York as an accommodation and review ship for the America's Cup Races at Newport, Rhode Island. However, several months later, on 7 December, while on another cruise, the *Arosa Star* was 'arrested' for debt at Bermuda. The Arosa Line had just gone bankrupt. In the following May, the ship was auctioned-off for $510,000 to the McCormick Shipping Corporation of Panama (she would actually sail under the banner of the Eastern Steamship Lines of

Midnight sailings from Bremerhaven: the Arosa Star *in the foreground with the United States Lines'* America *berthed further along.*

Miami), who had her refitted for three and four day cruises from Miami to Nassau. She worked this trade very successfully until the autumn of 1968, when new US Coast Guard safety regulations barred her from further American service.

Sold to the Western Steamship Company (another Panamanian firm) and renamed *La Janelle*, she was expected to go to some Central American lake for use as a hotel ship, in fact to be cut in pieces and reassembled at some inland location. While their project never materialized, her owners proposed that she become a hotel-restaurant on the American West Coast. While awaiting conversion, she was blown ashore during a hurricane at Port Hueneme, California, on 13 April 1970. Wrecked and half-sunk, she had to be scrapped on the spot.

The AROSA SUN

By 1955, Arosa progress was such that the Company looked for a third passenger ship. Their first, although rather unlikely intention was to buy the 6000-ton *Acadia*, a former American coastal liner that had been laid up since the War. This idea never came to pass. Instead, the 20,100-ton *Felix Roussel* of France's Messageries Maritimes had just been replaced by new tonnage and was put up for sale. The Arosa Line quickly bought her.

Built in 1930, the *Felix Roussel* had originally belonged to a rather odd breed of ships that were unique to the French – 'the square stackers'. A motorship, she had two very squat square funnels. While distinctive, it was hardly a feature of great beauty, but certainly eccentric. The ship worked the colonial Indo-China trade out of Marseilles and via the Suez. Managed by Britain's Bibby Line while serving as a troop ship during the war, she was eventually

The Arosa Star *was enlarged from the American cruise ship* Puerto Rico. *She finished her 39-year career by being wrecked along the California coast.*

returned to the French and rebuilt, 1948–50, with a single oval funnel. She went back on the Indo-China route until the end of 1954, when she was refitted at Trieste to a transatlantic standard with 60 in first class and 862 in tourist. Her maiden voyage, under a new name, *Arosa Sun*, in July 1955, took her from Trieste to New York via Palermo, Naples and Lisbon, and then to Quebec City, before crossing to Le Havre, Southampton and Bremerhaven. Thereafter, there were three Arosa passenger ships (*Arosa Kulm*, *Arosa Star* and *Arosa Sun*) on the Canadian trade.

The *Arosa Sun* did a considerable amount of off-season cruising, mostly to the Caribbean. However, some appraisals were less than encouraging. One passenger returned from a cruise and classified the ship as 'totally unsafe'. Her dwindling public image was further reduced on 15 March 1958. While off Colombia during a cruise from Miami, with 217 passengers aboard, she was immobilized by an engine room explosion. Two crewmen died and the ship had to be towed to Cristobal for repairs. Shortly afterward, there were protests from the staff, primarily emphasizing the low safety standards and unpaid wages. For the following winter season (1958–59), Arosa chartered the ship to the Caribbean Cruise Lines for a varied series of tropical trips (from New York, Norfolk, Morehead City, Charleston, Savannah, Mobile and Galveston), which never happened. That December, while delayed at Bremerhaven, the *Arosa Sun* was arrested for debt, following the collapse of her owners. Claims against her amounted to $2.3 million. An attempt to auction the

Victor Scrivens Coallection

twenty-nine-year-old ship failed at first. She was later transferred to a group of Swiss bankers, who planned to resell her for $1 million to Japanese scrappers. There were further reports that she might be sold instead to the Grimaldi-Siosa Lines for their Caribbean immigrant service. She was, in fact, sold to the Dutch, but for non-sailing purposes. Her new owners, the Koninklijke Nederlansche Hoogovens, used her as a floating workers' hostel at IJmuiden. She remained in this role until March 1974, when she was towed to Bilbao, Spain for scrapping. She was the last survivor of the former Arosa Line fleet.

The AROSA SKY

The *Arosa Sky* was the last and the largest member of the Arosa Line fleet. Bought for $6.5 million in early 1957, she saw only rather brief service with the Swiss owners. Laid down in 1939, at La Ciotat, France, she soon fell into Nazi hands after the invasion of France. While the enemy wanted to complete her, the French Underground masterminded a 'go slow' and even sabotaged parts of the construction. However, under the Vichy Régime, she was launched 14 June 1944, as the *Maréchal Petain* and towed to Port de Bouc for completion. Shortly thereafter, she was scuttled by the retreating Nazis. Promptly refloated after the war, she was returned to her builder's yard and completed as the patriotically-named *La Marseillaise*. Commissioned in August 1949, she was the queen of the Indo-China colonial trade, being both the largest and fastest of her day. She was also the flagship of the Messageries Maritimes fleet. However, because of the subsequent political changes in the East, her French career lasted a mere eight years.

The Arosa Line spent $1 million on the ship (giving her 64 first class and 834 tourist berths), renamed her *Arosa Sky* and then recommissioned her in May 1957. She was, however, placed in a new Arosa trade, running to New

The Arosa Sky, *the Arosa Line's flagship and last passenger ship, also had a white hull for a time. She is shown sailing from Boston during a charter cruise run.*

York from Bremerhaven via Le Havre and Southampton or Plymouth. The 1957–58 period was the peak for the Company, with four passenger ships under its houseflag. During the winter months, the *Arosa Sky* cruised from New York to the Caribbean as well as on charter sailings. She was nearly destroyed during one of these voyages when, on 8 January 1958, just before she arrived at Wilmington, North Carolina, a fire broke out. Five first class cabins were destroyed.

The *Arosa Sky* was an unprofitable ship. She barely broke even on the North Atlantic and then needed considerable improvements for competitive American cruising. Generally, the immigrant business on which Arosa Line so relied had declined considerably. Overall, the Company began to lose money and were forced to sell their 18,400-ton flagship in the autumn of 1958, after only fifteen months of service. She went to Italy's Costa Line for just over $8 million. She was delivered in November, just a month before the Arosa Company's financial collapse.

Renamed *Bianca C*, the ship was lavishly refitted at Genoa for 'line voyages' between Italy, Venezuela and the Caribbean, and also cruising, which included further charter voyages from New York in the winter of 1959–60. Unfortunately, her new career was equally short-lived. Again, she suffered from an ill quite common to French-built ships – fire. She burned out on 22 October 1961, while off St George's, Grenada, in the Caribbean. The empty, charred hulk sank two days later. Two lives were lost. Soon afterward, the Costa Line erected a commemorative statue at the harbour entrance to St George's. It remains in place to this day.

Chapter Nine

THE LAST SHIPS OF STATE

HOLLAND-AMERICA LINE

The ROTTERDAM

The fifties were, in some ways, reminiscent of the thirties for ocean liners. The idea of new, large national flagships, the 'ships of state', had been reawakened. The French were thinking of the biggest of all, the 66,000-ton *France*, which finally emerged in 1962. But others had ideas as well. The Italians were creating the *Leonardo Da Vinci*, at 33,000 tons, Cunard was talking of a 75,000-tonner called the *Q3*, to replace the ageing *Queen Mary*, the Germans were adding the rebuilt 32,000-ton *Bremen*, and even the Spanish were making twin 20,000-tonners. Just as in the thirties, with the building of the 36,000-ton *Nieuw Amsterdam*, the Dutch were not to be left out. The long overdue running-mate to the 'Darling of the Dutch' was at last ordered. In fact, she would even come from the same shipyards, the Rotterdam Drydock Company.

The design of this new ship, named *Rotterdam* from the start, was, for the most part, kept a tight secret. In reality, she was to be revolutionary: the first transatlantic liner to do away with the traditional smokestack and instead use twin uptakes side by side, placed aft. Even the officers of the other Holland-America liners were not told of the radical design. In 1958, Captain Cornelius van Herk was serving aboard the *Statendam*. He remembered taking on a 'very secret, very mysterious' case at Rotterdam for shipment to New York. Strict orders from the home

Holland-America's Rotterdam, *the first transatlantic liner to dispense with the traditional funnel, arriving at New York for the first time, in September 1959.*

Crown Princess Beatrix of the Netherlands was aboard the Rotterdam *for her maiden crossing, but disembarked into a waiting Dutch warship in the outer reaches of New York Harbour for her final entry into the City.*

Herbert G Frank Jr Collection

amazed', as Captain van Herk remembered. 'There were no smokestacks!' The *Rotterdam* was, at 38,645 gross tons, nearly 2000 tons larger than the earlier *Nieuw Amsterdam*. Yet, at 748 feet long, she was ten feet shorter than the older ship. She had a capacity of 1456 passengers in first and tourist class, which was 223 more than the full capacity of the three-class *Nieuw Amsterdam*. The new liner was indeed a superb ship of state. In her thirteen passenger decks were over fifteen public rooms (which made extensive use of woods such as Bangkok Teak, Japanese Ashwood, Olive and French Walnut), indoor and outdoor swimming pools, and the largest theatre afloat, seating 607.

Like her mother before her, in the case of the *Nieuw Amsterdam* in 1937, Her Majesty Queen Juliana consented to launch the new flagship at Rotterdam on 13 September 1958. A year later, the liner crossed to New York, this time with Crown Princess Beatrix on board as a passenger, to commemorate the occasion and to begin a formal visit to America. During her maiden call, the *Rotterdam* had a week's stay in New York, which was divided between time at the Company's old terminal in Hoboken and then across the Hudson at their still incomplete Pier 40 in Manhattan (finally opened in March 1963). Between April and October, she sailed between New York, Southampton, Le Havre and Rotterdam in company with the *Nieuw Amsterdam* and *Statendam*. For at least a few more years, weekly Friday afternoon sailings from Manhattan were the pattern. The *Rotterdam* was also designed for luxury cruising during the winters, taking 730 first class passengers in a specially reduced capacity. In her first winter programme, she made two luxury voyages. In December 1959, she went completely around the South American continent for forty-nine days, with fares beginning at $1395. Upon her return on 1 February, she set sail for a visit to four continents – North and South America, Africa and Europe – on a seventy-five day run, with fares starting at $2400. A year later, in January 1961, she began what was to become her tradition: annual circumnavigations of the globe taking approximately eighty days. Loyal passengers came year after year, prompting Holland-America to revise the itineraries and add new ports of call. In January 1983 the *Rotterdam* began the Company's Silver Jubilee world cruise, the twenty-fifth such voyage in their corporate history. Many lavish events were planned, as was befitting to such a voyage, one was a contest among the passengers in which the first prize was a Rolls Royce! Fares for that cruise began at $15,600.

According to Captain van Herk, who was master of the *Rotterdam* for some years, she tended to be a 'tough sea boat. However, she once took a dive in an Atlantic storm that sounded like a cannon firing and lifted the mooring

office were that the case was not to be opened. It contained a model of the new flagship as she would actually look when completed. During the crossing, some officers could not resist the obvious temptation. In the poor light of a deep cargo hold, they saw the *Rotterdam* for the first time. 'We were quite shocked, completely

Herbert G Frank Jr Collection

The Sky Room was fitted in the uppermost passenger deck aboard the Rotterdam.

lines over the ship's breakwater.' The *Rotterdam* has also survived at least two close calls. In October 1973, while docked at the Lisnave shipyard in Lisbon for her annual overhaul, she came close to being seriously damaged, even lost completely. Captain van Herk was with her at the time. 'We were in the 1,000,000-ton dry dock, sharing it with a supertanker. The tanker had had a tremendous explosion and the shipyard crews were burning a huge section out of her side. A gantry crane was being used to lift off a 500-ton section from the ship. The weight was obviously too great as the operator felt the entire crane shiver. He moved the crane further along the dock. Minutes later, the dock wall began to crack and collapse. Immediately, the dry dock began to flood. Our pressing concern was for the *Rotterdam*. The manholes in her double bottom were open. If the flooding continued, she would flood as well and possibly even sink. Again, if more of the dry dock wall collapsed, there could be a tidal wave of flooding that could cause the *Rotterdam* to smash into the opposite dock wall. Either way, she was in a very dangerous position. I ordered an "Abandon Ship" for the very few crew members who were on board. The Portuguese, on the other hand, were excitedly moving in haste and removing the gangways to the *Rotterdam*. In the end, all was well. The flooding was stopped before any great danger occurred. In fact, we were even able to save

Herbert G Frank Jr Collection

An intimate bar-lounge: the Cafe de la Paix aboard the Rotterdam.

the buckets of fresh blue paint, which were to be used on the ship's hull for the first time, replacing the previous grey colouring. The earlier grey had become a problem since periodic partial maintenance painting always left the hull in different colour shades.'

When the *Rotterdam* completed this major overhaul at Lisbon, she had a series of tests in the Tagus River. At one point, she tested full astern (reverse) and did a rather swift

11 knots for about twenty minutes.

The second narrow escape came in January 1976, at the beginning of her annual world cruise. Captain van Herk was again in command. 'We arrived off Casablanca, our first port of call out of the United States, several hours ahead of schedule. We were proceeding at reduced speed with the stabilizers withdrawn. The pilot was due on board at 7.00am I came on the bridge at 6.00am, as I always liked to familiarize myself with a harbour and its overall layout. Because of swells, we were asked by the pilot station to proceed at 4 knots to a point just off the breakwater. When we were about a third of a mile off this breakwater, all of us on the bridge heard a strange, very loud noise. We looked to starboard and saw the most tremendous wave coming toward the ship. With our bridge more than 85 feet above the water, I estimated the wave at over 100 feet high. We couldn't see the horizon. When this huge wave finally hit the *Rotterdam*, we were swung a full 35 degrees. However, because she is so solidly built, and because of just plain good luck, we straightened. The returning waves merged with the outgoing ones and had the effect of rebalancing the ship. Of course, there was damage, but luckily most of our passengers were still in bed. However, several beds were pulled out completely from the bulkheads. The concert piano in the Ritz-Carlton Lounge was found totally upside-down. All of the deck chairs on the Promenade Deck had broken away and finished up in the swimming pool. Three hundred of these chairs were ruined, turned into little pieces of wood. In our offices, papers were everywhere. The settee in my own cabin was turned upside-down as well. Most fortunately, however, there were not many serious injuries among the passengers or crew. Mostly, there were broken limbs and bones and lots of bruises.

'After the hit of that giant wave, we swung the *Rotterdam* around completely. My engineers advised that, should a second wave strike, we might suffer even worse injuries and that there could be a breakdown of engines and a loss of power. We couldn't afford further problems. We decided to cancel our call at Casablanca, abandoning all of the prearranged tours, the provisions we needed and even the 500 tons of bunker fuels. We sailed direct to our next port of call: Villefranche on the French Riviera. In closer inspection during that passage, we found that the *Rotterdam* had not suffered any serious structural damage. She was still a safe, strong ship. Of course, we were kept busy for days afterward. Numerous replacement pieces were needed, such as the 300 new deck chairs that were flown to Piraeus [Greece] to meet the ship.' No formal explanation of the incident was ever expressed. Captain van Herk, by then a thirty-year veteran at sea, still refers to it as a 'freak wave'.

There have of course, been glories for the *Rotterdam*. In

April 1982, she was used for a gala evening cruise in New York Harbour to celebrate the Dutch-American Bicentennial, the 200th anniversary of uninterrupted relations between Holland and the United States. Over 600 guests were on board for the official banquet, most of whom were greeted by the guest-of-honour, Her Majesty Queen Beatrix. In the Queen's honour (she is from the Royal House of Orange), orange-coloured fireworks were displayed in the Upper Bay.

The *Rotterdam* is still a well-reputed, well-maintained cruise ship. Now, over twenty-five and still in excellent condition and handsomely decorated, she has become something of a 'grand hotel' among the more modern cruise ships. She is, of course following in the pattern of the beloved earlier *Niew Amsterdam*. Through the years and through the changes, the *Rotterdam* has upheld Holland-America's one-time slogan: 'It's good to be on a well-run ship!'

ITALIAN LINE

The LEONARDO DA VINCI

Some ocean liners are possessed of a unique charm. The *Leonardo Da Vinci* was one of them. It may have had something to do with external beauty, the extraordinary good looks that have made ships like the *America* and *Nieuw Amsterdam* remain so well loved. Early in 1960, a six-foot-

A rare occasion at Genoa: both the Cristoforo Colombo *(left) and* Leonardo Da Vinci *in dry dock together. The two ships normally maintained Italian Line's express liner service to New York.*

long model of the new *Leonardo* sat in the main concourse of New York's Grand Central Terminal, covered by glass, lit up, and in shining perfection. Crowds gathered, and there was general enthusiasm over the design for the first major Italian liner of the sixties. The love affair had begun.

The *Leonardo Da Vinci* emerged primarily as a replacement for the ill-fated *Andrea Doria*. The Italian Line's Mediterranean-New York business was booming and the sisters *Augustus* and *Giulio Cesare* had to be swung off the South American trade to fill the gap. One part of the Company's management sat through the tedious court hearings of the *Doria* disaster. Another handled the regular operations while a third worked toward the design of the new ship. The plans of the *Augustus* and *Giulio Cesare* of 1951–52 and then the *Andrea Doria* and *Cristoforo Colombo* of 1953–54 were reviewed. The basic design concept would be similar, but with vast improvements – such as the elimination of the aft cargo space so as to create more

A dramatic view of the Leonardo Da Vinci, *Italy's 'ship of state' in the early sixties.*

151

Michael D J Lennon

A Scrimali

The burnt out wreck of the Leonardo da Vinci *at La Spezia in 1981. She is shown after having been deliberately sunk in the outer harbour and awaits the scrappers.*

The Leonardo Da Vinci *was repainted in white in 1965, following a pattern set by the then brand new* Michelangelo *and* Raffaello.

Italian Line was rightfully proud of the new flagship, with the end result that the tragic image of the *Doria* was slowly erased. There were some blemishes, however. Captain Narciso Fossati, who became Commodore of the Italian Line fleet, remarked, 'The *Da Vinci* did have her problems, mostly with stability. We had to put 3000 tons of iron in her double bottoms. Therefore, being heavier, she had a very high fuel consumption rate. I always remember her as a quiet roller at sea.'

The 33,000-ton *Leonardo*'s popularity was high, first on the express run in partnership with the *Cristoforo Colombo*, and then after they were superseded by the *Michelangelo* and *Raffaello*, a pair at over 45,000 tons each, which appeared in the spring and summer of 1965. The *Da Vinci*'s route thereafter included additional Mediterranean ports of call, in Majorca, Sicily, North Africa and Portugal, and also periodic cruises to the Caribbean and South America (her most adventurous trip was a forty-one-day jaunt from New York in February 1970, that took her through the Caribbean and Panama Canal to Hawaii). Her sleek black hull took on a more tropical flavour in 1966, when she was painted white overall. Captain Fossati was also aboard with some special cargo. 'In 1964, for the World's Fair at New York, the Pietà from the Vatican was carried aboard the *Da Vinci*. We put the ship in dry dock so that she would not move at all. A big crane lowered the case aboard, which was filled with plastic foam. It was lowered on to a rubber base placed in the bottom of the first class pool. The crate was specially floatable in case of

outdoor areas for passengers (including the six swimming pools, one of which had infra-red heating), the installation of far more private plumbing in the passenger cabins (even as much as eighty per cent in tourist class), and a look into the future with her steam turbine machinery, which could be easily converted to nuclear power. In short, she was the finest liner that Italy could produce. Launched from the Ansaldo shipyard at Genoa, on 7 December 1958, she left the Mediterranean on 30 June 1960 for her first run to New York. She arrived to a morning welcome of spraying fireboats, tugs, and buzzing helicopters, followed by elegant pierside parties, and then held open house. The

A Scrimali

Slowly disappearing, the remains of the Leonardo da Vinci *as her final demise is well underway.*

sinking. It was secured only by easily releasable snap hooks.'

By the early seventies, however, cruising became more of the *Leonardo*'s mainstay, especially as the Italian Line's transatlantic passenger loads began to drop. Embarrassing news articles contained comments about the large number of crew members compared with passengers, the $30,000 she cost each day to run (1973), and the costly subsidy ratio of over $700 given by the Italian Government for every traveller carried. Together with her running mates, the *Da Vinci* had indeed fallen on hard times. She was selected to close out the Italian North Atlantic passenger service in June 1976, and then sat idle for a time awaiting further work. In July 1977, she was reactivated by the newly-formed Italian Line Cruises International for the Miami-Nassau overnight shuttle service. Her managers were other Italians, the Costa Line. Little was done to the accommodation except that the liner now carried about nine hundred one-class passengers against the original 1326 in three classes. However, the sparkle was gone. She proved far too big for such a service, was in need of some costly repairs and, as one official put it, 'the *Da Vinci* burned more fuel at the dock than most ships do at sea.'

On 23 September, the one time national flagship was laid up permanently at La Spezia, perilously close to the largest Italian shipbreakers. Of course, she was the subject of speculation. At various times, she was to become an Italian exhibition ship, a floating casino and resort on the Thames, and even a revived cruise ship for the Panamanian-flag Trident Maritime Corporation, who

talked of recreating the luxury liner atmosphere of the thirties, while charging a minimum of $200 per day on runs from New York and Port Everglades to Rio and other sunshine ports. It all failed to materialize. Then, twenty years after that glorious maiden sailing, on 4 July 1980, she suffered a fire, which started in the chapel and raged for four days. Thousands watched from the shoreline, especially as the sky filled with heavy clouds of black smoke after the fire reached the fuel tanks. In the end, she had to be towed outside La Spezia's main harbour and left half-submerged in forty feet of water with a sixty-degree list. The *Leonardo* was finished, although heavily surrounded in controversy, since she was insured for $7.7 million yet worth little more than $1 million in scrap value. Her charred remains were scrapped in 1982.

FRENCH LINE

The FRANCE

The *France*, the last of the specially designed transatlantic superships, with hardly any expectation of cruising, has left behind a legendary, sumptuous, but perhaps somewhat inflated impression. Designed in the mid-fifties for what seemed to be a healthy trade, she steamed regally into New York Harbour on a cloudy winter's afternoon in February 1962, to cheers, excitement, praises, and uncertaintyu. It did not seem likely that the French might hope to recover their $80 million investment, or that she would be profitable even when filled to the very last upper-berth. Although she was, indeed, often booked to capacioty, the *France* was a subsidized ship, unable to earn her way for most of her French Line days. Perhaps more than Britain's subsequent *Queen Elizabeth 2*, the *France* was the last true ship of state, the floating national showcase of art, design, technology and size. To the French Government, and in particular to President De Gaulle himself, her purpose was to display the tricolour. Profit was not essential to her being. As with superliners in the thirties, including the exquisite *Normandie*, the profits were measured more in terms of prestige and goodwill. In these, the giant, luxurious *France* succeeded beautifully.

As she sailed into New York on that maiden visit, her most notable distinction was her winged, smoke-deflector stacks. While the Dutch *Rotterdam* had used twin uptakes aft, and Italy's *Michelangelo* and *Rafaello* had birdcage-like funnels, the *France*'s twin stacks were eye catching. They were special creations, just for her, that systematically pushed the smoke and soot away from the ship and, therefore, off the passenger decks below.

Internally, the *France* seemed to be a series of modern and ultra-modern public rooms, all attached to one another in sequence. The first class quarters were dominated by a series of expensive suites, ranging from

French Line

The last of the purpose-designed Atlantic superliners, the French Line's France *of 1962, is shown arriving at New York's Pier 88 for the first time.*

bed-sitting rooms to more elaborate arrangements that included private verandahs, dining rooms, warming kitchens, trunk and dressing rooms, and adjoining servants' quarters. For the rich, famous and well-travelled, first class on the *France* was unsurpassable. These passengers also had one other superb amenity, the circular Chambord Restaurant, perhaps the most exquisite public room on a post-war liner, and noted by one epicure as 'the best French restaurant in the world'. As on almost all previous French liners, a large staircase descended into the room. Otherwise, while the accommodation was generally spacious and always impeccable, the decor (particularly in tourist class) tended to be either too flashy or too austere. One critic wrote, 'there are far too many winged-chairs on board, making the ship appear like some functional space craft.' Frank Braynard, who attended the maiden festivities, added, 'She had a fantastic exterior that was not equalled by the interior. She was immediately equated with the brilliant *Normandie*, but that earlier ship was vastly superior. In the case of the *France*, the legend exceeded the reality.'

The *France* sailed for about ten months of each year on the North Atlantic, between Le Havre, Southampton and

154

Hapag-Lloyd Shipyards

Twilight of the Gods, on a grey winter's afternoon, in February 1973. Italy's Michelangelo *would be retired within two years; Britain's* Queen Elizabeth 2 *(in centre position) would endure as the last of her type; and the French* France *(right) would see just two further seasons on the run to Le Havre.*

The France *being towed, on 22 August 1979, after a long lay-up at Le Havre to a thorough facelift at Bremerhaven and then new life as the world's largest cruise-ship, the* Norway.

French Line

New York. In her early years, she made only very rare appearances in the Caribbean, usually on rather expensive two or three week cruises. In later years, she went on a special run to Rio for Carnival and then, in the early seventies, made two widely publicized cruises around the world. Realistically, she was not the most appropriate liner for the tropics. Being basically a transatlantic indoor ship, she had glass surrounding her aft deck pool, and rather limited open-air spaces.

I crossed in the *France* in the summer of 1973, just as the French Government were beginning to question her ever-increasing subsidies. To a new generation of politicians, it seemed a far wiser choice to support the new supersonic Concorde instead. On my sailing, the courtesy of free wine and caviar had disappeared, there were five hundred unfilled berths, and a number of souls like myself, were travelling on a $150 student fare in tourist class. A year later, in September, the Government decided that the *France* was simply too costly. Her 1100 crew members reacted poorly. They held the ship in the English Channel and then demanded a 35 per cent wage increase. Their methods did little but create a further nuisance. Eventually docked at Le Havre, the ship was later moved to an unused, backwater berth.

Many felt that the *France* might actually be scrapped. There were reports that she might become a hotel ship on the French Riviera or in the Caribbean, that the Arabs wanted her as a pilgrim ship, the Chinese as a trade-fair ship, and the Soviets for general liner service. There was

The Tourist Class Restaurant was equally desolate and uninviting during the France's *lay-up.*

even a suggestion that tycoon Aristotle Onassis wanted her as a present for his wife, the former Jacqueline Kennedy. The ship was sold finally to an Arab, Akram Ojjeh, for $22 million. He had an equally unrealistic plan for the ship: converting her to a casino and centre of French culture moored off Daytona Beach, Florida.

It was the Norwegians who saw a bright future in the ship. They already monopolized the American cruise trades and predicted ever better days ahead. Christian Kloster, the managing director of Klosters Rederi A/S of Oslo, parent company of the Miami-based Norwegian-Caribbean Lines, was among those who were supporting this bold venture of reviving the world's longest liner as a tropic cruise ship. 'By the late seventies, we were steadily searching for new tonnage, preferably bigger ships. We looked at the *Michelangelo* and *Raffaello*, and even at the *United States* [all laid up at the time], but the most impressive by far was the *France*, then still moored at Le Havre. She was of absolutely impeccable quality. Everything about her – from the hull plating to the engines – was top quality. After all, she had been a personal project of De Gaulle himself and therefore cost was incidental. According to our marine inspection teams, she was built to last for fifty years.

'We bought the *France* for $18 million [in 1979] and, realizing that she must have a very special identity, decided almost immediately to rename her as *Norway*. I

The France *freshly arrived at Bremerhaven, to begin her transformation into the* Norway. *While her funnels are still in the original French Line colours, she is shown flying the Norwegian colours.*

The long promenade decks, once lined with deck chairs, were barren and silent.

recall some brief suggestions like *Queen of Norway* or *Ocean Queen*, but simple *Norway* was perfect.

'The French Line was very cooperative from the start. We hired several of their personnel, including the former staff captain, who knew the 1035-foot liner intimately. They stayed with her during the refit at the Hapag-Lloyd yard at Bremerhaven and then through her maiden voyage.'

The vastly different *Norway* recrossed the Atlantic in May 1980, from Oslo to Miami via Southampton and New York. Painted externally in blues and whites, she had acquired a new, festive quality. Within, she was now a pleasure carnival of theatres, two decks of shops, a huge casino, bars, discos, pools and even an ice cream parlour. According to Christian Kloster, 'At present [early 1983], we have spent about $130 million on the *Norway* project. Considering that a brand new liner of half her size costs upwards of $125 million, we are quite pleased. To us, the *Norway* is now a new ship, with at least twenty-five years of service ahead. Blended with her very high quality, we believe in a very high standard of maintenance and consistent improvement.' In the summer of 1984, the *Norway* returned to Bremerhaven for further repairs and overhaul. In doing so, she made a rather nostalgic Atlantic crossing, to Southampton, Amsterdam and Hamburg, which certainly rekindled something of the earlier transatlantic era.

The celebrated Chambord Restaurant, the France*'s exquisite first class restaurant, was partially stripped and the furnishings were overlaid with canvas coverings for her five years of idleness in the backwaters of Le Havre.*

157

Sal Scannella Collection

ITALIAN LINE

The MICHELANGELO and RAFFAELLO

If the *France* was perhaps a bit misplaced on a declining North Atlantic, the Italians were even less sensible when, as late as 1965, they commissioned not one but two 45,000-tonners for the New York trade. In their ten years of service, neither ever earned a profit. Captain Narciso Fossati, the commodore of the Italian Line passenger fleet, added, 'The *Michelangelo* and *Raffaello* were, of course, good ships but they were built out of sheer politics – to give work to both the shipyards and the crews that manned them. They were the "make work" ships.'

The *Michelangelo* arrived first, in May 1965, and was followed by the *Raffaello* in July. Certainly the biggest liners to ply the post-war Mediterranean run, they ran a balanced express schedule between Naples, Genoa, Cannes, Gibraltar and New York. Occasionally, these schedules were extended to include Casablanca, Tenerife, Lisbon, Barcelona, Palermo and Palma de Majorca. These longer sailings had special appeal as roundtrip cruises and were advertised as Mediterranean 'Go-rounds'.

The first class swimming pool and adjoining children's pool were forward of the Michelangelo's twin funnels. Four other pools were aft, two each for cabin and tourist class.

158

The last of the Italian liners, the Michelangelo *and her twin sister, the* Raffaello, *had unique funnels – lattice cages with sweeping deflector tops.*

A dramatic stern view of the Michelangelo, *showing the vast lido deck spaces and the double pools for both cabin and tourist class.*

Despite their 46,000 tons and 902 feet, both the Michelangelo *(shown in drydock at Genoa) and the* Raffaello *were rather low in height. A disappointment in design, both ships had very few outside cabins.*

Aside from their financial woes, they had some other problems. The *Raffaello* had a rather serious engine room fire on 31 October 1965, and then, in May 1970, collided with a tanker in Algeciras Bay. However, the most serious incident was the lashing of the *Michelangelo* by huge waves in a severe Atlantic storm in April 1966. Captain Fossati was aboard the *Cristoforo Colombo* at the time. 'We were sailing between Venice and Piraeus, when we received radio news that the *Michelangelo* had been hit in the North Atlantic by at least one giant wave. We had the chairman of the Italian Line on board with us. The aluminium had crumbled under the extreme pressure of the wave, but it was miraculous that the entire bridge did not collapse. At the time of the incident, most of the passengers in the forward section had been moved aft. One couple refused, however, and they were lost, completely swept into the sea. Afterward, during the repairs at the Ansaldo yard at Genoa, the support

159

Lashed by a giant Atlantic wave during a westbound crossing in April 1966, the delayed Michelangelo *approaches her New York berth. Note that the forward guard walls on the bow are either mangled or missing. In the distance, the* Queen of Bermuda *is at dock.*

structure on the *Michelangelo* [and later on the *Raffaello* as well] was changed to steel.'

In the early seventies, with less and less Atlantic passengers, the twin superliners were sent on more frequent cruises, often to the Caribbean. However, their range was limited to their size. Often, they had to anchor off shore because of unsuitable docking facilities. The overall operations were complicated further by frequent, often erratic, strikes and job actions by the Italian seamen. Delays and cancelled sailings became commonplace. The

The forward superstructure of the Michelangelo *was twisted, crushed and partially collapsed.*

ships often sailed into New York days off their intended schedules.

Captain Fossati was with the liners at the very end. 'The *Michelangelo* and *Raffaello* had become highly unprofitable in the end and desperately needed Government assistance. They were kept running to the very last possible moment, however. I was aboard for the *Michelangelo*'s final transatlantic crossing from New York to Genoa in June 1975. It was, of course, a sad ending. I remember that the Duchess of Windsor was on board – an old, very frail lady, who rarely left her cabin throughout the voyage. It was her last trip to America and she left the ship at Cannes. Both the *Michelangelo* and *Raffaello* [withdrawn in April 1975] were kept at Genoa for a few months, for the convenience of possible buyers. Then, in September, I took them to La Spezia, where they were moored side by side, with double anchors out for protection. They sat at Port Venere, in the Gulf of La Spezia, very near to the big Italian scrapyards. They were, by then, completely stripped. All of the furniture and artwork had been removed and sent to warehouses [and later still, sold-off]. Nets were placed over the six outdoor pools. Only the instruments on the bridge remained. A maintenance crew of fifty looked after them and often showed prospective buyers around [the Soviets, Greeks and Norwegians being among them]. Two years later, in 1977, when they were sold to Iran, they were delivered by way of the Suez Canal by Italian crews of about fifty men each. Now [1983], as I understand it, they can never be used again. They are in very, very poor condition.'

Both intended as military accommodation ships, the *Michelangelo* was docked at Bandar Abbas and the *Raffaello* went to Bushire. Unfortunately, the *Raffaello* was bombed and partially sunk in February 1983, during an Iraqi bombing raid. The end of these two Italian liners is one of the saddest.

CHAPTER TEN

THE EMPTY NORTH ATLANTIC

POLISH OCEAN LINES

The STEFAN BATORY

In January 1980, when American actress Maureen Stapleton, who has a dread of flying, wanted to cross to London for a film commitment, she had to sail in a Polish freighter. The route was from Baltimore to Rotterdam (and then by ferry to England). In deepest winter, it has long since become the only way to cross the Atlantic by sea. By the late seventies, only two passenger ships remained in transatlantic service: Cunard's *Queen Elizabeth 2* out of New York and Poland's *Stefan Batory* from Montreal. Even at that, their services were limited, from April to late November at best. Otherwise, the Atlantic sea lanes are bare. Other, earlier services to areas such as the Mediterranean and Scandinavia are practically non-existent. Even passenger-carrying freighters are very few. When, after three months, Miss Stapleton returned to the United States, it was aboard a Soviet containership.

In the sixties, there was a recurrent story that the Poles were actually going to build a 20,000-tonner, to be called *Polonia*, that would replace the ageing, but extremely popular *Batory* of 1936. Somehow, such a brand new ship never came about. Instead, in the autumn of 1968, the state-owned Polish Ocean Lines bought the rather small and rather slow *Maasdam* from the Holland-America Line. To most observers, it was a rather surprising move. Sent to a Gdynia shipyard and renamed the *Stefan Batory*, the ship was given a refit that resulted in little more than a refined, modernized external look and some rearrangement and redecoration in the public rooms. The original, almost entirely tourist class atmosphere remained. Most of the cabins still lacked private toilet facilities. The general tone is almost as it was in 1952, when the ship first crossed as the economical *Maasdam*. However, she is impeccably maintained. The brass is always polished, the veneers always shine and the accommodation smells clean and fresh. To at least one Canadian passenger, who has sailed in the ship eleven times, the preference is clear: 'I always sail in the *Stefan Batory* because she is always immaculate. There's hardly a cleaner ship afloat.'

Frank Braynard has also been a frequent passenger.

'The *Stefan Batory* is the proudest ship on the Atlantic – from the giant lifering [a decorative piece] placed on the uppermost deck, to the last assistant in the dining room. The entire ship is class and style. She's a final reflection of an earlier era: a small, cosy, totally comfortable and charming Atlantic liner. She is, indeed, the last of an era. Even the lack of private facilities in the cabins has its charm. A steward will knock at your stateroom door to announce a hot bath. He will be carrying a large, fresh towel.'

The *Stefan Batory*, which began her Polish transatlantic service in the spring of 1969, has continued her service without interruption. Apart from the big, *QE2*, which is like a cruise ship, she is the last of her breed on the North Atlantic, certainly the last on the Canadian trade. She sails from April to October, between Gdynia, Rotterdam, London and Montreal. Occasionally, in midsummer, there are short cruises from Montreal along the St Lawrence and out to Newfoundland. For the remainder of the year, she cruises mostly from London, to the Canaries, the Mediterranean and the Black Sea, and even across to the Caribbean. These voyages are very popular and considered quite inexpensive. Minimum fares for a fifty-day midwinter Mediterranean trip in 1982 began at a mere $1,600.

In September 1981, I crossed aboard this ship, travelling from London to Montreal in nine days. The fare was $750, for an outside double, which I shared with a rather elderly Hungarian. During the crossing, I spent time with Captain Boleslaw Rakowski. We met in his dayroom, which adjoined the bridge. The Captain took great pride in pointing out a mural of the original *Batory* (1936–71), which hung above the sofa, as well as a painting from that earlier ship, and a stainless steel Art Deco floor lamp. A wooden model of the *Maasdam* rested on the desk.

The Captain, who joined the original *Batory* in 1948, spoke proudly of his current staff. 'Some fifty per cent of our 321 crew members had service in the earlier *Batory*.' He said that the tradition of excellent service, friendliness, cleanliness, is the Company's hallmark. It was certainly in evidence on his vessel. He felt that the success of the Polish Ocean Lines, if only with one passenger ship, is due to its

Luis Miguel Correia

The Stefan Batory, *the former Holland-America* Maasdam, *is the last liner to run transatlantic sailings into the St Lawrence.*

The Captain's Table during a westbound crossing in September 1981. Captain Boleslaw Rakowski is seated in the centre position and the author is to his immediate right.

high reputation in both Europe and England. I asked why the firm survives in transatlantic service when larger companies like Canadian Pacific, Cunard and even Holland-America have long ago abandoned the St Lawrence trade. He answered quickly: 'We have a strong ethnic clientele — Poles from both ends. Some are emigrating to Canada, while others are returning to the homeland for a visit and wanting lots of baggage space [furniture and other large items are often brought as gifts]. In addition, we are well known in Britain, both from the time of the old *Batory*, as a liner and a wartime troopship, and also as excellent travel value.'

We spoke too, of the future. He told me, 'The *Stefan Batory* will complete her last four-year survey in 1982. We will then retire her in 1986. By then, she will be ready – how do you say? – for razor blades. We are planning a new passenger vessel of about 18–19,000 tons, probably for service to New York rather than Montreal. She'll carry about 800 passengers. We are very interested in the American market, realizing the big Polish population in that country. However, we must be patient at this time. [Shortly after this conversation, all rumours regarding a possible new Polish liner ceased. However, at the time of writing, there has been some talk of acquiring another second-hand liner, namely the cruise ship *Mardi Gras*, Canadian Pacific's former *Empress of Canada*]. The *Stefan Batory* does not meet all US Coast Guard standards and therefore cannot enter American ports [this was basically a reflection of the then recently improved sanitary regulations]. We are now "shopping" for a shipyard to build such a new ship. If we build in Poland, which I personally think is unlikely because of our inexperience with similar types of vessel, she will be called *Polonia*. If we build outside, say in Finland or West Germany, she will be called *Batory*, a traditional, well-known name. We can trade on our heritage.'

There were 741 passengers aboard that late summer crossing (32 less than capacity): 572 were Polish followed by 64 with British passports, 32 Canadian, 24 American, 21 German, 12 Dutch, 6 Swiss, 2 each from Yugoslavia, Belgium and France, and individuals from Denmark, Israel, Australia and Ireland. Some 462 passengers had boarded at Gdynia, 140 at Rotterdam and 139 at London. About 188 passengers, mostly Poles, were making the round trip with a three-day stop in Montreal before sailing eastbound. In addition, there were 9 dogs in the kennels, located on the upper deck just aft of the funnel, and a mixture of 57 cars, campers and motorbikes in the twin cargo holds.

Daily life aboard the *Stefan Batory* is also in the tradition of the earlier Atlantic liners, leisurely, uninterrupted, and with little in the way of planned entertainment. A notation from my diary, for a Sunday evening, recorded, 'An evening recital of classical music, staged in the Grand Lounge, is the absolute highlight of the day. Remarkable differences in the mixture of people that attend: a rotund Dutch woman with a walking stick and ermine cape; Poles huddled together in endless conversation and smoking cigarettes with the strongest (and strangest) smells; English women – from Blackpool landladies in rhinestones to country types in tweed skirts and no-nonsense shoes; American and German students, made slightly more conspicuous by jeans and loose-fitting sweaters; some Canadian couples sitting half-asleep; and great clusters of Polish ladies – some in shiny synthetic dresses, others with the heavy, almost blackened features of latter-day Helena Rubinstein.'

Another special memory was an invitation to join the Captain for drinks and dinner. 'The request was for drinks at 5.45 in that little bar on Boat Deck. Every officer seemed to be present, all looking impeccable in their short tuxedoes. The Captain was truly the host: the first in greetings, taking drink orders, passing the peanuts. The mood was happy, the Master being the beam of conversation. The other invitees included a middle-aged Polish engineer and his wife, who is a living testament to famed Polish complexions. They were returning home, German shepherd included, to Victoria, British Columbia. The other guest was a seventy-five-year-old Polish Wartime Resistance leader. He was a small, fat-faced man, given to mad bursts of chuckling, who grew more jovial and offered more toasts with each successive vodka. He was wearing, across his left breast, a stretch of seventeen medals, all honours from the homeland for her heroic exploits between 1939 and 1944. He proudly added that there were six more at home, given by America and Canada, but not space to wear them. Now, well retired, he makes an annual pilgrimage to Poland, always aboard the *Stefan Batory*.

'A ship run in the old style, the *Stefan Batory* has its rituals. For example, the Captain always dines at first sitting. Precisely at 6.10, ten minutes after the dinner has begun in the restaurant below, the Chief Steward arrives. He motions, rather discreetly, to the Captain. The Captain and the other officers then rise, gently bringing to a close the cocktail session. We were escorted to the elevator, along the short central corridor. A stewardess sensed her poor timing, clutched her feather duster and armful of fresh linen, and literally bowed into disappearance. The elevator was waiting, its operator poised in rigid form. The Captain smiled and gently placed the four guests into the tiny elevator for the drop downward to the restaurant, located three decks below. He and his officers used the stairwell and, like magic, they were there to greet the elevator at the other end. Not a huff or a puff or sign of rapid pace. The Chief Steward then arranged the order of march into the restaurant, much like some wedding or graduation procession. "Remember, you are to the Captain's left", he said to me. Two waiters swung open the portside dining room doors. The band struck up the National Anthem. The passengers began to applaud. We marched to the Captain's Table. It was a gala night. All those present were in their best. A few passengers stood, pointed their cameras in our direction – click, flash – then sat and continued to applaud. The entire meal was prescribed. The drinks flowed, the beef was done to perfection and, just before dessert, a great ice-carving was delivered by two waiters and placed in the center of the table.'

At the time of writing, the *Stefan Batory* has a slightly reduced number of Atlantic crossings. It is considered rather likely that she will be replaced after 1986. It will be quite an achievement if her successor is as charming and as well-run.

CUNARD LINE

The QUEEN ELIZABETH 2

The *Queen Elizabeth 2* is a legendary ship. She is very often called the last of the transatlantic superliners. She is also the last of the big Cunarders, but, perhaps more importantly, the last liner to run a regular North Atlantic service out of New York (mostly between April and December). While she was still under construction, *Holiday* magazine called her the first ship that would seriously rival the reputation of the exquisite French

Normandie of 1935. This was something of an exaggeration. Instead, the QE2 as she is best known, is a handsome, well-appointed ship, but in fact more of a transatlantic cruise ship. Unlike her predecessors listed here, she is rather luxuriously one-class (technically, there are two general grades of accommodation, first and transatlantic class, but all with run-of-the-ship privileges) and has two outdoor pools, a casino, a health spa and a rather extraordinary daily schedule of entertainments and diversions (from guest lecturers on wine tasting to classes in aerobic dancing, seminars on stock investing, or Las Vegas-style cabarets). The *Queen's* transatlantic service is supported by those who are loyal to, or curious about, a supposedly grander, more leisurely era. In fact, the *Elizabeth 2* is far more comfortable than any of her Atlantic predecessors. Her clientele is divided among those who can recall (and sometimes yearn for) the earlier liners and those who want at least one last chance to ride in an Atlantic supership, 'a luxurious dinosaur', as someone called her.

Initially, in the early sixties, Cunard had a superliner project called the Q3, a very traditionally styled three-class ship of some 75,000 tons that was to replace the

veteran *Queen Mary*. However, that plan was far too late in the face of the jet invasion and the project was scrapped. The revised idea was for a two-class ship that could divide her economic life between six months or so on the Atlantic and the remainder in world-wide cruising. Of course, much as with the earlier *Queens*, considerable experimentation and enquiry were employed in planning for this new ship. Tests were run in the old *Queens*, notes

The last of the superliners, the Queen Elizabeth 2, *as seen in 1968, while still fitting-out at Clydebank.*

J K Byass

were taken on board other giant liners, such as the *France*, double-deck lounges were tested in Cunard's *Carmania* and *Franconia*, and there was even some examination of less obvious ships such as Norway's *Bergensfjord* and the Dutch *Rotterdam*. The new Cunarder was to be a blend of the very best of the past with some fresh, innovative and creative ideas. Along with her four pools (two are indoors), her enormous range of public rooms and even a twenty-four-hour grill room (since removed), every passenger cabin would have private facilities (so unlike almost all of the earlier Cunarders). Even the exterior would be different. The Company colours of orange-red and black stripes were not going to be used on the singular funnel-device (they were, in fact, added in the summer of 1982, much to the joy of many observers). Furthermore, unlike the earlier *Queen Mary* and *Queen Elizabeth*, as they were originally planned, she would sail alone and independently. No sister ship or running mate was ever planned.

The *QE2* was ordered, quite sensibly, from the John Brown yard at Clydebank that had built the two previous *Queens*. The order was placed in 1964 and the first keel plates laid a year later, on 5 June. As she began to develop, great secrecy surrounded the choice of a name for this latest Cunard giant. Reports hinted that she might be called *Winston Churchill*, *Britannia*, *William Shakespeare* or even *Queen Mary II*. Just as with the *Queen Mary*, her name was first revealed at the launching. Her Majesty Queen Elizabeth II happily sent the ship down the ways, on 20 September 1967 (and two days before the *Queen Mary's* final sailing from New York), as the *Queen Elizabeth 2*. The ship is, in fact, named for her predecessor, the original *Elizabeth* of 1940, and not the Queen herself.

As part of her legendary status, the new *Queen* has almost always been surrounded with controversy, headlines and frequent embarrassment. When she left the Clyde for the first time, on 26 November 1968, very serious (and threatening) turbine problems and other defects were noted on the trial runs. Most obviously, Cunard could not accept the ship without further repair and modification. Captain Robin Woodall joined the liner just in time for her first trials. 'We had a run to the Canaries with 1300 Cunard personnel and their families on-board. It was a test trip. We would have everyone ask for boiled eggs at the same time just to see what happened.'

When the *Queen* docked at Southampton for the first time, on 2 January 1969, the Cunard Company refused her. She was quite simply faulty and certainly not up to contractual specifications. A rather elaborate, well publicized maiden voyage to New York via the Caribbean had to be cancelled. She went to the shipyard for well over two months. In March, there was a new set

During her first season on the North Atlantic, the QE2 called at Le Havre instead of Cherbourg. In this view, dated September 30th 1969, the Swedish-American Gripsholm is docked just in front of the big Cunarder and the French Line freighter Magellan is to the right of the Queen's stern.

of trials, in which she averaged an impressive 32.6 knots on the speed runs. Then, with the final alterations and repairs made, Cunard accepted their $80 million ship on 18 April. The delays had cost over $10 million.

Seven months after the original *Elizabeth* left New York for the last time, the *QE2* steamed into port, in May 1969, for a rousing reception. She was given the last of the busy, noisy, triumphant maiden receptions in New York Harbour. Of course, with the first wave of passengers and visitors alike, the newest Cunarder was appraised. Some thought her to be a superb example of contemporary ocean liner design and decoration; others were deeply disappointed that she hardly resembled that earlier generation of wood-panelled passenger ships at all. Much like the *Queen Mary* and others during the thirties, the *Elizabeth 2* was something of a groundbreaker, certainly a ship that had to be suited to the competitive and pressing demands of the decade ahead.

The *Queen* settled into a balanced life: sailing between Southampton, Cherbourg and New York, and then on cruises in the off-season. Rumours and the occasional press report suggest that, even in those early years, she was, in fact, a huge white elephant. In reality, her earliest years were not impressive, at least for the accountants. At best, she served as a lingering example of a ship of state, a prestige liner that represented not just a company, but a nation. However, in more recent years, the *QE2* has been

called profitable. Her transatlantic voyages are, in fact, the more successful of her divided operations. Her 1983 season was said to be her best ever. In high summer, she is often booked to capacity. In addition to the loyalist travellers, Cunard has developed a rather extensive series of package plans, from tours of Britain to homeward passages. Most recently, a twelve-day package tour that included a crossing on the *Queen*, a trip in the other direction on Concorde and a stay at a good New York City hotel might cost less than $1,500.

In general, cruises have not been as successful for the *Queen*. Quite simply, the competition in North America is especially strong. Her journeys are diverse, however. There are three-day voyages to 'nowhere', costing some $400, to two weeks in the Caribbean or along the Norwegian fjords, or a three-month cruise around the world, usually beginning in January. One of the *Queen's* more dubious distinctions is to offer the most expensive ocean liner accommodations of all time. The rate for four passengers in the ultra-sumptuous Queen Mary or Queen Elizabet Suite on her 1985 world cruise was advertised at almost $310,000.

The *Queen* also runs the occasional special or charter voyage. Captain Woodall was aboard for the 'YPO Cruise', a charter from the Young Presidents Organization of America. 'The group consisted of top management, all of whom reached their positions before the age of forty-five. To them, expense was no object. We sailed out of Southampton to the Mediterranean with 1200

The Queen Mary Suite and its twin, the Queen Elizabeth Suite, rank as the most expensive accommodation ever offered aboard a liner.

Port of Le Havre Authority

Cunard Line

on board, including the Duke of Bedford. There seemed to be an endless array of fantastic entertainment. A special rendezvous was arranged (and specially paid for) with the American aircraft carrier USS *John F. Kennedy*. The carrier was moored a quarter of a mile off the *QE2* as twenty-six jet fighters gave a thrilling air show. We also had the Royal Marine Band on board, as well as a daredevil motorcycle team.'

The planning for the *Queen*'s travels is quite special, especially for the longer sailings. In September 1973, Captain Woodall was given 'a thick folder of airline tickets, a fistful of dollars and a case of charts.' He travelled for 52 days, to 28 cities, covered 38,700 air miles and spent 92½ hours in aircraft seats. His mission to prepare for the *QE2*'s first world cruise, which was scheduled to sail in January 1975. 'I visited the projected ports of call and outlined the *Queen*'s requirements, which included such items as the disposal of 10 tons of garbage a day, a daily need of 1000 tons of fresh water and the overall general reception of 1400 passengers [her cruise capacity] and 1000 crew. We even had to take a close look at the Panama Canal. There were 18 inches clearance in the locks, between the 963-foot long ship and the pontoons. The Canal is 110 feet across; the *QE2* is 105 feet in width. Most fortunately, the ship has exceptional steering ability.'

The *QE2* has certainly made her share of headlines. In January 1971, while on a Caribbean cruise, she rescued survivors from the burning French liner *Antilles*, while off the island of Mustique. A year later, she endured one of the North Atlantic's worst recorded storms. Her passengers were given special certificates to mark the event.

STORM CERTIFICATE

This is to record that on her North Atlantic voyage, leaving New York on 16 April 1972, for Southampton, England, RMS *Queen Elizabeth 2*, of 65,863 gross tons, encountered exceptionally severe weather in position Latitude 42°18' North, Longitude 55°52' West.

During this storm, winds reached speeds in excess of 100 mph. Combined with heavy swells, waves were encountered at 50 feet in height.

This weather caused even the *Queen Elizabeth 2*, with exceptional size and sea-keeping qualities, to lie hove to for 21½ hours between 17 and 19 April 1972, until the storm abated.

I commend all passengers in sharing this unique experience with great cheerfulness and calm.

Mortimer Hehir
Captain

Unfortunately, even worse press attention was ahead.

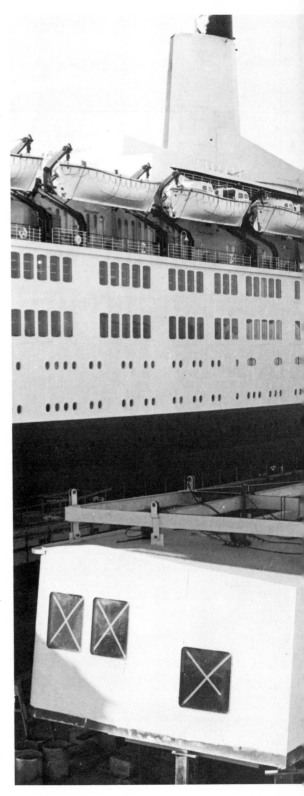

On 1 April 1974, while some 280 miles south-west of Bermuda, the *Queen* was immobilized with boiler troubles. Powerless and adrift, the 1654 passengers were transferred at sea two days later to the Norwegian cruiseship *Sea Venture*. On 7 April, the *QE2* was towed to Bermuda for initial repairs. Again, a special certificate was presented to her passengers:

CERTIFICATE OF AN UNUSUAL EVENT ON THE HIGH SEAS

The *Queen Elizabeth 2* left New York at 2100 hours running into heavy weather and the misfortune of engine trouble, leaving the ship without power. The officers and crew of the *Queen Elizabeth 2* worked tirelessly for many hours, until the final decision had to be made to transfer her passengers.

The MS *Sea Venture* was made aware of the situation at 1100 hours while at Hamilton, Bermuda, on 2 April 1974, receiving a request asking for assistance from Captain Peter Jackson, Master of the *Queen Elizabeth 2*. This was immediately taken up by Captain Torbjorn Hauge, master of the MS *Sea Venture*, with permission of Flagship Cruises Inc. and Cunard Line.

Before departing at 1348 hours, from Bermuda, passengers were given the option of staying in hotels in Bermuda or remaining aboard. 202 hardy souls left with the officers and crew of the MS *Sea Venture* to assist in these difficulties.

The MS *Sea Venture* hove to at 0330 hours position North 29 Degrees 43 Mins West 67 Degrees 32 Mins and immediately started to prepare for the transfer of 1654 passengers from the *Queen Elizabeth 2* to the MS *Sea Venture*. The final operation concluded at 1745 hours.

We are very proud of our 202 passengers who joined us in this most important operation, and we appreciate the cooperation of passengers of the *Queen Elizabeth 2*, making things run as smoothly as they did. The crews of the MS *Sea Venture* and the *Queen Elizabeth 2* came forward in our hour of need.

This certificate states that the passengers of the *Queen Elizabeth 2* were in good health and after the transfer to the MS *Sea Venture*, settled down for the overnight voyage to Bermuda.

From time immemorial, tradition of the seamen of all nations has not changed, holding a bond only common to those who go down to the sea in ships.

Torbjorn Hauge
Master
MS *Sea Venture*

The prefabricated upper-level of the QE2's Queen Mary Penthouse is about to be lifted aboard the liner during her refit at Bayonne, New Jersey, in December 1978.

Cunard Line

In December 1975, during her annual Christmas Caribbean cruise, the *Queen* was damaged on a coral reef at Nassau. The damage was sufficient to warrant a special direct sailing to the Newport News yard in Virginia, from where her disappointed passengers were sent home. On 23 July 1976, after an engine room fire, her westbound passage had to be cancelled and the ship was forced to return to Southampton. She was lashed by another huge North Atlantic storm in September 1978, and there was yet another mechanical breakdown in the Channel in September 1982.

The *Queen's* most dangerous duty, however, was perhaps the call from the British Government for the Falklands War in May 1982. Like most contemporary passenger ship owners, Cunard could not have guessed that the *QE2* would be used as a troop ship. At a rate of some $225,000 per day, the liner was chartered to the British Government to transport 3000 troops from Southampton to the troubled Falklands via Ascension. Enormous interest and press coverage surrounded the *Queen*. There were reports that the Argentinians would make a special effort to sink her. Certainly, she would be a prime target in the age of sophisticated, aerial warfare. However, her role was nothing less than heroic. She returned to Southampton to a grand welcome, in mid-June. Reconditioned and refitted, she resumed her Atlantic schedule in early August.

As she completed her post-Falklands dry docking, even the *Queen's* exterior had been changed. Her black hull was redone in a milky grey and the funnel was given the orange-red stripes of the earlier Cunard liners. The new stack colouring was well received, but the change to the hull was disappointing. Mostly, the earlier coats of black bled through the pale grey. Within a year, by the summer of 1983, the *QE2* again had a black hull.

In 1984, the *Queen Elizabeth 2* turned fifteen, which has been technically mid-life for a liner. Cunard was investigating the possibilities of converting her to a diesel-powered ship, which may well extend her lifespan to as much as forty years, but which might cost as much as $50 million. The estimated cost for a brand new liner, say in the 45,000-ton range, would be about $150 million. Cunard has estimated that the replacement value of the *Queen* with a duplicate ship of the same size and capacity would be as much as $350 million. Most likely, there will never again be a superliner on the Atlantic run.

The big era of the transatlantic liner is, of course, well past. The *QE2* and the little *Stefan Batory* are the last of a long and distinguished family of ships, from the earlier Cunarders and others such as the *Île de France*, *United States*, *Bremen* and *Rotterdam*, to the smaller, less well remembered ships such as the *Media*, *Prinses Margriet* and *Groote Beer*. Cruising has, of course, created an entirely new

Cunard Line

Just after her special service to the Falklands in 1982, the Queen Elizabeth 2 *was repainted in a light grey hull and, for the first time in her career, was given the traditional Cunard funnel colours of orange-red and black. The grey hull colouring has, in fact, been changed back to black. In this dramatic final view, the last of the Atlantic superliners is outbound in Lower New York Bay, bound for a nostalgic five-day crossing to Cherbourg and Southampton.*

generation of passenger ships, often more luxurious and more comfortable than their Atlantic predecessors. But, these last Atlantic liners are an immortal group, lingering memories of a luxuriant age and its ending.

Hail and Farewell to THE LAST ATLANTIC LINERS!

SPECIFICATIONS OF THE LAST
ATLANTIC LINERS

Alexandr Pushkin (Soviet Union)
Built by Mathias-Thesen Werft Shipyard, Wismar, East Germany, 1965. 19,860 gross tons; 577 feet long; 77 feet wide. Sulzer diesels, twin screw. Service speed 20 knots. 666 passengers (86 first class, 580 tourist class).

America (United States Line). ex-*USS West Point*, later *Australis, America, Italis* and *Noga*.
Built by Newport News Shipbuilding & Drydock Company, Newport News, Virginia, 1940. 33,532 gross tons; 723 feet long; 93 feet wide. Steam turbines, twin screw. Service speed 22 knots. 1046 passengers (516 first class, 530 tourist class).

Andrea Doria (Italian Line)
Built by Ansaldo SpA, Genoa, Italy, 1953. 29,083 gross tons; 700 feet long; 90 feet wide. Steam turbines, twin screw. Service speed 23 knots. 1241 passengers (218 first class, 320 cabin class, 703 tourist class).

Aquitania (Cunard)
Built by John Brown & Company Limited, Clydebank, Scotland, 1914. 45,647 gross tons; 901 feet long; 97 feet wide. Steam triple-expansion turbines, quadruple screw. Service speed 23½ knots. Approximately 2200 post-war austerity berths.

Argentina (Home Line), ex-*Bergensfjord*, later *Jerusalem*
Built by Cammell Laird & Company Limited, Birkenhead, England, 1913. 11,015 gross tons; 530 feet long; 61 feet wide. Steam turbines, twin screw. Service speed 15 knots. 1001 passengers (32 first class, 969 tourist class).

Arkadia (Greek Line), ex-*New Australia*, ex-*Monarch of Bermuda*
Built by Vickers-Armstrong Shipbuilders Limited, Newcastle, England, 1931. 20,259 gross tons; 590 feet long; 84 feet wide. Steam turbo-electric, quadruple screw. Service speed 19 knots. 1300 passengers (150 first class, 1150 tourist class).

Arosa Kulm (Arosa Line), ex-*Protea*, ex-*City of Athens*, ex-*Ville d'Anvers*, ex-*American Banker*, ex-*Cantigny*
Built by American International Shipbuilding Corporation, Hog Island, Pennsylvania, 1920. 8929 gross tons; 448 feet long; 58 feet wide. Steam turbines, single screw. Service speed 14½ knots. 965 passengers (46 first class, 919 tourist class).

Arosa Sky (Arosa Line), ex-*La Marseillaise*, ex-*Maréchal Petain*, later *Bianca C*

Built by Societé Provençale de Constructions Navales, La Ciotat, France, 1939-49. 17,408 gross tons; 594 feet long; 75 feet wide. Sulzer diesels, triple screw. Service speed 21 knots. 898 passengers (64 first class, 834 tourist class).

Arosa Star (Arosa Line), ex-*Puerto Rico*, ex-*Borinquen*, later *La Janelle*
Built by Bethlehem Steel Company, Quincy, Massachusetts, 1931. 9070 gross tons; 466 feet long; 60 feet wide. Steam turbines, single screw. Service speed 15 knots. 806 passengers (38 first class, 768 tourist class).

Arosa Sun (Arosa Line), ex-*Felix Roussel*
Built by Ateliers et Chantiers de la Loire, St Nazaire, France, 1930. 20,126 gross tons; 598 feet long; 68 feet wide. Sulzer diesels, twin screw. Service speed 16½ knots. 1049 passengers (100 first class, 949 tourist class).

Ascania (Cunard)
Built by Armstrong-Whitworth Company Limited, Newcastle-upon-Tyne, England, 1925. 14,440 gross tons; 538 feet long; 65 feet wide. Steam turbines, twin screw. Service speed 15 knots. 696 passengers (198 first class, 498 tourist class).

Atlantic (American Export Line), ex-*Badger Mariner*, later *Universe Campus*, then *Universe*
Built by Sun Shipbuilding & Drydock Company, Chester, Pennsylvania, 1953. 14,138 gross tons; 564 feet long; 76 feet wide. Steam turbines, single screw. Service speed 20 knots. 880 passengers (40 first class, 840 tourist class).

Atlantic (Home Line), ex-*Matsonia*, ex-*Malolo*, later *Queen Frederica* (National Hellenic Line, then Chandris Group)
Built by William Cramp & Sons Ship & Engine Building Company, Philadelphia, Pennyslavia, 1927. 20,553 gross tons; 582 feet long; 83 feet wide. Steam turbines, twin screw. Service speed 21 knots. 1178 passengers (349 first class, 203 cabin class, 626 tourist class); 1179 passengers (132 first class, 116 cabin class, 931 tourist class, and later 174 first class, 1005 tourist class) as *Queen Frederica*.

Augustus (Italian Line), later *Great Sea*, then *Ocean King*
Built by Cantieri Riuniti dell' Adriatico, Trieste, Italy, 1952. 27,090 gross tons; 680 feet long; 87 feet wide. Fiat diesels, twin screw. Service speed 21 knots. 1172 passengers (180 first class, 280 cabin class, 714 tourist class).

Batory (Polish Ocean Line)
Built by Cantieri Riuniti dell' Adriatico, Trieste, Italy, 1936.

14,287 gross tons; 526 feet long; 71 feet wide. Sulzer diesels geared to twin screws. Service speed 18 knots. 816 passengers (76 first class, 740 tourist class).

Bergensfjord (Norwegian America Line), later *De Grasse, Rasa Sayang, Golden Moon,* and *Rasa Sayang*
Built by Swan, Hunter & Wigham Richardson Limited, Wallsend-on-Tyne, England, 1956. 18,739 gross tons; 578 feet long; 72 feet wide. Stork diesels, twin screw. Service speed 20 knots. 878 passengers (126 first class, 752 tourist class).

Berlin –see *Gripsholm*

Brasil – see *Drottningholm*

Bremen (North German Lloyd), ex-*Pasteur,* later *Regina Magna, Saudi Phil I,* and *Filipinas Saudi I*
Built by Chantiers de L'Atlantique, St Nazaire, France, 1939. 32,336 gross tons; 697 feet long; 88 feet wide. Steam turbines, quadruple screw. Service speed 23 knots. 1122 passengers (216 first class, 906 tourist class).

Britannic (Cunard)
Built by Harland & Wolff Limited, Belfast, Northern Ireland, 1930. 27,666 gross tons; 712 feet long; 82 feet wide. B&W type diesels, twin screw. Service speed 18 knots. 993 passengers (429 first class, 564 tourist class).

Carinthia (Cunard), later *Fairland,* then *Fairsea*
Built by John Brown & Company Limited, Clydebank, Scotland, 1956. 21,947 gross tons; 608 feet long; 80 feet wide. Steam turbines, twin screw. Service speed 19½ knots. 868 passengers (154 first class, 714 tourist class).

Carmania – see *Saxonia*

Caronia (Cunard), later *Colombia,* then *Caribia*
Built by John Brown & Company Limited, Clydebank. Scotland, 1948. 34,172 gross tons; 715 feet long; 91 feet wide; 31-foot draft. Steam turbines, twin screw. 932 passengers (581 first class, 351 cabin class).

Constitution (American Export Line), later *Oceanic Constitution,* then *Constitution*
Built by Bethlehem Steel Company, Quincy, Massachusetts, 1951. 30,293 gross tons; 683 feet long; 89 feet wide; 30-foot draft. Steam turbines, twin screw. Service speed 23 knots. 1000 passengers (295 first class, 375 cabin class, 330 tourist class).

Conte Bigancamano (Italian Line), ex-USS *Hermitage,* ex-*Conte Biancamano*
Built by William Beardmore & Company, Glasgow, Scotland, 1925. 23,842 gross tons; 665 feet long; 76 feet wide. Steam turbines, twin screw. Service speed 18 knots. 1578 passengers (215 first class, 333 cabin class, 1030 tourist class).

Conte Grande (Italian Line), ex-USS *Monticello,* ex-*Conte Grande*
Built by Stablimento Tecnico, Trieste, Italy, 1928. 23,562 gross tons; 667 feet long; 78 feet wide. Steam turbines, twin screw. Service speed 18 knots. 1379 passengers (261 first class, 338 cabin class, 780 tourist class).

Covadonga (Spanish Line), ex-*Monasterio de la Rabida*
Built by Compania Euskalduna, Bilbao, Spain, 1953. 10,226 gross tons; 487 feet long; 62 feet wide. Sulzer diesel, single

screw. Service speed 16½ knots. 353 passengers (105 first class, 248 tourist class).

Cristoforo Colombo (Italian Line)
Built by Ansaldo SpA, Genoa, Italy, 1953. 29,191 gross tons; 700 feet long; 90 feet wide. Steam turbines, twin screw. Service speed 23 knots. 1246 passengers (301 first class, 242 cabin class, 703 tourist class).

De Grasse (French Line), later *Empress of Australia* (Canadian Pacific), then *Venezuela*
Built by Cammell Laird & Company Limited, Birkenhead, England, 1924. 18,435 (19,370 as *Empress of Australia*) gross tons; 574 feet long; 71 feet wide; 29-foot draft. Steam turbines, twin screw. Service speed 16 knots. 970 passengers (500 first class, 470 tourist class); 664 passengers (220 first class, 444 tourist class) as *Empress of Australia.*

Drottningholm (Swedish-American Line), ex-*Virginian,* later *Brasil, Homeland* (Home Line)
Built by Alexander Stephen & Sons Limited, Glasgow, Scotland, 1905. 10,249 (10,043 as *Brasil/Homeland*) gross tons; 538 feet long; 60 feet wide. Steam turbines, triple screw. Service speed 18 knots. 1386 passengers (532 first class, 854 tourist class); 942 passengers (96 first class, 846 tourist class) as *Brasil/Homeland.*

Empress of Australia – see *De Grasse*

Empress of Britain (Canadian Pacific), later *Queen Anna Maria* (Greek Line), then *Carnivale*
Built by Fairfield Shipbuilding & Engineering Company, Glasgow, Scotland, 1956. 25,516 (21,716 as *Queen Anna Maria*) gross tons; 640 feet long; 85 feet wide. Steam turbines, twin screw. Service speed 20 knots. 1054 passengers (160 first class, 894 tourist class); 1254 passengers (109 first class, 1145 tourist class) as *Queen Anna Maria.*

Empress of Canada (1928; Canadian Pacific), ex-*Duchess of Richmond*
Built by John Brown & Company Limited, Clydebank, Scotland, 1928. 20,448 gross tons; 600 feet long; 75 feet wide. Steam turbines, twin screw. Service speed 18 knots. 700 passengers (400 first class, 300 tourist class).

Empress of Canada (1961; Canadian Pacific), later *Mardi Gras*
Built by Vickers-Armstrong Shipbuilders Limited, Newcastle-upon-Tyne, England, 1961. 27,284 gross tons; 650 feet long; 87 feet wide. Steam turbines, twin screw. Service speed 20 knots. 1056 passengers (200 first class, 856 tourist class).

Empress of England (Canadian Pacific), later *Ocean Monarch*
Built by Vickers-Armstrong Shipbuilders Limited, Newcastle-upon-Tyne, England, 1957. 25,585 gross tons; 640 feet long; 85 feet wide. Steam turbines, twin screw. Service speed 20 knots. 1058 passengers (160 first class, 898 tourist class).

Empress of France (Canadian Pacific), ex-*Duchess of Bedford*
Built by John Brown & Company Limited, Clydebank, Scotland, 1928. 20,235 gross tons; 600 feet long; 75 feet wide.

Steam turbines, twin screw. Service speed 18 knots. 700 passengers (400 first class, 300 tourist class).

Empress of Scotland (Canadian Pacific), ex-*Empress of Japan*, later *Hanseatic* (Hamburg-Atlantic Line)
Built by Fairfield Shipbuilding & Engineering Company, Glasgow, Scotland, 1930. 26,313 gross tons; 666 feet long; 83 feet wide (30,029 gross tons; 672 feet long as *Hanseatic*). Steam turbines, twin screw. Service speed 21 knots. 708 passengers (458 first class, 250 tourist class); 1252 passengers (85 first class, 11167 tourist class) as *Hanseatic*.

Europa – see *Kungsholm* (1953)

Excalibur (American Export Line), ex-USS *Duchess*, later *Oriental Jade*

Excambion (American Export Line), ex- USS *Queens*, later *Texas Clipper*

Exeter (American Export Line), ex-USS *Shelby*, later *Oriental Pearl*

Exochorda (American Export Line), ex-USS *Dauphin*, later *Stevens*

All four ships built by Bethlehem Steel Company, Sparrows Point, Maryland, 1944. 9644 gross tons; 473 feet long; 66 feet wide. Steam turbines, single screw. Service speed 17 knots. 125 first class passengers.

Flandre (French Line), later *Carla C*
Built by Ateliers et Chantiers de France, Dunkirk, France, 1952. 20,477 gross tons; 600 feet long; 80 feet wide; 26-foot draft. Steam turbines, twin screw. Service speed 22 knots. 743 passengers (232 first class, 511 tourist class).

France (French Line), later *Norway*
Built by Chantiers de l'Atlantique, St Nazaire, France, 1961. 66,348 gross tons; 1035 feet long; 110 feet wide. Steam turbines, quadruple screw. Service speed 31 knots. 1944 passengers (501 first class, 1443 tourist class).

Franconia (1923; Cunard)
Built by John Brown & Company Limited, Clydebank, Scotland, 1923. 20,341 gross tons; 623 feet long; 73 feet wide. Steam turbines, twin screw. Service speed 16 knots. 850 passengers (250 first class, 600 tourist class).

Franconia (1955) – *Ivernia*

Georgic (Cunard)
Built by Harland & Wolff Limited, Belfast, Northern Ireland, 1932. 27,469 gross tons; 711 feet long; 82 feet wide. B&W type diesels, twin screw. Service speed 18 knots. 1962 one-class passengers.

Giulio Cesare (Italian Line)
Built by Cantieri Riuniti dell' Adriatico, Monfalcone, Italy, 1951. 27,078 gross tons; 681 feet long; 87 feet wide. Fiat diesels, twin screw. Service speed 21 knots. 1183 passengers (181 first class, 288 cabin class, 714 tourist class).

Gripsholm (1925; Swedish-American Line), later *Berlin* (North German Lloyd)
Built by Sir W G Armstrong-Whitworth & Company, Newcastle, England, 1925. 19,105 gross tons; 590 feet long; 74 feet wide. B&W diesels, twin screw. Service speed 16½

knots. 920 passengers (210 first class, 710 tourist class); 976 passengers (98 first class, 878 tourist class) as *Berlin*.

Gripsholm (1957; Swedish-American Line), later *Navarino*, then *Samantha*
Built by Ansaldo SpA, Genoa, Italy, 1957. 23,191 gross tons; 631 feet long; 82 feet wide. Gotaverken diesels, twin screw. Service speed 19 knots. 842 passengers (214 first class, 628 tourist class).

Groote Beer (Netherlands Government), ex-*Costa Rica Victory*, later *Marianna IV*, *Groote Beer*, and *Marianna IV*
Built by Permanente Shipyard No 1, Richmond, California, 1944. 9190 gross tons; 455 long; 62 feet wide. Steam turbines, single screw. Service speed 16 knots. 800 one-class passengers.

Guadalupe (Spanish Line), ex-*Monasteris de Guadalupe*
Built by Societa Espanola de Construccion Naval, Bilbao, Spain, 1953. 10,226 gross tons; 487 feet long; 62 feet wide. Sulzer diesel, single screw. Service speed 16½ knots. 349 passengers (105 first class, 244 tourist class).

Hanseatic – see *Empress of Scotland*

Homeland – see *Drottningholm*

Homeric (Home Line), ex-*Mariposa*
Built by Bethlehem Steel Company, Quincy, Massachusetts, 1931. 24,907 gross tons; 638 feet long; 79 feet wide. Steam turbines, twin screw. Service speed 20 knots. 1243 passengers (147 first class, 1096 tourist class).

Ile de France (French Line), later *Furanzu Maru*
Built by Chantiers de L'Atlantique, St Nazaire, France, 1927. 44,356 gross tons; 792 feet long; 91 feet wide. Steam turbines, quadruple screw. Service speed 23½ knots. 1345 passengers (541 first class, 577 cabin class, 227 tourist class).

Independence (American Export Line), later *Oceanic Independence*, then *Independence*
Built by Bethlehem Steel Company, Quincy, Massachusetts, 1951. 30,293 gross tons; 683 feet long; 89 feet wide; 30-foot draft. Steam turbines, twin screw. Service speed 23 knots. 1000 passengers (295 first class, 375 cabin class, 330 tourist class).

Italia (Home Line), ex-USS *John Ericsson*, ex-*Kungsholm*
Built by Blohm & Voss, Hamburg, Germany, 1928. 21,532 gross tons; 609 feet long; 78 feet wide. B&W diesels, twin screw. Service speed 17 knots. 1319 passengers (213 first class, 1106 tourist class).

Ivernia (Cunard), later *Franconia*, then *Feodor Shalyapin*
Built by John Brown & Company Limited, Clydebank, Scotland, 1955. 21,717 gross tons; 608 feet long; 80 feet wide. Steam turbines, twin screw. Service speed 19½ knots. 925 passengers (125 first class, 800 tourist class).

Klek – see under *Visevica*

Kungsholm (1953; Swedish-American Line), later *Europa* (North German Lloyd), *Columbus C*, and *Costa Columbus*
Built by De Schelde, Flushing, Holland, 1953. 21,141 (21,514 as *Europa*) gross tons; 600 feet long; 77 feet wide. B&W diesels, twin screw. Service speed 19 knots. 802 passengers

(176 first class, 626 tourist class); 843 passengers (122 first class, 721 tourist class) as *Europa*.

Kungsholm (1966; Swedish-American Line), later *Sea Princess*
Built by John Brown & Company, (Clydebank), Ltd, Scotland, 1966. 26,678 gross tons; 660 feet long; 86 feet wide. Gotaverken diesels, twin screw. Service speed 21 knots. 750 passengers (108 first class, 642 tourist class).

Laurentia (Donaldson Line), ex-*Medina Victory*
Built by Permanente Shipyard No 1, Richmond, California, 1945. 8349 gross tons; 455 feet long; 62 feet wide. Steam turbines, single screw. Service speed 15 knots. 55 first class passengers.

Leonardo da Vinci (Italian Line)
Built by Ansaldo SpA, Genoa, Italy, 1960. 33,340 gross tons; 761 feet long; 92 feet wide. Steam turbines, twin screw. Service speed 23 knots. 1326 passengers (413 first class, 342 cabin class, 571 tourist class).

Liberté (French Line), ex-*Europa*
Built by Blohm & Voss, Hamburg, Germany, 1930. 51,839 gross tons; 936 feet long; 102 feet wide; 34-foot draft. Steam turbines, quadruple screw. Speed 24 knots. 1502 passengers (555 first class, 497 cabin class, 450 tourist class).

Lismoria (Donaldson Line), ex-*Taos Victory*, later *Neon*
Built by California Shipbuilding Corporation, Los Angeles, California, 1945. 8323 gross tons; 455 feet long; 62 feet wide. Steam turbines, single screw. Service speed 15 knots. 55 first class passengers.

Maasdam (Holland-America Line), later *Stefan Batory* (Polish Ocean Lines)
Built by Wilton-Fijenoord, Schiedam, Holland, 1952. 15,024 (15,043 as *Stefan Batory*) gross tons; 503 feet long; 69 feet wide. Steam turbines, single screw. Service speed 16½ knots. 875 passengers (39 first class, 836 tourist class); 773 tourist class only as *Stefan Batory*.

Mauretania (Cunard)
Built by Cammell Laird & Company Limited, Birkenhead, England, 1939. 35,655 gross tons; 772 feet long; 89 feet wide; 30-foot draft. Steam turbines, twin screw. Service speed 23 knots. 1140 passengers (470 first class, 370 cabin class, 300 tourist class).

Media (Cunard), later *Flavia*, then *Flavian*
Built by John Brown & Company Limited, Clydebank, Scotland, 1947. 13,345 gross tons; 531 feet long; 70 feet wide; 30-foot draft. Steam turbines, twin screw. Service speed 18 knots. 250 first class passengers.

Michelangelo (Italian Line)
Built by the Ansaldo SpA, Genoa, Italy, 1965. 45,911 gross tons; 902 feet long; 102 feet wide. Steam turbines, twin screw. Service speed 26½ knots. 1775 passengers (535 first class, 550 cabin class, 690 tourist class).

Mikhail Lermontov (Soviet Union)
Built by Mathias-Thesen Werft Shipyard, Wismar, East Germany, 1971. 19,872 gross tons; 578 feet long; 77 feet

wide. Sulzer diesels, twin screw. Service speed 20 knots. 700 one-class passengers.

Nea Hellas (Greek Line), ex-*Tuscania*, later *New York*
Built by Fairfield Shipbuilding & Engineering Company, Glasgow, Scotland, 1922. 16,991 gross tons; 578 feet long; 70 feet wide. Steam turbines, twin screw. Service speed 16 knots. 1370 passengers (70 first class, 1300 tourist class).

Neptunia (Greek Line), ex-*Johan de Witt*
Built by Netherlands Shipbuilding Company, Amsterdam, Holland, 1920. 10,519 gross tons; 523 feet long; 59 feet wide. Triple-expansion engines, twin screw. Service speed 15 knots. 787 passengers (39 first class, 748 tourist class).

New York – see *Nea Hellas*

Newfoundland (Furness-Warren), later *George Anson*
Built by Vickers-Armstrong Shipbuilders Limited, Newcastle, England, 1947. 7438 gross tons; 440 feet long; 61 feet wide. Steam turbines, single screw. Service speed 15 knots. 154 passengers (62 first class, 92 tourist class).

Nieuw Amsterdam (Holland-America Line)
Built by the Rotterdam Drydock Company, Rotterdam, Holland, 1938. 36,667 gross tons; 758 feet long; 88 feet wide. Steam turbines, twin screw. Service speed 21 knots. 1187 passengers (552 first class, 426 cabin class, 209 tourist class).

Noordam (Holland-America Line), later *Océanien*
Built by P Smit, Jr Shipbuilding, Rotterdam, Holland, 1938. 10,726 gross tons; 501 feet long; 64 feet wide. B&W type diesels, twin screw. Service speed 17 knots. 148 first class passengers.

Nova Scotia (Furness-Warren Line), later *Francis Drake*
Built by Vickers-Armstrong Shipbuilders Limited, Newcastle, England, 1948. 7437 gross tons; 440 feet long; 61 feet wide. Steam turbines, single screw. Service speed 15 knots. 154 passengers (62 first class, 92 tourist class).

Olympia (Greek Line), later *Caribe I*
Built by Alexander Stephen & Sons Limited, Glasgow, Scotland, 1953. 22,979 gross tons; 611 feet long; 79 feet wide. Steam turbines, twin screw. Service speed 22 knots. 1307 passengers (138 first class, 1169 tourist class).

Oslofjord (Norwegian America Line), later *Fulvia*
Built by Netherlands Shipbuilding Company, Amsterdam, Holland, 1949. 16,844 gross tons; 577 feet long; 72 feet wide. Stork diesels, twin screw. Service speed 20 knots. 646 passengers (179 first class, 467 tourist class).

Parthia (Cunard), later *Remuera*, then *Aramac*
Built by Harland & Wolff Limited, Belfast, Northern Ireland, 1948. 13,362 gross tons; 531 feet long; 70 feet wide; 30-foot draft. Steam turbines, twin screw. Service speed 18 knots. 250 first class passengers.

Prins Willem van Oranje (Oranje Line), later *Ferdinand Freiligrath, Freijo Universal Honolulu*, and *August 8th*
Built by Boele's Shipbuilding & Engineering Company, Bolnes, Holland, 1953. 7328 gross tons; 462 feet long; 62 feet wide. Werkspor-Lugt diesel, single screw. Service speed 17 knots. 60 one-class passengers.

Prinses Irene (Oranje Line), later *Tjut Njak Dhien*

Built by De Merwede Shipbuilding Yard, Hardinxveld, Holland, 1959. 8526 gross tons; 456 feet long; 61 feet wide. MAN type diesel, single screw. Service speed 17 knots. 116 one-class passengers.

Prinses Margriet (Oranje Line), later *Enna G*
Built by De Merwede Shipbuilding Yard, Hardinxveld, Holland, 1961. 9336 gross tons; 456 feet long; 61 feet wide. MAN-type diesel, single screw. Service speed 17 knots. 111 one-class passengers.

Queen Anna Maria – see *Empress of Britain*

Queen Elizabeth (Cunard), later *Seawise University*
Built by John Brown & Company Limited, Clydebank, Scotland, 1940. 83,673 gross tons; 1031 feet long; 119 feet wide; 39-foot draft. Steam turbines, quadruple screw. Service speed 28½ knots. 2233 passengers (823 first class, 662 cabin class, 798 tourist class).

Queen Elizabeth 2 (Cunard)
Built by Upper Clyde Shipbuilders Limited (formerly John Brown & Company), Clydebank, Scotland, 1969. 65,863 gross tons (later increased to 67,107); 963 feet long; 105 feet wide. Steam turbines, twin screw. Service speed 28½ knots. 1820 maximum passengers.

Queen Frederica – see *Atlantic* (Home Line)

Queen Mary (Cunard)
Built by John Brown & Company Limited, Clydebank, Scotland, 1936. 81,237 gross tons; 1019 feet long; 119 feet wide; 39-foot draft. Steam turbines, quadruple screw. Service speed 28½ knots. 1957 passengers (711 first class, 707 cabin class, 577 tourist class).

Raffaello (Italian Line)
Built by Cantieri Riuniti dell'Adriatico, Trieste, Italy, 1965. 45,933 gross tons; 902 feet long; 102 feet wide. Steam turbines, twin screw. Service speed 26½ knots. 1775 passengers (535 first class, 550 cabin class, 690 tourist class).

Rotterdam (Holland-America Line)
Built by Rotterdam Drydock Company, Rotterdam, Holland, 1959. 38,645 gross tons; 748 feet long; 94 feet wide. Steam turbines, twin screw. Service speed 20½ knots. 1356 passengers (301 first class, 1055 tourist class).

Ryndam (Holland-America Line), later *Waterman*, *Ryndam*, and *Atlas*
Built by Wilton-Fijenoord, Schiedam, Holland, 1951. 15,015 gross tons; 503 feet long; 69 feet wide. Steam turbines, twin screw. Service speed 16½ knots. 875 passengers (39 first class, 836 tourist class).

Sagafjord (Norwegian America Line)
Built by Societe des Forges et Chantiers de la Méditerranée, Toulon, France, 1965. 24,002 gross tons; 615 feet long; 82 feet wide. Sulzer diesels, twin screw. Service speed 20 knots. 789 passengers (70 first class, 719 tourist class).

Samaria (Cunard)
Built by Cammell Laird & Company Limited, Birkenhead, England, 1921. 19,848 gross tons; 624 feet long; 73 feet wide. Steam turbines, twin screw. Service speed 16 knots. 900 passengers (250 first class, 650 tourist class).

Santa Maria (Companhia Colonial)
Built by Cockerill Ougree, Shipyard, Hoboken, Belgium, 1953. 20,906 gross tons; 609 feet long; 76 feet wide. Steam turbines, twin screw. Service speed 20 knots. 1078 passengers (156 first class, 226 cabin class, 696 third class).

Saturnia (Italian Line), ex-USS *Frances Y Slanger*, ex-*Saturnia*
Built by Cantieri Navali Triestino, Monfalcone, Italy, 1927. 24,346 gross tons; 630 feet long; 80 feet wide. Sulzer diesels, twin screw. Service speed 19 knots. 1479 passengers (255 first class, 270 cabin class, 954 tourist class).

Saxonia (Cunard), later *Carmania*, then *Leonid Sobinov*
Built by John Brown & Company Limited, Clydebank, Scotland, 1954. 21,637 gross tons; 608 feet long; 80 feet wide. Steam turbines, twin screw. Service speed 19½ knots. 925 passengers (125 first class, 800 tourist class).

Scythia (Cunard)
Built by Vickers-Armstrong Shipbuilders Limited, Barrow-in-Furness, England, 1920. 19,930 gross tons; 624 feet long; 73 feet wide. Steam turbines, twin screw. Service speed 16 knots. 878 passengers (248 first class, 630 tourist class.

Shalom (Zim Israel Navigation), later *Hanseatic*
Built by Chantiers de L'Atlantique, St Nazaire, France, 1964. 25,320 gross tons; 629 feet long; 82 feet wide. Steam turbines, twin screw. Service speed 20 knots. 1090 passengers (72 first class, 1018 tourist class).

Sobieski (Polish Ocean Line), later *Gruzia*
Built by Swan, Hunter & Wigham Richardson Limited, Newcastle, England, 1939. 11,030 gross tons; 511 feet long; 67 feet wide. B&W diesels geared to twin screw. Service speed 16 knots. 940 passengers (70 first class, 270 cabin class, 600 tourist class).

Statendam (Holland-America Line), later *Rhapsody*
Built by Wilton-Fijenoord, Schiedam, Holland, 1957. 24,294 gross tons; 642 feet long; 81 feet wide. Steam turbines, twin screw. Service speed 19 knots. 952 passengers (84 first class, 868 tourist class).

Stavangerfjord (Norwegian America Line)
Built by Cammell Laird & Company Limited, Birkenhead, England, 1918. 14,015 gross tons; 553 feet long; 64 feet wide. Steam quadruple-expansion engines and turbines, twin screw. Service speed 16½ knots. 675 passengers (90 first class, 172 cabin class, 413 tourist class).

Stefan Batory – see *Maasdam*

Stockholm (Swedish-American Line), later *Volkerfreundschaft*
Built by A/B Gotaverken, Gothenburg, Sweden, 1948. 12,644 gross tons; 525 feet long; 69 feet wide. Gotaverken diesels, twin screw. Service speed 19 knots. 608 passengers (24 first class, 584 tourist class).

Sylvania (Cunard), later *Fairwind*
Built by John Brown & Company Limited, Clydebank, Scotland, 1957. 21,989 gross tons; 608 feet long; 80 feet wide. Steam turbines, twin screw. Service speed 19½ knots. 878 passengers (154 first class, 724 tourist class).

Tohubic – see under *Visevica*

United States (United States Line)
Built by Newport News Shipbuilding & Drydock Company, Newport News, Virginia, 1952. 53,329 gross tons; 990 feet long; 101 feet long; 28-foot draft. Steam turbines, quadruple screw. Service speed 30–33 knots. 1930 passengers (871 first class, 508 cabin class, 551 tourist class).

Veendam (Holland-America Line)
Built by Harland & Wolff Limited, Govan, Glasgow, Scotland, 1923. 15,652 gross tons; 579 feet long; 67 feet wide. Steam turbines, twin screw. Service speed 15 knots. 586 passengers (223 first class, 363 tourist class).

Vera Cruz (Compania Colonial)
Built by Cockerill-Ougree Shipyard, Hoboken, Belgium, 1952. 21,765 gross tons; 610 feet long; 75 feet wide. Steam turbines, twin screw. Service speed 20 knots. 1296 passengers (150 first class, 250 cabin class, 896 third class).

Visevica (Jugolinija), later *Abu Hosna*

Klek (Jugolinija), later *Abu Alia*

Tuhobic (Jugolinija), later *Abu Rashid*

Zuir (Jugolinija), later *Abu Yussuf I*

All built by Brodogradiliste 'III Maj', Rijeka, Yugoslavia, 1964–65. 6750 gross tons; 492 feet long; 65 feet wide. Sulzer diesel, single screw. Service speed 18 knots. 50 passengers (20 first class, 30 tourist class).

Vistafjord (Norwegian American Line)
Built by Swan, Hunter & Wigham Richardson Limited, Newcastle, England, 1973. 24,292 gross tons; 628 feet long; 82 feet wide, Sulzer diesels, twin screw. Service speed 20 knots. 660 first class passengers.

Volendam (Holland-America Line)
Built by Harland & Wolff Limited, Govan, Glasgow, Scotland, 1922. 15,434 gross tons; 579 feet long; 67 feet wide. Steam turbines, twin screw. Service speed 14 knots. 1693 one-class passengers.

Vulcania (Italian Line), later *Caribia*
Built by Cantieri Navali Triestino, Monfalcone, Italy, 1928. 24,496 gross tons; 631 feet long; 80 feet wide. Fiat diesels, twin screw. Service speed 19 knots. 1452 passengers (232 first class, 262 cabin class, 958 tourist class).

Waterman (Netherlands Government), ex-*La Grande Victory*, later *Margarita*
Built by Oregon Shipbuilding Corporation, Portland, Oregon, 1945. 9176 gross tons; 455 feet long; 62 feet wide. Steam turbines, single screw. Service speed 16 knots. 800 one-class passengers.

Westerdam (Holland-America Line)
Built by Wilton-Fijenoord, Schiedam, Holland, 1940–46. 12,149 gross tons; 516 feet long; 66 feet wide. MAN type diesel, twin screw. Service speed 16 knots. 134 first class passengers.

Zuiderkruis (Netherlands Government), ex *Cranston Victory*
Built by Oregon Shipbuilding Corporation, Portland, Oregon, 1944. 9178 gross tons; 455 feet long; 62 feet wide. Steam turbines, single screw. Service speed 16 knots. 800 one-class passengers.

Zvir – see under *Visevica*

FIFTY LARGEST TRANSATLANTIC
LINERS FROM 1945

ship	gross tonnage	company	ship	gross tonnage	company
Queen Elizabeth	83,673	Cunard Line	Conte Grande	23,562	Italian Line
Queen Mary	81,237	Cunard Line	Gripsholm (1957)	23,191	Swedish-American Line
Queen Elizabeth 2	67,107	Cunard Line	Olympia	22,979	Greek Line
France	66,348	French Line	Sylvania	21,989	Cunard Line
United States	53,329	United States Lines	Carinthia	21,947	Cunard Line
Liberté	51,839	French Line	Vera Cruz	21,765	Companhia Colonial
Raffaello	45,933	Italian Line	Ivernia (later		
Michelangelo	45,911	Italian Line	Franconia)	21,717	Cunard Line
Aquitania	45,647	Cunard Line	Italia	21,532	Home Lines
Île de France	44,356	French Line	Europa		
Rotterdam	38,645	Holland-America Line	(ex-Kungsholm,		
Nieuw Amsterdam	36,667	Holland-America Line	1953)	21,514	North German Lloyd
Mauretania	35,655	Cunard Line	Saxonia (later		
Caronia	34,172	Cunard Line	Carmania)	21,367	Cunard Line
America	33,532	United States Lines	Santa Maria	20,906	Companhia Colonial
Leonardo Da Vinci	33,340	Italian Line	Flandre	20,477	French Line
Bremen	32,336	North German Lloyd	Empress of France	20,448	Canadian Pacific
Independence	30,293	American Export Lines			
Constitution	30,293	American Export Lines			
Hanseatic	30,029	Hamburg-Atlantic Line			
(ex-Empress of					
Scotland)	(26,313)	Canadian Pacific			
Cristoforo Colombo	29,191	Italian Line			
Andrea Doria	29,083	Italian Line			
Britannic	27,666	Cunard Line			
Georgic	27,469	Cunard Line			
Empress of Canada					
(1961)	27,284	Canadian Pacific			
Augustus	27,090	Italian Line			
Giulio Cesare	27,078	Italian Line			
Kungsholm (1966)	26,678	Swedish-American Line			
Empress of England	25,585	Canadian Pacific			
Empress of Britain	25,516	Canadian Pacific			
(later Queen Anna					
Maria)		Greek Line			
Shalom	25,320	Zim Lines			
Homeric	24,907	Home Lines			
Vulcania	24,496	Italian Line			
Saturnia	24,346	Italian Line			
Statendam	24,294	Holland-America Line			
Vistafjord	24,292	Norwegian America Line			
Sagafjord	24,002	Norwegian America Line			
Conte Biancamano	23,842	Italian Line			

FIFTY LONGEST TRANSATLANTIC
LINERS FROM 1945

ship	length	company	ship	length	company
France	1035'	French Line	Scythia	624'	Cunard Line
Queen Elizabeth	1031'	Cunard Line	Samaria	624'	Cunard Line
Queen Mary	1018'	Cunard Line	Franconia (1983)	623'	Cunard Line
United States	990'	United States Lines	Sagafjord	615'	Norwegian America Line
Queen Elizabeth 2	963'	Cunard Line	Olympia	611'	Greek Line
Liberté	936'	French Line	Vera Cruz	610'	Companhia Colonial
Michelangelo	902'	Italian Line	Santa Maria	609'	Companhia Colonial
Raffaello	902'	Italian Line	Italia	609'	Home Lines
Aquitania	901'	Cunard Line	Saxonia		
Île de France	792'	French Line	(later Carmania)	608'	Cunard Line
Mauretania	772'	Cunard Line	Ivernia		
Leonardo Da Vinci	761'	Italian Line	(later Franconia)	608'	Cunard Line
Nieuw Amsterdam	758'	Holland-America Line	Carinthia	608'	Cunard Line
Rotterdam	748'	Holland-America Line			
America	723'	United States Lines			
Caronia	715'	Cunard Line			
Britannic	712'	Cunard Line			
Georgic	711'	Cunard Line			
Andrea Doria	700'	Italian Line			
Cristoforo Colombo	700'	Italian Line			
Bremen	697'	North German Lloyd			
Constitution	683'	American Export Lines			
Independence	683'	American Export Lines			
Giulio Cesare	681'	Italian Line			
Augustus	680'	Italian Line			
Hanseatic	672'	Hamberg-Atlantic Line			
(ex-Empress of Scotland)	(666')	Canadian Pacific			
Conte Grande	667'	Italian Line			
Conte Biancamano	665'	Italian Line			
Kungsholm (1966)	660'	Swedish-American Line			
Empress of Canada (1961)	650'	Canadian Pacific			
Statendam	642'	Holland-America Line			
Empress of Britain (later Queen Anna Maria)	640'	Canadian Pacific / Greek Line			
Empress of England	640'	Canadian Pacific			
Homeric	638'	Home Lines			
Gripsholm (1957)	631'	Swedish-American Line			
Vulcania	631'	Italian Line			
Satumia	630'	Italian Line			
Shalom	629'	Zim Lines			
Vistafjord	628'	Norwegian America Line			

CHRONOLOGY OF SIGNIFICANT
TRANSATLANTIC LINER EVENTS

August 1945
First commercial transatlantic crossing since the war, made by Norwegian America *Stavangerfjord*.

June 1946
Holland-America Line resumes transatlantic passenger service with *Westerdam*.

September 1946
Swedish American *Stockholm* launched; first new post-war liner for North Atlantic service.

October 1946
Queen Elizabeth commissioned following war duties.

November 1946
America recommissioned following war service.

January 1947
Italian Line resumes transatlantic liner service with *Saturnia*.

July 1947
Queen Mary recommissioned after war service.

August 1947
Cunard *Media* completed; first new transatlantic passenger ship to enter service.

October 1947
Nieuw Amsterdam recommissioned following war service.

January 1949
Cunard *Caronia* commissioned; first large liner designed mostly for cruising.

May 1949
Home Lines begin North Atlantic passenger operations.

July 1949
Île De France recommissioned after war duties.

December 1949
Cunard *Aquitania* retired; last four-stacker.

August 1950
French *Liberté* recommissioned.

January 1951
Polish *Batory* withdrawn from transatlantic service through political troubles in the United States.

July 1951
Holland America *Ryndam* introduces tourist class dominance of passenger accommodations.

July 1952
United States sweeps the North Atlantic and takes the Blue Ribband from *Queen Mary;* last record-breaker.

January 1955
North German Lloyd resumes transatlantic passenger service with *Berlin*.

July 1956
Italian *Andrea Doria* sinks off Nantucket after collision with Swedish *Stockholm*.

October 1958
First commercial jet aircraft service across the Atlantic.

November 1958
Île de France retired.

September 1959
Rotterdam commissioned; first Atlantic liner to dispense with conventional funnel.

December 1960
Cunard's *Britannic* retired; last of the original White Star Line fleet.

January 1961
Portuguese *Santa Maria* hijacked by political rebels during transatlantic crossing.

November 1961
French *Liberté* retired.

February 1962
France commissioned; last of the purposely designed transatlantic superliners.

February 1963
Queen Elizabeth makes first cruise in the history of the Cunard *Queens*.

October 1963
Home Lines ceases transatlantic passenger services.

April 1966
Soviets resume North Atlantic passenger service (first since 1949) with *Alexandr Pushkin* to Montreal.

September 1967
Queen Mary retired from transatlantic service; last three-stacker.

October 1968
Cunard ends its Canadian passenger service.

November 1968
Zim Lines ceases Atlantic passenger operations.

September 1968
American Export Lines ceases Atlantic liner services.

October 1968
Queen Elizabeth retired from transatlantic service.

May 1969
Queen Elizabeth 2 commissioned; last of the superliners.

November 1969
United States withdrawn; United States Lines ends
transatlantic passenger service.

May 1971
Queen Mary opens as hotel and museum ship at Long Beach,
California.

September 1971
Holland-America Line and North German Lloyd cease
transatlantic operations.

November 1971
Canadian Pacific ends Atlantic liner service.

January 1972
Former *Queen Elizabeth*, as the *Seawise University*, destroyed by
fire at Hong Kong.

March 1973
Spanish Line ceases North Atlantic passenger operations.

May 1973
Soviets open irregular Atlantic service to New York with
Mikhail Lermontov.

September 1974
France withdrawn; French Line ends Atlantic liner runs.

January 1975
Greek Line ceases all passenger operations.

December 1975
Swedish-American Line ends passenger service.

June 1976
Italian Line ends transatlantic passenger service.

May 1980
France recommissioned as cruise ship *Norway*.

1981
Jugolinija ends transatlantic passenger operations; termination
of all regular liner service to the Mediterranean area.

Soviets withdraw from all Atlantic liner service.

SAMPLE TRANSATLANTIC SAILING
SCHEDULE FROM NEW YORK

Saturday, July 11th 1959

Westerdam, Holland-America; Rotterdam — Noon 5th Street, Hoboken

Sunday, July 12th

No sailings

Monday, July 13th

Constitution, American Export; Mediterranean — Noon 84 HR, West 44th St

Tuesday, July 14th

Atlantic, American Banner; Amsterdam — 11.59 pm 97 HR, West 57th St

Wednesday, July 15th

Queen Mary, Cunard; Southampton — 1.30 pm 90 HR, West 50th St
Statendam, Holland-America; Rotterdam — Noon 5th Street, Hoboken

Thursday, July 16th

Berlin, North German Lloyd; Bremerhaven — 11.00 am 88 HR, West 48th St
United States, United States Lines; Bremerhaven — Noon 86 HR, West 46th St
Guadalupe, Spanish Line; Spain — Noon 15 ER, Maiden Lane
Zion, Zim Lines; Haifa — 6.00 pm Kent St, Brooklyn

Friday, July 17th

Nieuw Amsterdam, Holland-America; Rotterdam — Noon 5th Street, Hoboken
Andes, Royal Mail Lines; Southampton — Noon 97 HR, West 57th St
Parthia, Cunard; Liverpool — 3.30 pm 92 HR, West 52nd St
America, United States Lines; Bremerhaven — 4.00 pm 86 HR, West 46th St

Saturday, July 18th

Liberté, French Line; Le Havre — 11.30 am 88 HR, West 48th St
Kungsholm, Swedish-American; Gothenburg — 4.30 pm 97 HR, West 57th St

SAMPLE LIST OF
TRANSATLANTIC CROSSINGS
June 1961

Date	Ship	Ports	Date	Ship	Ports
1	Bergensfjord	Kristiansand, Copenhagen, Oslo	16	Saturnia	Lisbon, Gibraltar, Naples, Palermo,
1	Maasdam	Cóbh, Southampton, Rotterdam			Patras, Dubrovnik, Venice, Trieste
2*	Empress of England	Greenock, Liverpool	16*	Ivernia	Le Havre, Southampton
2	Leonardo da Vinci	Gibraltar, Naples, Cannes, Genoa	16	Statendam	Southampton, Le Havre, Rotterdam
2	Nieuw Amsterdam	Southampton, Le Havre, Rotterdam	16	Jerusalem	Gibraltar, Marseilles, Naples, Haifa
2*	Saxonia	Le Havre, Southampton	16	Parthia	Liverpool
2	Media	Greenock, Liverpool	17	Independence	Algeciras, Naples, Genoa, Cannes
3	Constitution	Algeciras, Cannes, Genoa, Naples	19	Berlin	Southampton, Bremerhaven
3	Bremen	Cherbourg, Southampton,	21	Queen Elizabeth	Cherbourg, Southampton
		Bremerhaven	21	Bremen	Cherbourg, Southampton,
4*	Ryndam	Southampton, Le Havre, Rotterdam			Bremerhaven
5	Groote Beer	Southampton, Le Havre, Rotterdam	21	Kungsholm	Copenhagen, Gothenburg
6	Queen Frederica	Gibraltar, Naples, Messina, Piraeus	21	Stavangerfjord	Kristiansand, Copenhagen, Oslo
6	Gripsholm	Gothenburg	22*	Empress of England	Greenock, Liverpool
7	Queen Elizabeth	Cherbourg, Southampton	22	Zuiderkruis	Rotterdam
7	Oslofjord	Bergen	23	Constitution	Algeciras, Cannes, Genoa, Naples
7	Excalibur	Cadiz, Barcelona, Marseilles, Naples,	23	Leonardo da Vinci	Gibraltar, Naples, Cannes, Genoa
		Alexandria, Beirut, Piraeus	23	Nieuw Amsterdam	Southampton, Le Havre, Rotterdam
8	United States	Le Havre, Southampton,	23*	Saxonia	Le Havre, Southampton
		Bremerhaven	24	United States	Le Havre, Southampton
9*	Empress of Britain	Greenock, Liverpool	24	Westerdam	Rotterdam
9*	Carinthia	Greenock, Liverpool	26	Maasdam	Cóbh, Southampton, Rotterdam
9	Flandre	Southampton, Le Havre	27	Augustus	Gibraltar, Barcelona, Genoa, Naples
9	Sylvania	Cóbh, Liverpool	28	Queen Mary	Cherbourg, Southampton
9*	Arkadia	Cóbh, Le Havre, London,	28	Groote Beer	Rotterdam
		Amsterdam, Bremerhaven	28	Exeter	Cadiz, Barcelona, Marseilles, Naples,
9	Rotterdam	Southampton, Le Havre, Rotterdam			Alexandria, Beirut, Piraeus
9	Zion	Madeira, Gibraltar, Piraeus, Haifa	29	Liberté	Plymouth, Le Havre
10	Cristoforo Colombo	Gibraltar, Naples, Cannes, Genoa	29*	Empress of Britain	Greenock, Liverpool
10	Olympia	Lisbon, Naples, Messina, Piraeus	29*	Ryndam	Southampton, Le Havre, Rotterdam
10	Noordam	Rotterdam	30	America	Cóbh, Le Havre, Southampton,
11	Hanseatic	Southampton, Le Havre, Cuxhaven			Bremerhaven
13	America	Cóbh, Le Havre, Southampton	30*	Homeric	Southampton, Le Havre
13	Liberté	Plymouth, Le Havre	30*	Carinthia	Liverpool
13*	Batory	Southampton, Copenhagen, Gdynia	30*	Arkadia	Cóbh, Le Havre, London,
13**	Newfoundland	Liverpool			Amsterdam, Bremerhaven
14*	Homeric	Southampton, Le Havre	30	Rotterdam	Southampton, Le Havre, Rotterdam
14	Queen Mary	Cherbourg, Southampton	30	Israel	Madeira, Gibraltar, Piraeus, Haifa
14	Atlantic	Algeciras, Naples, Piraeus, Haifa	30	Media	Liverpool
15	Mauretania	Cóbh, Le Havre, Southampton	30**	Nova Scotia	Liverpool
16*	Empress of Canada	Greenock, Liverpool			

*Denotes sailings from Montreal: **sailings from Boston.
All other sailings from New York.

PASSENGER SHIPS' COLOURING

AMERICAN EXPORT LINES: black hull (white on *Independence*, *Constitution* and *Atlantic* after 1960); funnels with blue top, white band surrounded by thin red stripes and buff base.

AROSA LINE: black hull (changed to white on some ships); funnels with black top, thin black band and buff base.

CANADIAN PACIFIC STEAMSHIPS: white hull; yellow funnels with red and white chequer (colours later changed to green and white).

CHANDRIS LINES: white hull; blue funnels with black top band and white 'X'.

COMPANHIA COLONIAL: grey hull; yellow funnel with thick centre white band and twin green stripes.

CUNARD LINE: black hull (*Caronia* was done in shades of green, as were several later ships, as well as in white); funnel in orange-red with twin black stripes and black top. *QE2*'s funnel was painted all white with a black top from 1969 until 1982.

DONALDSON LINE: black hull; black funnel with white stripe.

FRENCH LINE: black hull; red funnel with black top.

FURNESS-WARREN LINE: black hull; red funnel with black top, black stripe and black base.

GREEK LINE: white hull (some earlier ships had black hulls); funnels with black top, blue centre and yellow base. Golden trident in centre.

HAMBURG-ATLANTIC LINE: black hull; red funnels with black top and white Maltese crosses.

HOLLAND-AMERICA LINE: black and later grey hulls; yellow funnels with green stripes and white centre.

HOME LINES: white hull; yellow funnels with blue top and blue disc encircling a golden crown.

ITALIAN LINE: black and later white hulls; white funnels with red top, white band and then thin green band.

JUGOLINIJA: grey hulls; blue funnels with black top and centre white band with large red star.

NATIONAL HELLENIC AMERICAN LINE: white hull; yellow funnels with blue top and blue disc encircling a golden crown (same as for Home Lines).

NETHERLANDS GOVERNMENT: grey hulls; yellow funnels with blue stripe, then white band, then red stripe.

NORTH GERMAN LLOYD: black hulls; mustard colored funnels.

NORWEGIAN AMERICA LINE: grey hulls; yellow funnels with red, white, blue, white and then red stripes in centre.

ORANJE LINE: grey hulls; orange funnels with blue diamond with white 'AV' monogram.

POLISH OCEAN LINES: grey and black hulls; buff coloured funnels with red band bearing shield and trident device of houseflag.

SOVIET PASSENGER SHIPS: white or black hulls; white funnels with golden hammer and sickle on red band.

SPANISH LINE: black hulls; all black funnels.

SWEDISH AMERICAN LINE: white hulls; yellow funnels with blue disc encircling three golden crowns.

UNITED STATES LINES: black hulls; red, white and blue-topped funnels.

ZIM LINES: white hulls; white funnels with two blue stripes and seven golden stars.

BIBLIOGRAPHY

Armstrong, Warren. *Atlantic Highway*. London: George G Harrap & Company Limited, 1961.

Arnott, Captain Robert Harry. *Captain of the Queen*. Sevenoaks, Kent: New English Library, 1982.

Bisset, Sir James. *Commodore: War, Peace and Big Ships*. London: Angus & Robertson Limited, 1961.

Bonsor, N R P. *North Atlantic Seaway*. Prescot, Lancashire: T Stephenson & Sons Limited, 1955.

Bonsor, N R P. *North Atlantic Seaway, Volumes 1–5* (revised). Jersey, Channel Islands: Brookside Publications, 1975–80.

Braynard, Frank O & Miller, William H. *Fifty Famous Liners*. Cambridge: Patrick Stephens Limited, 1982.

Brinnin, John Malcolm. *The Sway of the Grand Saloon*. New York: Delacorte Press, 1971.

Cairis, Nicholas T. *North Atlantic Passenger Liners Since 1900*. London: Ian Allan Limited, 1972.

Coleman, Terry. *The Liners*. New York: G P Putnam's Sons, 1977.

Crowdy, Michael (editor). *Marine News* (Journal, 1964–84). Kendal, Cumbria: World Ship Society.

Dodman, Frank E. *Ships of the Cunard Line*. London: Adlard Coles Limited, 1955.

Dunn, Laurence. *British Passenger Liners*. Southampton: Adlard Coles Limited, 1959.

Dunn, Laurence. *Passenger Liners*. Southampton: Adlard Coles Limited, 1961.

Dunn, Laurence. *Passenger Liners* (revised). Southampton: Adlard Coles Limited, 1965.

Eisele, Peter (editor). *Steamboat Bill* (Journal, 1966–84). New York: Steamship Historical Society of America Inc.

Emmons, Frederick. *The Atlantic Liners 1925–70*. New York: Bonanza Books, 1972.

Hyde, Francis E. *Cunard and the North Atlantic 1840–1973*. London: The Macmillan Press Limited, 1975.

Kludas, Arnold. *Great Passenger Ships of the World, Volumes 1–5*. Cambridge: Patrick Stephens Limited, 1972–76.

Kludas, Arnold. *Passenger Ships & Cruise Liners of the World*. Herford, West Germany: Koehlers Verlagesellschaft MBH, 1983.

Lacey, Robert, *The Queens of the North Atlantic*. London: Sidgwick & Jackson Limited, 1973.

MacLean, Commodore Donald. *Queen's Company*. London: Hutchinson & Company, 1965.

Maxtone-Graham, John. *The Only Way To Cross*. New York: The Macmillan Company, 1972.

Miller, William H. *Transatlantic Liners 1945–80*. Newton Abbot, Devon: David & Charles Limited, 1981.

Mitchell, W H. *The Cunard Line: A Post-War History*. Deal, Kent: Marinart Limited, 1975.

Potter, Neil & Frost, Jack. *The Mary, The Inevitable Ship*. London: George G Harrap & Company Limited, 1961.

Potter, Neil & Frost, Jack. *The Elizabeth*. London: George G Harrap & Company Limited, 1965.

van Herk, Cornelius. *The Ships of the Holland-America Line*. Haarlem: Historische Boekhandel Erato, 1981.

Wall, Robert. *Ocean Liners*. New York: E P Dutton, 1977.

INDEX

Entries in *italics* refer to illustrations